STARTER
VEGETABLE
GARDENS

STARTER
VEGETABLE
GARDENS

24 NO-FAIL PLANS *for* Small Organic Gardens

BARBARA PLEASANT

Storey Publishing

The mission of Storey Publishing is to serve our customers by
publishing practical information that encourages
personal independence in harmony with the environment.

EDITED BY Sarah Guare Slattery, Carleen Madigan, Gwen Steege, and Fern Bradley
COVER DESIGN BY Erin Dawson
BOOK DESIGN BY Dan O. Williams and Erin Dawson
TEXT PRODUCTION BY Erin Dawson and Jennifer Jepson Smith
INDEXED BY Christine R. Lindemer, Boston Road Communications

COVER PHOTOGRAPHY BY © Catalina.m/Shutterstock, front, bottom; courtesy of Barbara Pleasant, author's;
© Magdalena Bujak/Alamy Stock Photo, spine; © Zbynek Pospisil/iStock.com, front, top
INTERIOR PHOTOGRAPHY BY © John Gruen, except © Barbara Pleasant, 47, 85, 86, 116, 124, 155, 161
ADDITIONAL STOCK PHOTOGRAPHY BY © age footstock, 192; © Alexs/stock.adobe.com, 163 l.; © Ben44/
Alamy Stock Photo, 55; © binabina/iStock.com, 75; © Ekaterina Kiseleva/iStock.com, 118; © encierro/
stock.adobe.com, 120; © Fokusiert/iStock.com, 173; © IRYNA KAZLOVA/iStock.com, 110; © iztverichka/
stock.adobe.com, 126; © kunewave/stock.adobe.com, 163 r.; © Loraliu/stock.adobe.com, 101; Markus Spiske/
Unsplash, 154; © Nancy J. Ondra/stock.adobe.com, 145; © noorhaswan/stock.adobe.com, 121; © Phil
Degginger/Alamy Stock Photo, 59; © pidjoe/iStock.com, 69; © P_Wei/iStock.com, 147; © RyanJLane/iStock.com,
141; © sarahlucillegore/stock.adobe.com, 31; © tamifreed/stock.adobe.com, 2; © TeresaJaneD/Alamy Stock
Photo, 43; © Tim Gainey/Alamy Stock Photo, 35; © V. J. Matthew/stock.adobe.com, 71; © Vera Kuttelvaserova
Stuchelova/123RF.com, 139; © YuriyS/iStock.com, 34
PHOTO STYLING BY Lisa Newman
ILLUSTRATIONS BY Alison Kolesar

Text © 2010, 2023 by Barbara Pleasant

Storey books are available at special discounts when purchased in bulk for premiums and sales promotions
as well as for fund-raising or educational use. Special editions or book excerpts can also be created to specifi-
cation. For details, please call 800-827-8673, or send an email to sales@storey.com.

Storey Publishing
210 MASS MoCA Way
North Adams, MA 01247
storey.com

Printed in China through World Print
10 9 8 7 6 5 4 3 2 1

Library of Congress Cataloging-in-Publication Data on file

*To Madison,
and a new generation
of gardeners*

CONTENTS

PART 2:
ESSENTIAL TECHNIQUES AND MORE PLANTING PLANS

CHAPTER 5
DECIDING WHAT TO GROW 100

CHAPTER 6
DESIGNING BEAUTIFUL FOOD GARDENS 104

CHAPTER 7
WORKING WITH SEEDS AND SEEDLINGS 108

CHAPTER 8
SUPPORTING YOUR PLANTS 130

PART 3:
PICK-OF-THE-CROP VEGGIE VARIETIES

TOP VARIETIES FOR YOUR GARDEN, CROP BY CROP 196

GARDENER'S BASIC LINGO 222

WHICH PLANTING PLANS ARE RIGHT FOR YOU? 225

SOURCES FOR SEEDS AND PLANTS 226

METRIC CONVERSIONS 226

INDEX 227

DIGGING IN

Planting a garden is hope in action. As you tuck in seedlings or pat seeds into soft soil, you hope they will grow. But maybe you also feel a little anxious because, truth be told, you're just learning to tell a radish from a rutabaga. Relax. You *can* grow a successful organic food garden right now, this season. This book will get you started with simple, delectable garden plans and the instructions to see them through to a bountiful harvest. Next season, when you're ready for a little more challenge, you can graduate to specialized planting plans to expand your cultivated space, grow a pet crop like gourmet potatoes, or add more herbs and flowers for a garden that's as beautiful as it is practical.

Tending your garden will be more pleasure than struggle. Granted, there will be some bending and lifting involved, but you wanted a hobby that you could enjoy outdoors, moving around, right? The work won't be terribly hard. While I cannot guarantee that every crop in your garden will succeed any more than I can promise you a summer without hail, I can say this with certainty: Growing at least some of your own food will change your life for the better.

DIG THIS!

Food gardens can be as pretty as they are productive. Including colorful flowers looks great and attracts butterflies and bees as well as scores of pest-eating beneficial insects such as lady beetles.

HOW TO USE THIS BOOK

This book is intended to be of enduring value to three groups: new gardeners ready to jump into food gardening with both feet, experienced gardeners who are coaching new gardeners, and seasoned greenies who can grow prize-winning roses or peonies but are stumped on the fine points of growing a gourmet salad garden. In pursuit of this goal, the book is divided into three parts.

Part 1:
Developing Your Garden Plan

New gardeners are often told to start small, but how exactly is that done? The first section of this book takes the confusion out of this process by showing planting plans for three different Growing Gardens, each of which starts very small and simple and gradually expands to approximately double its initial size over a three-year period. Check out all three Growing Gardens if you're having trouble visualizing how a robust food garden can fit in your yard. Each uses a different soil-building strategy to transform underutilized space into a fertile new garden.

The Easy-Care Bag Garden (page 16) is sized for one or two people to plant and maintain, and it starts out with a no-dig approach: bags of potting soil arranged on top of lawn grass or untilled earth. At maturity, it supports two dozen delicious food plants.

A Bountiful Border (page 42) uses design principles borrowed from formal flower borders, with emphasis on building superior soil through deep digging. These balanced planting plans are ideal for gardeners who prefer the order that comes with formal style.

The Front-Yard Food Supply (page 64) transforms a small front yard into a beautiful tapestry of colorful beans, tomatoes, and chard. Eye appeal is built in from the first season, and soil quality improves as the beds receive regular helpings of compost and mulch. As the garden evolves, there are plenty of opportunities to add personal touches with handmade trellises and artful accessories.

For Growing Garden graduates and other experienced gardeners who simply want to enjoy plenty of great garden food, Part 1 also includes plans for three different **Family Food Gardens** (page 89). Designed for short-, moderate-, and long-summer climates, these plans make the most of regional crops with proven track records for delivering great results.

Part 2:
Essential Techniques and More Planting Plans

Every passing gardening season teaches me new things, so learning to be a better gardener is not the exclusive turf of beginners. That's the double-duty goal of Part 2: to help new gardeners learn basic skills, from planting seeds to harvesting crops at the best time, while providing interesting twists (and valuable pointers) for food gardeners who need a quick refresher course. Even folks who have hoed 10 seasons of beans might pick up a tip or two reading over the seed-starting instructions for vivid Paintbrush Beds (page 126). The Beneficial Border (page 168) may give experienced growers new insights into the world of bugs.

As you get to know your climate, site, and soil, you'll encounter certain challenges, be they drought, disease, or stubbornly infertile soil. Reacting to problems gets old fast, so instead this section invites you to build your gardening skills, which will improve your ability to prevent many problems—and manage them better when they do occur. Explore the practical possibilities here, whether you're installing your first soaker hose in the Marinara Medley garden (page 142) or piling on mulch in the Managed Mulch garden (page 150).

Part 3:
Pick-of-the-Crop Veggie Varieties

Choosing strong varieties is vital to growing a healthy garden. Can you simply buy packets of seeds off the rack at the store? (Yes.) Or should you order seeds from a specialty seed company? (Yes, there, too.) But whether you're stocking up on cheap seeds, ordering gourmet or historical strains, or looking for a variety to address a specific problem, be sure to check out Part 3. In these pages, I review the best old and new varieties for your garden. Read before you buy, and you'll be several steps closer to finding the perfect varieties for your garden.

Extra Help

When you're just getting started, sometimes you can feel a bit confused about precisely what gardening terms like "cover crop," "hardening off," and "intercropping" mean. Don't let the lingo discourage you! If you encounter unfamiliar words or phrases in the instructions for planting a garden, turn to Gardener's Basic Lingo starting on page 222 to learn what's what.

Finally, this is meant to be an idea book, so Which Planting Plans Are Right for You? on page 225 should not be missed. There you'll find lists of the garden plans in this book keyed to your wants, needs, and whims. If food gardening doesn't feel like fun, these lists may lead you to think in new directions as you look at all the uncharted territory you have yet to explore. In gardening as in life, there is always something new to learn.

DEVELOPING YOUR GARDEN PLAN

Pay attention to what you're doing, and don't get in over your head. This is the best way to learn anything new, whether you're learning to bake bread, set up a new computer, or grow your own great-tasting food. New gardeners are often told to start small and let their space grow with their experience, but that really doesn't give you much to go on. Which crops should you try first? When and how should you plant them?

STARTING SMALL AND GROWING YEAR BY YEAR

One worry-free way to start your first vegetable garden is to follow a "recipe" provided by an experienced gardener, and that's just what this section of the book provides: ingredient lists, step-by-step instructions, and illustrated planting plans that show you exactly what to plant where. These gardens are practically foolproof!

To make the process of establishing a vegetable garden even more manageable, I've created plans and instructions for three different Growing Gardens. Each one "grows" in size and scope over a three-year period—and I've provided all the details of what you need to do in year one, year two, and year three to achieve great results. The year one plan for each garden is small and simple. In year two and year three, you'll add more beds and crops until you have a garden that's double or even triple in size from when you started.

Each garden is different in style and uses a different soil-preparation technique—you can choose the one that appeals most to you. With any of these gardens, you have the choice of staying small or gradually expanding to something bigger as you gain experience over time. For example, you may decide that the year two layout of a particular garden is as large as you need and stop there. And if you feel ambitious, it's fine to skip right over the first year plan for any of these gardens and start with the year two or year three version instead.

SHOULD YOU BUILD RAISED BEDS?

You've probably heard that building raised beds is a good idea, both to make gardening easier and to improve the appearance of your garden. If you want raised beds, wait until the soil has been improved for three years to add wood, plastic, brick, or stone framing. It's easier to dig deep when you're not straddling framing materials, and deep soil improvement is a major mission in any garden's early years. When you're happy with the looks and feel of your soil 12 inches deep, you can start creating permanent raised beds. Keep in mind that deep beds and raised beds aren't the same thing. Deep beds are improved to 16 inches or more below the surface. They are more drought resistant by nature compared to raised beds, which stick up above the ground. The ideal situation in many cases is to have slightly raised beds (about 6 inches) atop deep beds, with permanent pathways between the beds. When you get your garden to this point (allow a few years), you can grow just about anything.

The Growing Gardens at a Glance

The Easy-Care Bag Garden (page 16). Starting in year one with bags of planting mix arranged on top of the ground, your Easy-Care Bag Garden will grow into a garden brimming with more than 20 vegetables and culinary herbs by year three. It's the perfect size for one person to manage.

A Bountiful Border (page 42). This beautiful and highly productive garden benefits from double-digging, a soil-improvement method. Over three years, new beds are added to form a lush border where bright annual flowers mingle with sun-ripened tomatoes and gourmet greens.

The Front-Yard Food Supply (page 64). Is it fitting to grow a food garden in your front yard? Of course! This garden gradually transforms a typical front yard into a feast for the eyes and the palate. You and your neighbors will love it.

Big, Bold Plans

For gardeners who want to jump into food gardening fast, I've also created ready-to-use regional garden plans that I call **Family Food Gardens**. These gardens will provide a season-long supply of food for four people, and the planting plans are tailored to short-, moderate-, and long-summer climates.

SIZING UP YOUR SITE AND SOIL

The sun is the main power supply for all garden plants, and most vegetables need all the sun they can get. Areas that receive less than six hours of sun are better used for shade-tolerant flowers than for edible plants; spots that receive six to eight hours of sun will do for lettuce and bush beans—two veggies with some tolerance of shade. Ten hours or more of sun is needed to bring out the best flavor and nutrition in tomatoes and many other crops and to keep them growing on schedule.

Bulldozers often do bad things to good sites when houses are built, so chances are good that the soil in your yard is only feebly fit for vegetable gardening. Don't worry! Every garden has to start somewhere, and any soil can be transformed in just a few years by adding organic matter (decomposed plant material) at every opportunity.

Organic matter is sold under many different names: compost, composted manure, humus, planting mix, or soil conditioner. (See What's Inside the Bag? on page 23 for tips on buying organic soil amendments.) Regular additions of organic matter improve the soil's texture and its ability to hold on to essential nutrients until they are needed by plants.

A Tip on Soil Testing

Unless you have reason to believe that your soil may be contaminated with lead or other pollutants, you don't need to have your soil tested before you start a new garden. Instead, begin doing everything you can to boost the organic matter content of your soil, digging in compost between plantings and mulching between plants with biodegradable materials. If you do want to have a soil test done, you can usually arrange one for about $20 through your state-sponsored soil testing lab. Contact your local Cooperative Extension office to request a mail-in soil testing kit.

Learning Step by Step

Wherever you start, following the garden plans provided here will help you learn food gardening basics while allowing time for your soil to improve. Each garden starts out simple and includes detailed step-by-step directions for beginners. As you look over the plans and the accompanying instructions, remember to consult the Gardener's Basic Lingo section starting on page 222 if you come across any terms you don't understand. Learning the lingo is one of the key steps in garden success.

By year three the planting plans become more complex as the gardens develop. Remember that you can refer back to the instructions for the first- and second-year versions of the garden if you've forgotten the details of techniques such as planting parsley seeds or onion seedlings. Pay attention and don't get in over your head. Expand your space as your soil improves and you gain experience. It's the no-fail way to start an organic food garden.

CHAPTER ONE

THE EASY-CARE BAG GARDEN

Designed to bring good things to eat to a city backyard or an oversize suburban lawn, this easy-to-install garden requires no prior experience. You can set up the first-year rendition in a single weekend, and even after you expand the garden in year two and year three, it remains a doable project for a gardener working alone who also has a full-time job or takes care of young children. This garden is big enough to keep you in fresh food all summer but not so big that it will take over your life.

YEAR ONE
PAGE 21

YEAR TWO
PAGE 28

YEAR THREE
PAGE 35

Bag gardening couldn't be easier. You simply set out purchased bags of topsoil, cut open the bags, and plant seeds and seedlings right in the topsoil. The Easy-Care Bag Garden is a one-person garden, and in year one, it will take one person only a few hours each week to keep up with watering, weeding, planting, and picking.

By the second year, the garden is fully functional as a food garden for a single person, with 15 vegetables and 5 herbs producing steadily from early summer to late fall. If you want more vegetables, you can expand the garden when you're ready. You're in charge, because this is intended to remain a one-person garden.

As the garden grows, you'll see how well your site and soil support popular garden plants like tomatoes and snap beans. You will also learn the preferred growing season for broccoli and its close cabbage-family relatives, which tend to prefer fall over spring in most (but not all!) climates. You will discover whether harvesting and eating garden-fresh potatoes and rutabagas rates as superspecial or just so-so in your book, and your experiences will help you customize your crop list for seasons to come.

When you're ready for new adventures, experiment by fitting planting plans from Part 2 such as Strictly from Seed (page 118) and the Good-for-You Garden (page 183) into the footprint of your Easy-Care Bag Garden. Browse the variety descriptions in Part 3 as well, and choose a few to try. This will make your garden more interesting with every passing season.

Scarlet runner beans and snap peas anchor the edge of the bag garden in its first year.

YEAR-BY-YEAR OVERVIEW

YEAR ONE

Large bags of planting mix define space for three permanent beds. Bags laid end to end create a narrow bed just right for a trellis. In the other beds, the bags create beds 3 feet wide (a good width for stepping over). The 2-foot-wide pathways between beds are easy to maintain with a mower.

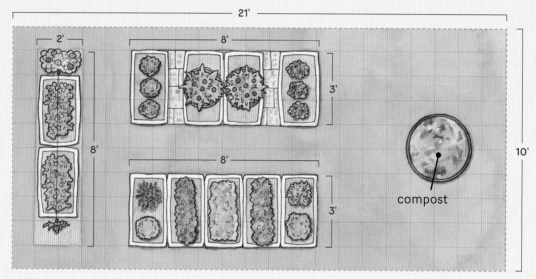

ONE SQUARE = 1 FOOT

YIELD

SPRING CROPS
- **lettuce:** 2–3 lbs.
- **snap peas:** 3–4 lbs.

SUMMER CROPS
- **bush snap beans:** 4 lbs.
- **tomatoes:** 16–20 lbs.

FALL CROPS
- **arugula and bok choy:** 3 lbs. each
- **kale:** 4 lbs.
- **spinach:** 1 lb.

HERBS
- **basil and parsley:** about 12 bunches each
- **oregano, rosemary, sage, and thyme:** a year's supply

The circular bed is a natural focal point, so have fun with it! Eventually, you might decide to use it as a permanent home for your collection of kitchen herbs or put up a trellis for heavy-bearing pole beans.

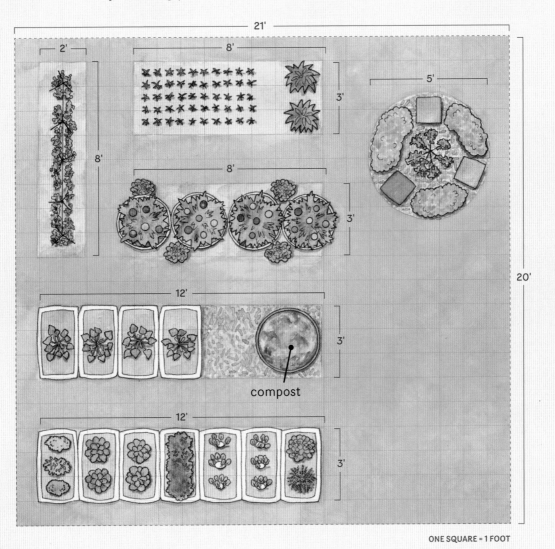

compost

ONE SQUARE = 1 FOOT

YIELD

SPRING CROPS
- lettuce: 7 lbs.
- snap or snow peas: 3 lbs.
- kale: 5 lbs.
- kohlrabi: 6 bulbs
- potatoes: 4 lbs.
- onions: about 50

SUMMER CROPS
- pole snap beans: 20 lbs.
- bush snap beans: 15 lbs.
- tomatoes: 30–40 lbs.
- peppers: 5–6 lbs.
- summer squash: 20 lbs.

FALL CROPS
- arugula: 6 lbs.
- salad greens: 10 lbs.
- carrots: 12 lbs.
- Chinese cabbage: 12 lbs.
- rutabagas: 5 roots
- garlic: 20 bulbs (harvested the following season)

HERBS
- basil: about 25 bunches
- oregano, rosemary, sage, and thyme: a year's supply

YEAR THREE

The garden triples in size over three years, from 64 to 168 square feet of bed space. But even at its maximum, this garden remains a manageable project for a food-minded gardener working alone.

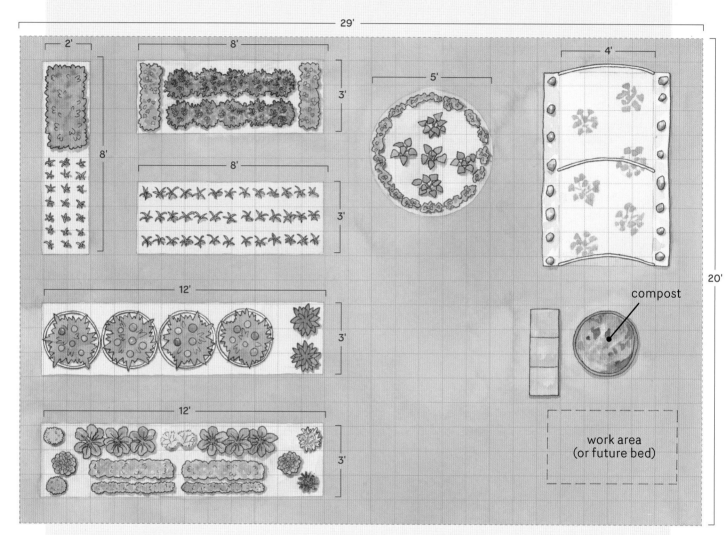

ONE SQUARE = 1 FOOT

YIELD

SPRING CROPS
- **lettuce:** 3–4 lbs.
- **snap or snow peas:** 3–4 lbs.
- **potatoes:** 20 lbs.
- **onions:** about 25
- **beets:** 8 lbs.
- **chard:** 12 lbs.

SUMMER CROPS
- **bush snap beans:** 16 lbs.
- **tomatoes:** 30–40 lbs.
- **peppers:** 4–6 lbs.
- **squash:** 35 lbs.

FALL CROPS
- **salad greens:** 7 lbs.
- **broccoli:** 6 lbs.
- **mizuna, red mustard, or mixed Asian greens:** 20 lbs.
- **carrots:** 4 lbs.
- **turnips:** 10 lbs.
- **garlic:** about 45 bulbs (harvested the following season)

HERBS
- **basil:** about 50 bunches
- **cilantro:** about 10 bunches
- **dill, oregano, rosemary, sage, and thyme:** a year's supply

YEAR ONE
GARDEN PLAN

Turning a patch of sun-drenched lawn into an edible garden may be one of the best things you will ever do in your life, and here we begin in the easiest way imaginable—by arranging bags of topsoil over the new garden site and planting right into them.

Growing vegetables in bags of topsoil is almost too easy to believe, but it really works! Many new gardeners who have tried it have been so amazed with the results that they use the bag method over and over. Whether you use bags for one season or three, gardening in bags offers several benefits to first-time gardeners.

- No need to dig up and remove the grass. In the course of a season, the bags will smother the grass beneath them. This can be a huge savings in time and labor!

- No aggravation from seedling-killing cutworms, which are actually caterpillars commonly found in soil where lawn grass is growing. The bags serve as barriers to keep them out.

- Few (if any) weeds, because bagged soils and planting mixes are steam-sterilized to kill weed seeds.

- In late fall, you can gather up the fragile bags and dig the contents into your new permanent beds.

TELL ME MORE!
COMPOST IN YOUR GARDEN

Every garden needs a place to make compost from vegetable trimmings, weeds, and pulled plants. If you place your compost in a spot where you're planning to add a new bed in the future, earthworms and other compost creatures will kick-start the soil-improvement process. Enclosed composters made from recycled plastic work like garden garbage cans by keeping rotting debris out of sight. Most models are animal resistant, making them a great choice for urban or suburban yards. You can also compost in a small pen made from garden fencing attached to stakes. Both types of compost enclosures are easy to move from one spot to another as your garden expands.

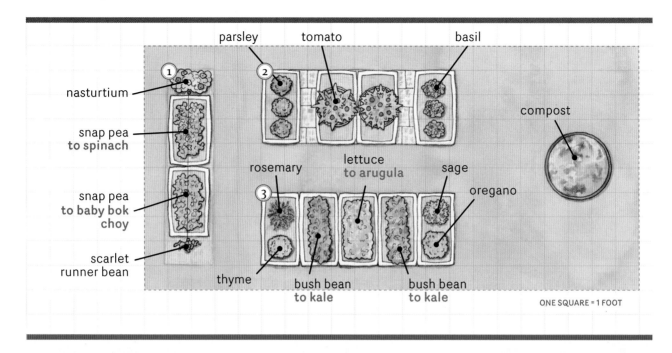

ONE SQUARE = 1 FOOT

NAME
The Easy-Care Bag Garden: Year One

FOOTPRINT
8 × 19 feet

SKILL LEVEL
Fine for first-timers

WHEN TO PLANT

Midspring: snap peas, lettuce, and parsley

Late spring: basil, tomatoes, bush snap beans, rosemary, thyme, oregano, sage, nasturtiums, and scarlet runner beans

Late summer: kale, spinach, arugula, and baby bok choy

THE PLANTS

BED ①

O Baby bok choy, 1 packet seeds
O Nasturtium, 1 packet seeds
O Scarlet runner bean, 1 packet seeds
O Snap pea, 1 packet seeds
O Spinach, 1 packet seeds

BED ②

O Basil, 1 packet seeds or 3 seedlings
O Parsley, 1 packet seeds or 3 seedlings
O Tomato, 2 seedlings

BED ③

O Arugula, 1 packet seeds
O Kale, 1 packet seeds
O Mixed lettuce, 2 packets seeds
O Oregano, 1 plant
O Rosemary, 1 plant
O Sage, 1 plant
O Snap bean (bush variety), 1 packet seeds
O Thyme, 1 plant

THE STUFF

FOR THE BEDS

- Eleven 40-pound bags of organic topsoil or tree and shrub planting mix
- Cardboard or newspaper to smother grass between bags
- One 2-pound box of organic vegetable garden fertilizer
- Stone or small board
- Organic mulch such as shredded leaves (see Chapter 10)

FOR THE PEA TRELLIS

- Two 6-foot-long wood or metal posts
- Cotton string, jute or hemp twine, or polyester garden netting

FOR THE TOMATOES

- Two 5-foot-tall tomato cages

FOR THE COMPOST AREA

- One stationary composter, or a pen made from plastic fencing attached to stakes

TOOLS

- Wheelbarrow, cart, or wagon for moving bags of soil
- Spade or shovel
- Digging fork
- Sledgehammer or hammer
- Utility knife
- Hand trowel
- Long-bladed knife or screwdriver
- Scissors or pruning shears

WHAT'S INSIDE THE BAG?

Most garden centers sell a dizzying array of bagged soil mixes and soil amendments, so choosing one can be confusing! To make the problem worse, there are no strict standards for what qualifies as "compost" or "shrub planting mix." The best way to know what you're getting is to look beyond the label and examine what's inside the bag. Many garden centers set aside broken bags so customers can examine the contents, or you can buy a few sample bags and bring them home.

★ For most soil-building purposes, a mixture that looks and feels fluffy, with plenty of tidbits of decomposed leaves or wood chips, offers more organic matter than a heavier mixture that includes mostly gritty soil. Light-textured composts are usually the best choice for digging into soil as a long-lasting source of organic matter.

★ For the fast bag beds in this garden, though, look for products that do include some gritty soil, because plant roots prefer a mixture of soil and organic matter to organic matter alone. A bag of such soil will feel heavier than one that's mostly organic matter (assuming that both are equally wet or dry). Ordinary bagged topsoil or inexpensive tree and shrub planting mix will do quite nicely for the first two years of the Easy-Care Bag Garden—or for any spot where you want to set up a new veggie bed fast.

★ A final sticking point: Soil amendments may be sold by weight or by volume. Throughout this book I have listed weights. A 40-pound bag is the large size typically sold at garden centers and home stores, while 20-pound bags are the smaller ones.

YEAR ONE
PLANTING AND CARE

EARLY SPRING

After bags are set in place, use a utility knife to prepare them for planting.

A 2-inch rim of plastic on the surface of each bag prevents soil spillage and helps retain moisture.

1 **Prepare your site.** Select a site and arrange the bags as shown in the garden plan on page 22. Before positioning the bags in Bed 2, cover the ground between the tomato and herb bags with four to six sheets of damp newspaper or a single thickness of well-dampened cardboard to deter weeds. The bags will hold the covering in place. Set up your composter or assemble your composting enclosure.

2 **Do a little digging.** Use the spade or shovel and digging fork to remove grass and weeds from the ends of Bed 1; toss all plant debris in the compost. The same tools work well for breaking up the stripped soil, loosening it at least 8 inches deep. Mix two handfuls of organic fertilizer into each end of the bed.

3 **Prepare the bags for planting.** Install the posts for the pea trellis in Bed 1 by pounding them into the ground at the ends of the bags (see How to Pound a Post on page 132). Use the utility knife to cut out a large rectangular window on the upper surface of each bag, leaving the sides and 2 inches of each top edge intact, like a picture frame. Lightly dust the surface of the soil inside the bags with organic fertilizer and mix in with a trowel. (Skip this if the bag's label says that fertilizer has been added.) Stab each bag about a dozen times with a knife or screwdriver to pierce drainage holes in the bottom. Plant roots will also use these holes to grow down into the soil below the bags.

4 **Weave the trellis.** Install the trellis netting or string between the posts. If using string, start by tying a horizontal line between the posts, no more than 6 inches above the soil's surface. Then tie more horizontal lines at least 6 inches apart (so there's room to reach through the trellis when harvesting) until the top string is 4 feet from the ground. Create a trellis grid by weaving more string vertically in and out through the horizontal strings.

TRELLIS REINFORCEMENTS

A single slender stick or bamboo rod lashed to the tops of the two end posts of a trellis adds substantial stability, which makes it easier to weave the net of strings. Another option is to use sticks in place of string for some of the trellis' vertical lines. After you tie off the horizontal strings, weave slender sticks or bamboo rods between the strings. Push the ends of the sticks a few inches into the ground. Then go back and lash the horizontal strings to your vertical sticks.

MIDSPRING

5 Sow peas. One month before your last spring frost date, plant pea seeds in the soil in the bags, sowing one row on either side of the trellis. Poke seeds into the soil 1 inch deep and 2 to 3 inches apart.

Left: With the string trellis in place, you will know exactly where to plant your snap peas.

Right: After poking pea seeds into the soil, pat the surface with the palm of your hand to fill in the holes.

6 Sow parsley. In Bed 2, cut away the upper surface on three sides of the bag to be planted with parsley, leaving the plastic attached along one short edge. Apply fertilizer and make drainage holes as you did in Step 3. Plant about 25 parsley seeds ¼ inch deep and ½ inch apart (fewer than half will germinate). Pat lightly to firm the soil over the seeds, then spritz with a light spray of water until thoroughly moist. Fold out the plastic flap over the seeded area, and hold it in place with a stone or small board. The plastic flap will help keep the soil moist until the parsley seeds germinate, which usually takes one to

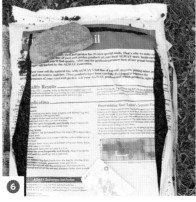

Left: Planting parsley seeds in rows makes it easier to track their germination.

Right: A flap of plastic helps keep the soil moist for slow-sprouting parsley seeds.

two weeks. After a week or so, check daily to see whether parsley has sprouted. As soon as seeds germinate, you'll need to lift and cut away the plastic flap. (If you buy seedlings, see Step 8.)

7 **Sow lettuce.** In Bed 3, prepare the center bag (lettuce) as in Step 3. Lettuce seeds sprout faster than parsley, so they don't need to be covered with a plastic flap. After applying fertilizer and making drainage holes, scatter the lettuce seeds over the soil's surface so that they are about 1 inch apart. Pat them into place with your hand, barely covering them with soil. Keep the soil moist until the seeds germinate. Two to three weeks later, fill any gaps in the planting with small pinches of seeds.

8 **Plant herbs.** As soon as they're available at garden centers, buy rosemary, thyme, sage, and oregano plants for Bed 3. Prepare the end bags in the bed as in Step 3. Keep the plants watered until you're ready to set them out. Plant them at even spacing, with each plant about 10 inches in from the edge of the bag. Position each herb in its planting hole so that the base of the main stem is no deeper than it grew in the container. After filling in the hole, water well and use scissors or pruning shears to snip off any broken branches. (*Note:* If you purchased parsley plants for Bed 2, plant them now, too.)

LATE SPRING

9 **Sow beans and more.** After the last frost date passes, cut away the tops of the remaining bags, sprinkle on fertilizer, and make drainage holes. In Bed 3, poke 10 to 15 bush bean seeds into each of the two bags, 1 inch deep and 6 inches apart. In Bed 2, sow pinches of basil seeds ½ inch deep and 10 inches apart or plant the basil seedlings. In Bed 1, plant five or so nasturtium seeds 1 inch deep and 2 inches apart at one end of the trellis; plant five scarlet runner bean seeds 1 inch deep and 2 inches apart at the other end.

10 **Plant tomatoes.** Water tomato seedlings, and try to handle them by the roots rather than the stem as you transplant them into Bed 2. Set the plants deep, as shown on the facing page. Water well. Install tomato cages soon after you set out the plants (see How to Cage a Tomato on page 132).

THROUGHOUT SUMMER

11 **Water when needed.** Since plastic helps retain moisture, your bag garden may not need as much watering as plants growing in the ground would. But even so, be sure to water your plants during periods of warm, dry weather. See Chapter 9 to learn about wise watering practices.

IS THERE A PERFECT TOMATO?

Probably not. Cherry, plum, and saladette tomatoes are generally easier to grow than large-fruited beefsteaks. Hybrids are generally more dependable and fast-maturing than heirloom varieties, though there are exceptions to every rule. Tomato varieties are discussed in detail on page 220, but keep in mind that you are always wise to diversify. Even if you're growing only two plants, choose two different varieties to keep things interesting in your garden and on your table.

To transplant a tomato seedling: (A) Gently slip it from its container without squeezing the main stem. (B) Use scissors or clippers to snip off the lowest leaves. (C, D) Place the plant at an angle so the bottom part of the stem is buried. Supplemental roots will grow from the buried section of stem, helping the plant grow faster and produce bigger, better crops.

12 **Enjoy the harvest often.** Visit your garden at least every other day to harvest what's ready for your table. Be sure to gather peas every other day, because they quickly go from perfect to starchy. See Chapter 14 for more tips on harvesting your vegetables and herbs at their peak.

LATE SUMMER

13 **Sow fall crops.** Pull up and compost tattered peas, bush beans, and lettuce. Scatter a dusting of organic fertilizer over the soil's surface, and lightly mix it in with a hand trowel. Sow bok choy and spinach in Bed 1 and kale and arugula in Bed 3. Plant the seeds ¼ inch deep and 3 to 4 inches apart, in rows at least 8 inches apart. Keep the soil moist until the seeds germinate.

FALL

14 **Start garden cleanup.** A heavy frost will end the season for the runner beans, tomatoes, basil, and nasturtiums, but cold nights actually improve the flavor of leafy greens. As exposure to cold damages more and more crops, pull up old plant debris and throw it into the compost. Once a bag is vacant, gather up the plastic and dispose of it in the garbage, leaving the topsoil or planting mix in place. Don't try to remove bags where perennial herbs are growing, though! Leave them in place through winter.

EARLY WINTER

15 **Put the garden to bed.** As time and weather permit, dig the topsoil into the beds, cultivating the soil at least 12 inches deep. Then mulch over the beds with any organic mulch you can get your hands on, from shredded leaves to dry grass clippings. Spread the mulch 3 to 4 inches deep; leave it in place until the soil begins to warm in spring.

Plant roots have no trouble growing through drainage holes into the soil below.

YEAR TWO
GARDEN PLAN

Picking up where you left off last fall, your Easy-Care Bag Garden will double in size as you set up more bags and turn the compost area into a circular planting bed for peas and salad greens. Expect a faster pace, because you will have twice as many veggies to tend, including peppers and superproductive summer squash.

Learning to grow new crops is part of what makes gardening fun. This growing season, you'll be introduced to the cabbage family—an incredibly diverse clan of related cool-season crops. You'll start with the easiest to grow of all the cabbage-family cousins, kale and kohlrabi. Planting and tending them will be excellent preparation for future crops of more challenging broccoli or cauliflower.

There are also secrets afoot belowground in this garden, where soil that has benefited from a full year of improvement is used to support bulb onions—your first root crop. Like other root crops, onions require the improved drainage and fertility of organically enriched soil, and they need more root space than is available in bags. Long-bearing pole beans and tomatoes benefit from the bag-to-bed transition, too. With the bigger and better root space available to them in an actual bed, expect your tomatoes to grow stronger and produce longer than they did in your first-year garden.

This year's garden plan is intended to make the most of the growing season by keeping every bed busy until late fall, putting fresh food on your table for five months or more. All of the 22 veggies and herbs are easy to grow, and you can keep on top of routine watering, weeding, and other tasks by working in your garden for an hour or so three times a week.

THE STUFF

FOR THE BEDS
- Eleven 40-pound bags of topsoil or tree and shrub planting mix
- One 5- to 7-pound package of organic vegetable garden fertilizer
- One bale of straw

FOR THE BEAN AND PEA TRELLISES
- Twenty-four 8-foot-long bamboo poles or 1 × 2 pieces of lumber
- Cotton string or jute or hemp twine
- Three 18- to 24-inch-diameter stone or concrete stepping-stones

FOR THE TOMATOES
- Four 5-foot-tall tomato cages

FOR THE COMPOST AREA
- One stationary composter, or a pen made from plastic fencing attached to stakes

TOOLS
- Wheelbarrow, cart, or wagon for moving bags of soil
- Utility knife
- Long-bladed knife or screwdriver
- Hand trowel
- Spade, shovel, or digging fork
- Soil rake
- Clean, sharp knife (for cutting potatoes)

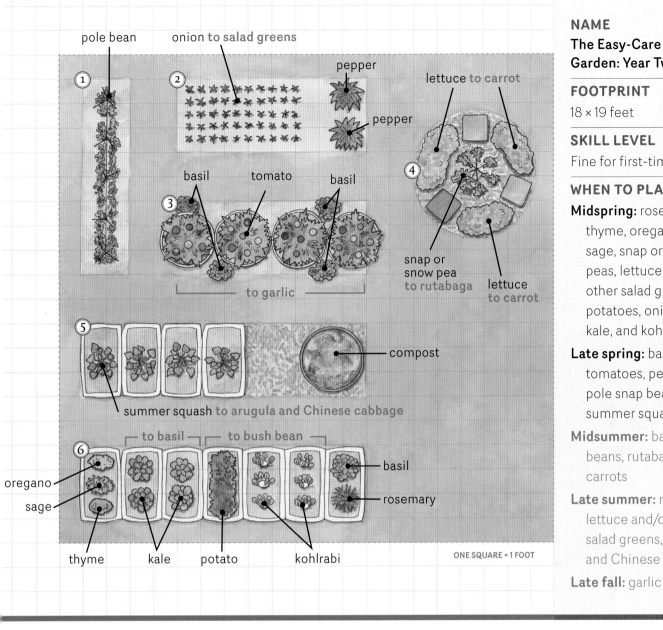

pole bean

onion **to salad greens**

pepper

pepper

lettuce **to carrot**

basil

tomato

basil

④

snap or
snow pea
to rutabaga

lettuce
to carrot

③

to garlic

⑤

compost

summer squash **to arugula and Chinese cabbage**

to basil

to bush bean

⑥

basil

oregano

rosemary

sage

thyme

kale

potato

kohlrabi

ONE SQUARE = 1 FOOT

NAME
The Easy-Care Bag Garden: Year Two

FOOTPRINT
18 × 19 feet

SKILL LEVEL
Fine for first-timers

WHEN TO PLANT
Midspring: rosemary, thyme, oregano, sage, snap or snow peas, lettuce and/or other salad greens, potatoes, onions, kale, and kohlrabi

Late spring: basil, tomatoes, peppers, pole snap beans, and summer squash

Midsummer: basil, bush beans, rutabagas, and carrots

Late summer: more lettuce and/or other salad greens, arugula, and Chinese cabbage

Late fall: garlic

THE PLANTS

BED ①
- Snap bean (pole variety), 1 packet seeds

BED ②
- Lettuce and/or other salad greens, 2 packets seeds
- Onion, 50 seedlings or ½ pound sets
- Pepper, 2 seedlings

BED ③
- Basil, 1 packet seeds or 4 seedlings

- Seed garlic, ½ pound or about 3 bulbs
- Tomato, 4 seedlings

BED ④
- Carrot, 1 packet seeds
- Lettuce and/or other salad greens, 1 packet seeds
- Rutabaga, 1 packet seeds
- Snap or snow pea, 1 packet seeds

BED ⑤
- Arugula, 1 packet seeds
- Chinese cabbage, 1 packet seeds

- Summer squash, 2 packets seeds or 4 seedlings

BED ⑥
- Basil, 1 packet seeds and 1 seedling
- Kale, 4 seedlings
- Kohlrabi, 6 seedlings
- Oregano, 1 plant
- Red potatoes, 3 small (from grocery store)
- Rosemary, 1 plant
- Sage, 1 plant
- Snap bean (bush variety), 1 packet seeds
- Thyme, 1 plant

YEAR TWO
PLANTING AND CARE

MIDSPRING

① Set up new beds. About four weeks before your last frost, mark spaces for Beds 5 and 6 and arrange bags on the ground as shown in the garden plan on page 29. Cut, fertilize, and perforate the bags as described in Step 3 on page 24.

② Transplant herbs. Dig up thyme and other perennial herbs that survived winter and move them to their new planting spots in Bed 6. Try to keep the soil intact around the plants' roots as you work, and water them thoroughly when you're finished with the job. Set out new herb plants as needed (if some from last year's garden died during winter). Then go back and remove the plastic from Bed 3 and work the bag's contents into the soil beneath.

③ Prepare established beds. Apply a light dusting of organic fertilizer to Beds 1, 2, and 3. Use a spade, shovel, or digging fork to mix in the fertilizer along with the weathered winter mulch. Rake to level the soil surface.

④ Move the composting area. Relocate the compost to its new spot. In the old composting area (now Bed 4), spread the decomposed material into a 5-foot-wide circle. Rake out undecomposed chunks and put them in the new compost pile; dig in the rest.

⑤ Build a tripod. In the middle of Bed 4, erect a 30-inch-diameter tripod using five bamboo or wood poles, bound together near the top with string. Push the bases of the poles 2 inches into the ground. Tie the string to a pole about 3 inches above soil level, weave it horizontally among the poles, and tie off the end. Tie and weave two more strings at 6-inch intervals. Plant pea seeds all around the tripod.

TIPS FOR SUCCESS

★ Onion sets (small dormant bulbs) are more likely to bolt (produce flowers and seeds) than pencil-size seedlings. If you must use sets, plant them later, just before your last frost date. Exposure to chilly weather often triggers bolting in any onion, whether they're grown from sets or seedlings.

★ Consider small-fruited peppers rather than big bells, which often set fruit poorly in hot weather. For example, banana-type peppers are famous for bearing heavy crops, and they come in both sweet and hot varieties (see page 214).

★ When planting carrots in hot weather, cover the seeded area with boards raised up on rocks or bricks a few inches above the soil to prevent sunlight from drying the germinating seeds. Be patient, because, like parsley, carrots need two weeks or more to complete the sprouting process.

6 **Plant salad greens.** Rake up the soil outside the tripod into three evenly spaced mounds about 10 inches tall. Install the stepping-stones between the mounds by setting them on firm soil. Then use the rake to flatten the top of each mound to prepare it for planting. Sow one of the mounds with lettuce, smooth-leafed spinach, or mixtures of salad greens called mesclun (see page 209).

7 **Plant potatoes, kohlrabi, and kale.** Cut the potatoes in half and let them dry in a warm, sunny place for a day or two before planting. Set them 2 inches deep at even intervals in the center bag in Bed 6. Set out kohlrabi seedlings about 8 inches apart and kale seedlings about 12 inches apart.

Kale seedlings spaced a foot apart

8 **Plant onions.** In Bed 2, plant onion seedlings or sets 2 inches deep and 6 inches apart in five parallel rows, so that the plants are 6 inches apart in all directions. Onion seedlings that are more than 6 inches tall will stay upright better if you first trim back the tops with scissors or pruning shears. While you plant, avoid walking on the soil where peppers will be planted later.

When transplanting onion seedlings, firm the soil with your hands to ensure good contact between roots and soil.

9 **Sow more salad.** Two weeks later, sow another mound in Bed 4 with lettuce, spinach, or mesclun. Then two weeks after that, sow the third mound.

Stepping-stones provide access to trellised peas and small plantings of lettuce.

10 Plant tomatoes and more. When the soil feels warm to your bare feet, set out tomato seedlings 2 feet apart, starting 1 foot away from the ends of Bed 3. Set out basil and pepper seedlings, and set out either four squash seeds or one squash seedling per bag. If you sow seeds, wait until the seedlings sprout and develop three leaves, then thin to one seedling per bag.

11 Distribute mulch. Use about half of the bale of straw to mulch the potatoes, spreading a layer 3 inches deep. Spread 2 inches of mulch beneath and between the kohlrabi and kale. Use more straw to mulch over the front edge of Bed 6, which will hide the bags from view.

12 Make a bean trellis. Starting at the center of Bed 1, arrange poles in five tripods, three poles each. Push the poles an inch or two into the ground as you set up the tripods, and loosely bind the top of each one with string. Lay a pole across the tops of two of the tripods, and lash the tripods to it with more string. Repeat with the remaining tripods. Poke bean seeds into the soil 1 inch deep and 4 inches apart along both sides of the trellis.

Pole beans quickly twine their way up a trellis made from bamboo poles.

MIDSUMMER

13 **Start the fall crops.** Pull up the peas and the last of the spring lettuce and other salad crops in Bed 4, and take down the trellis. Dig a moderate dusting of organic fertilizer into the soil before planting rutabaga seeds ¼ inch deep and 3 inches apart in the center of the bed. Rutabaga seeds sprout quickly. Watch for seedlings, and thin plants to 12 inches apart. Plant carrot seeds in the renovated mounds. To get good germination in hot weather, sow the tiny seeds thickly, and cover the seeded bed with an old blanket to keep the soil moist.

14 **Dig the potatoes.** In Bed 6, harvest potatoes when the viney stems begin to lose their green color and die back; pull kohlrabi when they are the size of tennis balls. Replace the potatoes and kohlrabi with bush beans (in short-season areas, choose a fast-maturing filet bean). Replace the kale with a second sowing of basil.

15 **Dig the onions.** When the leaves of your onion plants topple over, pull or dig the bulbs and cure the pulled bulbs in a warm, dry place for two weeks before trimming off the tops and roots. If any plants produced flowering stalks, eat those bulbs right away; they won't keep worth a flip.

LATE SUMMER

16 **Sow fall salad greens.** Once nighttime temperatures cool down, sow lettuce and other salad greens in place of the onions in Bed 2. At about this time, your summer squash plants in Bed 5 may slow down or stop producing, so pull and compost them. Replant two of the bags with arugula and the other two with Chinese cabbage.

LATE FALL

17 **Put the garden to bed.** Pull up tomatoes in Bed 3 after they are damaged or killed by frost. Replace them with garlic cloves, planted 6 inches apart and 4 inches deep with their pointed ends up. Mulch the planted area with at least 2 inches of grass clippings, weathered hay, or shredded leaves. By next summer, each clove will mature into a big, new bulb. Clean up and bed down the rest of the garden as you did last year (see page 27).

17

YEAR THREE
GARDEN PLAN

With more than 170 square feet of cultivated space, the Easy-Care Bag Garden in year three provides plenty of room to grow many of the vegetables you got to know from the past two years, plus colorful, weather-resilient chard, cheerful sunflowers, and easy-to-store winter squash.

Chard livens up the front of the garden with its dramatic presence, which may be rivaled when tall sunflowers burst into bloom in Bed 4 in midsummer. The new bed in this year's garden will play host to an exciting mix of summer squash and winter squash. Both types of squash belong to the same species, *Cucurbita pepo*, so they help pollinate one another. And for an insect-free start, you shield the young winter squash plants with a special structure called a row cover tunnel. Once the squash is well established, you'll move the tunnel to protect fall broccoli from the many insects that would like to eat it before you do. Expect to spend four to five enjoyable hours a week maintaining this garden, with more time needed during the late-summer harvest season.

TELL ME MORE!
SMOTHERED BY SQUASH

Instead of using bags to expand the garden this time around, vigorous squash plants take on the task of breaking in new space. Broad squash leaves shade the soil well, so any weeds that manage to sprout will be small and spindly. By the time the squash plants are in full production, you will wade into a jungle of foliage to gather your crop.

After you pull the spent squash plants and add them to the compost, you can decide whether to dig Bed 7 (to amend and improve the soil) or use the bag method the following spring. In fact, you can use bags in your garden any time you like—I've heard from people who like them so much that they plan never to stop using this easy method.

THE STUFF

FOR THE BEDS

- ○ Ten 25-pound bags of compost
- ○ One 5- to 7-pound package of organic vegetable garden fertilizer

FOR THE TOMATOES

- ○ Four 5-foot-tall tomato cages

FOR THE SQUASH

- ○ Three 7-foot pieces of 9-gauge wire for row cover support hoops
- ○ One 8×12-foot piece of lightweight row cover
- ○ Boards, bricks, or stones

FOR THE COMPOST AREA

- ○ One stationary composter, or a pen made from plastic fencing attached to stakes

TOOLS

- ○ Wheelbarrow, cart, or wagon for moving bags of compost
- ○ Spade or shovel
- ○ Digging fork
- ○ Soil rake
- ○ Clean, sharp knife (for cutting potatoes)

NAME

The Easy-Care Bag Garden: Year Three

FOOTPRINT

18 × 27 feet

SKILL LEVEL

Beyond beginner

WHEN TO PLANT

Midspring: potatoes, peas, beets, onions, chard, dill, cilantro, lettuce, rosemary, thyme, oregano, and sage

Late spring: basil, tomatoes, peppers, snap beans, sunflowers, more cilantro, and squash

Midsummer: broccoli

Late summer: more lettuce or other salad greens, turnips, Asian greens, carrots, and a mixed cover crop of bush snap beans and red mustard

Late fall: garlic

THE PLANTS

BED ①

- ○ Beet, 1 packet seeds
- ○ Mizuna, red mustard, or mixed Asian greens, 1 packet seeds
- ○ Onion, about 20 seedlings (½ bunch)

BED ②

- ○ Lettuce or other salad greens, 2 packets seeds
- ○ Seed potatoes, 5 small
- ○ Snap or snow pea (bush variety), 1 packet seeds
- ○ Turnip, 1 packet seeds

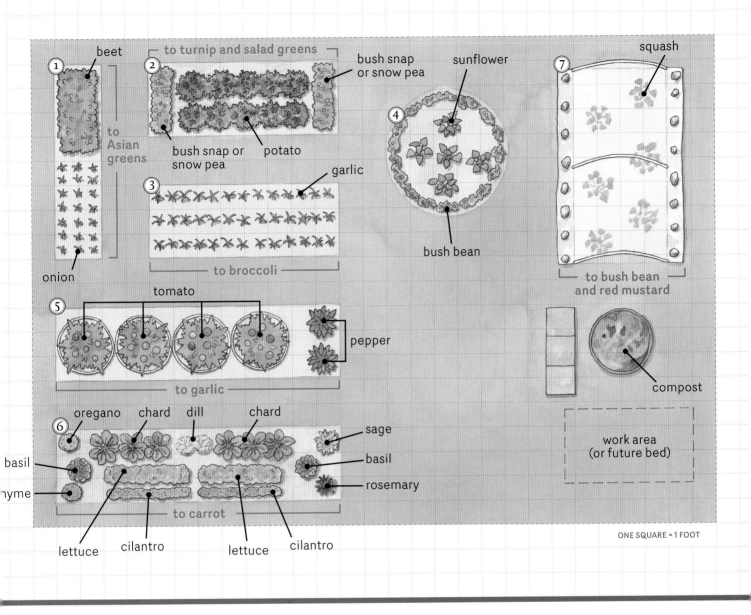

ONE SQUARE = 1 FOOT

BED ③
- ○ Broccoli, 1 packet seeds or 12 seedlings

BED ④
- ○ Snap bean (bush variety), 1 packet seeds
- ○ Sunflower, 1 packet seeds

BED ⑤
- ○ Pepper, 2 seedlings
- ○ Seed garlic, 1 pound or about 4 large bulbs
- ○ Tomato, 4 seedlings of assorted varieties

BED ⑥
- ○ Basil, 1 packet seeds or 2 seedlings
- ○ Carrot, 1 packet seeds
- ○ Cilantro, 1 packet seeds
- ○ Dill, 1 packet seeds
- ○ Mixed lettuce, 1 packet seeds
- ○ Oregano, 1 plant
- ○ Red or multicolored chard, 1 packet seeds or 6 seedlings
- ○ Rosemary, 1 plant
- ○ Sage, 1 plant
- ○ Thyme, 1 plant

BED ⑦
- ○ Red mustard, 1 packet seeds
- ○ Snap bean (bush variety), 1 packet seeds
- ○ Squash, 3 packets seeds or 6 seedlings in assorted types: summer squash (zucchini, yellow squash, pattypan), acorn squash, spaghetti squash, and sweet potato (delicata) squash

YEAR THREE
PLANTING AND CARE

LATE WINTER

1 **Prepare for a new season.** Gather up and dispose of any old plastic bags, and cover all cultivated beds with a 2-inch-deep blanket of compost. Relocate the compost area to its new spot. In the old composting area in Bed 5, spread the decomposed material down the bed. Move the stepping-stones from Bed 4 to the new composting area.

2 **Dig a new bed.** As weather permits, dig and turn the soil in the new bed (Bed 7), shaking out and composting chunks of grass or weeds. Then work in 4 inches of compost. If you prefer to work with more bags, you will need seven of them.

MIDSPRING

3 **Plant onions and beets.** About four weeks before your last frost, plant a matrix of onion seedlings 2 inches deep and 6 inches apart in Bed 1. Water well to settle the soil around the roots. Sow beet seeds in three parallel rows spaced 6 inches apart, planting the seeds ½ inch deep and 2 inches apart. Beets sometimes germinate erratically, so plan to go back two weeks later to both thin the seedlings (which emerge in pairs or clumps, see page 128) and to plant more seeds if there are any gaps in the rows.

4 **Plant potatoes and peas.** Cut the potatoes in half and let them dry in a warm, sunny place for a day or two before planting. Set them 2 inches deep and 12 inches apart in Bed 2, flanked by double rows (two rows spaced 6 inches apart) of bush snap or snow peas. These short, bushy varieties don't need a trellis when grown close together, but a few twiggy sticks stuck into the row between plants will help them stay upright when they become heavy with pods.

5 **Plant greens and herbs.** In Bed 6, plant lettuce, dill, cilantro, and chard seeds. (Plant the chard the same way you planted the beets.)

Dry branch prunings provide ample support for peas that have a bushy growth habit.

4

6 Move perennial herbs. Dig up the herbs from last year's bag in Bed 6. Remove the plastic and dig the planting mix from the bed into the soil beneath. Replant the herbs as shown in the plan on page 37. Try to keep the soil packed around the plants' roots as you work, and water them thoroughly when you're finished with the job. If any of the herb plants died, discard them and plant new ones instead. Now is also the time to plant rosemary in this bed.

LATE SPRING

7 Make a second sowing. One week before your last frost, make a second sowing of lettuce and cilantro.

8 Plant tomatoes and more. When the soil feels warm to your bare feet, set out tomatoes and peppers in Bed 5 and basil in Bed 6. Water well.

⑨ Sow the circle. Plant about 10 sunflower seeds 5 inches apart in the middle of Bed 4. Plant bush bean seeds in a circle around the sunflowers.

⑩ Set up the squash bed. In Bed 7, use a spade or shovel to make six planting holes arranged in a zigzag pattern, as shown in the planting plan on page 37. Place a large shovelful of compost and a handful of organic fertilizer in each hole, then mix them in thoroughly. Plant three squash seeds, or one seedling, in each prepared planting spot. Push the ends of the wire hoops into the ground to form three evenly spaced arches over the squash. Unfold or unroll the row cover and drape it over the arches. Secure the edges of the row cover with boards, bricks, or stones or by burying them. Open the cover to weed and thin, and remove it entirely when the plants start to bloom to allow insects to pollinate the flowers.

MIDSUMMER

⑪ Harvest garlic. Dig or pull the garlic plants in Bed 3 when one-third of the leaves appear to be fading but most of the leaves are still green. After the garlic has been set aside to cure, cover the bed with a heavy dusting of organic fertilizer (about 12 handfuls) and a 2-inch blanket of compost. Mix in thoroughly with a digging fork, water well, and set out broccoli seedlings during a period of cloudy weather. Move the row cover tunnel from the squash to your baby broccoli.

When closed at the ends, this row cover tunnel will protect broccoli from insect pests.

⑪

WHAT TO EXPECT FROM GARLIC

In late spring, the varieties of garlic known as hardneck garlic produce a curled flower stalk, called a scape, which is a rare and wonderful gourmet vegetable. Use a sharp knife to cut the base of the scape just as it forms a full curl. Clip off the blossom end (unless it is very young and tender), and cut the scapes into bite-size pieces before using them as a substitute for onions *and* garlic in recipes. Blanch and freeze extra scapes to use during winter. (To learn more about the different varieties of garlic and their growing needs, see page 206.)

Carefully avoid bruising garlic bulbs as you pull them from the ground, and spread the plants in a warm place to dry. After two weeks, trim off the roots and the tops, and rub off excess dirt with your hands. Cured this way, garlic will store at normal room temperature for months.

LATE SUMMER

12 **Plant fall greens.** Replace spring beets and onions in Bed 1 with mizuna, red mustard, and other Asian greens, and replace potatoes and peas in Bed 2 with salad greens in front of a turnip backdrop. Replace spring lettuce and cilantro in Bed 6 with carrots.

13 **Plant a cover crop.** After you collect the winter squash harvest from Bed 7, you can keep the soil busy growing a cover crop such as bush beans or dwarf peas mixed with red mustard to improve the soil (see Custom Cover Cropping at right).

LATE FALL

14 **Dream of next year.** Remove the tomato cages and pull up tomatoes after they have been killed by frost. Now you're ready to make your own plan for next season, which will probably be a repeat of your previous years' successes along with a few new adventures. Just remember that if you want to grow garlic again, plant it in fall.

CUSTOM COVER CROPPING

You can buy special cover crop seed mixes, but instead I like to use odds and ends from my seed collection and create my own custom cover crop blends. If you try this, aim for a mix of one-third legumes and two-thirds leafy greens. If you have whole wheat, rye, or oat berries in your pantry, you can add a few of those in your cover crop mix, too. Most of the cover crop plants will be killed by cold weather during winter, but others will survive until spring. Dig up any survivors, shake off the soil, and compost them to cycle the nutrients taken up by the plants back into your garden. Expired cover crops can be left on the surface as mulch or turned under when the soil warms in spring.

CHAPTER TWO

A BOUNTIFUL BORDER

Abundant rewards await gardeners who blur the lines between flowers and good things to eat, which is exactly what happens when you transform part of your lawn into a Bountiful Border. Traditionally, a border is a special boundary bed in which ornamental shrubs and perennial flowers are arranged in lush layers with the tallest in back, like players on a stage. Apply the same design principles to vegetables and herbs, and the result is a feast for the eyes and the palate.

In the Bountiful Border, dramatic plants like red-stemmed chard and multicolored snap beans share bed space with frilly salad greens or variegated herbs. Groups of upright onions serve as texture accents. Over time, edging plants are added to dress the border's curving front edge and attract beneficial insects at the same time. As you grow this garden, you will see how simple it is to have it all: beauty, nutrition, flavor, and bumper crops of natural wonder.

A border is an intensive type of garden, and the success of any type of border depends on excellent soil. Building good soil takes time, but here you'll push the process ahead by double-digging—a method that will improve plant performance immediately and for many seasons to come. By the time the Bountiful Border reaches its mature size (100 square feet of cultivated space) in year three, the soil in the original beds will be so soft with organic matter that you will be able to dig into it with your hands alone. Like the Easy-Care Bag Garden (see page 16), this tasty border can easily be maintained by one motivated gardener working a few hours each week.

DIG THIS!

If the most spacious part of your yard is to the side of your house, use the spot for this border. At its mature size, this garden forms an edible outdoor "room."

YEAR-BY-YEAR OVERVIEW

YEAR ONE

A row of double-dug 3-foot-wide beds creates the border's backbone. Large containers provide planting space and visual interest while smothering the grass beneath them.

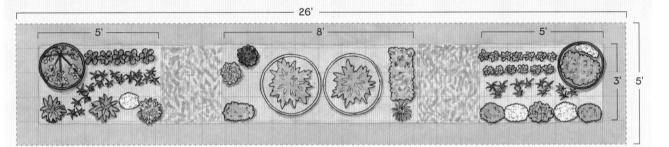

ONE SQUARE = 1 FOOT

YIELD

SPRING CROPS
- **lettuce:** 1–2 lbs.
- **mesclun:** 1–2 lbs.
- **snap peas:** 1 lb.
- **onions:** about 32
- **chard:** 10 lbs.

SUMMER CROPS
- **bush snap beans:** 6 lbs.
- **tomatoes:** 16–20 lbs.
- **peppers:** 4–6 lbs.

FALL CROPS
- **arugula:** 3–4 lbs.
- **mustard:** 4 lbs.

HERBS
- **basil:** 15 bunches
- **parsley:** 10 bunches
- **cilantro:** 5 bunches
- **garlic chives, sage, and thyme:** a year's supply

YEAR TWO

The border takes on wings with two new side beds that structure the garden's mature shape. With the pair of planters anchoring the edges, the garden's symmetrical plantings set a formal style.

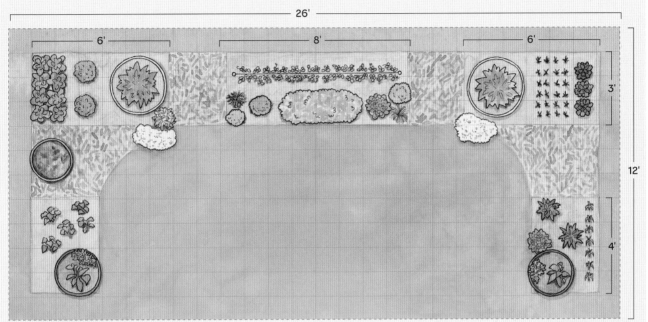

ONE SQUARE = 1 FOOT

YIELD

SPRING CROPS
- **salad greens:** 3-4 lbs.
- **snow peas:** 6 lbs.
- **collards:** 4-5 lbs.
- **kale:** 3-4 lbs.
- **scallions:** about 15
- **leeks:** 7 or 8 shanks

SUMMER CROPS
- **pole snap beans:** 20 lbs.
- **bush snap beans:** 5 lbs.
- **tomatoes:** 16-20 lbs.
- **peppers:** 4-6 lbs.
- **eggplant:** 4-6 lbs.
- **cucumbers:** 6-8 lbs.

FALL CROPS
- **salad greens:** 3-4 lbs.
- **tatsoi:** 3-4 lbs.
- **rutabagas:** 4 roots
- **shallots:** 25 bulbs (harvested the following season)
- **garlic:** 20 bulbs (harvested the following season)

HERBS
- **basil:** 10 bunches
- **parsley:** 10 bunches
- **garlic chives, Greek oregano, lemon thyme, marjoram, rosemary, sage, and assorted mints:** a year's supply

As the front edge softens into a curve, the garden takes on the intimate feel of a true border. Open spaces paved with bark or wood chip mulch provide easy access for planting and picking.

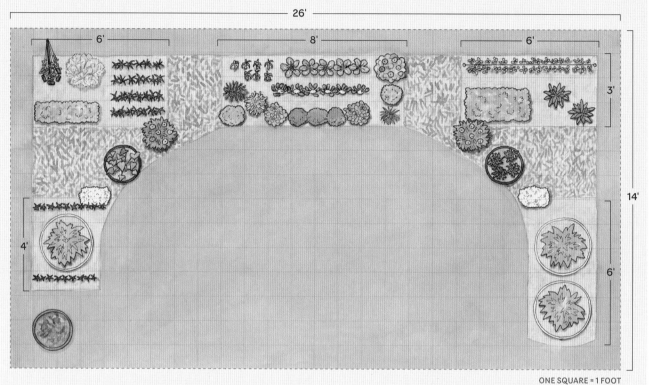

ONE SQUARE = 1 FOOT

YIELD

SPRING CROPS

- **salad greens:**
  6 lbs.
- **snap peas:**
  3–4 lbs.
- **leeks:** about 12 shanks
- **onions:** about 20 bulbs

SUMMER CROPS

- **bush snap beans:**
  4–5 lbs.
- **runner beans:**
  1 lb.
- **tomatoes:**
  25–30 lbs.
- **peppers:**
  4–6 lbs.
- **chard:** 10 lbs.
- **cucumbers:**
  5–7 lbs.

FALL CROPS

- **Asian greens:**
  3 lbs.
- **kale:** 6 lbs.
- **red mustard:**
  2 lbs.
- **spinach:** 1–2 lbs.
- **rutabagas:** 4 roots
- **garlic:** about 20 bulbs
  (harvested the following
  season)

HERBS

- **basil:** 10 bunches
- **parsley:** 15 bunches
- **dill, garlic chives,
  Greek oregano, thyme,
  assorted mints,
  rosemary, and sage:**
  a year's supply

YEAR ONE
GARDEN PLAN

Double-digging is a classic soil-preparation technique, and you'll use it here to create a vibrant, no-fail garden packed with more flavors, colors, and textures than you ever imagined might fit into such a small patch of ground.

The practice of double-digging soil dates back a thousand years or more. The method works its magic by introducing air into the subsoil, which in turn opens up new worlds to soil microorganisms and plant roots. In field trials, vegetables grown in double-dug beds consistently outperform those grown in soil cultivated in conventional ways.

Can you double-dig without breaking your back? Yes, you can, but only if you work a little at a time and use a sharp spade. Also practice good lifting technique, which means bending your knees to make your thighs and torso do most of the work. The payoff for diligent digging is well worthwhile, and you'll end up with stronger muscles, too!

You will also gain valuable knowledge about your garden's subsoil—the hard, dense, or sometimes rocky layer you often hit as you double-dig. In addition, tree roots, buried boulders, or other obstructions will come out of hiding as you work. Before you dig, be sure you know the locations of buried utility lines.

SPADE SHARPENING

Garden spades work best when they have a sharp edge that will cut through roots and other obstructions. At least once a year, use an inexpensive mill file (also called a flat or draw file) to sharpen your spade. Draw the file outward and off the edge of the blade about 30 strokes, then flip the blade and do the same to the other side. Repeat. Now you're ready to dig again.

HOW TO DOUBLE-DIG

1 Starting at one end of a bed from which you've removed sod or surface weeds, dig out the top 8 to 10 inches of soil in a 2-foot-wide band. Toss the soil into a pile near the other end of the bed.

2 Use a digging fork to perforate and loosen the next 8 to 10 inches of soil, which is probably compacted subsoil.

3 Refill the trench with topsoil taken from the next 2-foot section of the bed.

4 Repeat steps 2 and 3 until you reach the end of the bed. Use the soil from the first trench to fill the last trench. Distribute any extra topsoil evenly over the bed.

Double-dug beds naturally sit higher than surrounding soil because they hold so much air by volume. Walking on double-dug beds can quickly undo all your hard work by squeezing out air. As long as you regularly add organic matter to the top few inches of soil (by mulching or adding compost), the benefits of your double-digging project will last for years.

THE STUFF

FOR THE BEDS

- O Four 40-pound bags of composted manure
- O Six 40-pound bags of yard-waste compost
- O Two 40-pound bags of hardwood or wood chip mulch
- O Newspaper or cardboard
- O Two half-barrel planters at least 16 inches in diameter
- O Two 40-pound bags of organic potting soil

FOR THE POTTED TRELLISES

- O Twelve 5-foot slender sticks or bamboo poles
- O Cotton string or jute or hemp twine

FOR THE TOMATOES

- O Two 5-foot-tall tomato cages

FOR THE COMPOST AREA

- O One stationary composter, or a pen made from plastic fencing attached to stakes

TOOLS

- O Spade or shovel
- O Digging fork
- O Wheelbarrow, cart, or wagon for moving bags of soil amendments
- O Hand trowel

NAME

A Bountiful Border: Year One

FOOTPRINT

3 × 24 feet

SKILL LEVEL

Fine for first-timers

WHEN TO PLANT

Midspring: snap peas, mesclun, onions, garlic chives, lemon thyme, sage, parsley, chard, lettuce, and sweet alyssum

Late spring: basil, tomatoes, peppers, and bush snap beans

Midsummer: sunflowers and scarlet runner beans

Late summer: mustard, cilantro, and arugula

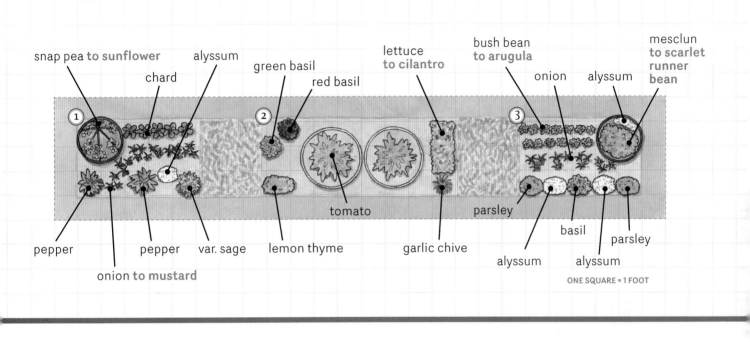

snap pea **to sunflower**　chard　alyssum　green basil　red basil　lettuce **to cilantro**　bush bean **to arugula**　onion　alyssum　mesclun **to scarlet runner bean**

pepper　onion **to mustard**　pepper　var. sage　lemon thyme　tomato　garlic chive　parsley　alyssum　basil　alyssum　parsley

ONE SQUARE = 1 FOOT

THE PLANTS

BED ①
- Chard, 1 packet seeds
- Dwarf sunflower, 1 packet seeds
- Mustard, 1 packet seeds
- Onion, 20 seedlings
- Pepper, 2 seedlings
- Sage (variegated), 1 plant
- Snap pea, 1 packet seeds
- Sweet alyssum, 1 seedling (buy a 4- or 6-pack)

BED ②
- Cilantro, 1 packet seeds
- Garlic chives, 3 plants (one clump)
- Green-leaved basil, 1 plant
- Lemon thyme, 2 plants
- Mixed lettuce, 1 packet seeds
- Red-leaved basil, 1 plant
- Tomato, 2 seedlings

BED ③
- Arugula, 1 packet seeds
- Basil, 1 plant
- Mesclun (mixed salad greens), 1 packet seeds
- Onion, 12 seedlings
- Parsley, 2 seedlings
- Scarlet runner bean, 1 packet seeds
- Snap bean (bush variety), 1 packet seeds
- Sweet alyssum, 3 seedlings

YEAR ONE
PLANTING AND CARE

EARLY SPRING

The easiest way to get rid of grass without digging is to smother it with a double mulch of newspaper topped with organic matter.

1 **Prepare the site.** Select a site and mark the locations of the three beds. Use the spade or shovel and digging fork to remove grass and weeds from the beds. Toss them into the compost. Cover the ground between the beds with four to six sheets of damp newspaper or a single thickness of well-dampened cardboard, and cover with 2 to 3 inches of hardwood or wood chip mulch (or another organic mulch material).

2 **Double-dig the end beds.** Starting at the edges closest to the garden's center, double-dig Beds 1 and 3 except for the spaces where the planters will be located. In those corners, lightly cultivate the soil and then set the empty planters in place. Fill planters to within 1 inch of the brim with potting soil.

3 **Double-dig Bed 2.** When you're finished, sprinkle on a generous dusting of organic fertilizer and spread two bags of composted manure evenly over the bed. Top the manure with a 2-inch layer of yard-waste compost (about three bags). Without stepping in the bed, lightly turn the top 10 inches of soil once or twice to mix in the fertilizer and soil amendments. Water well.

MIDSPRING

4 **Plant trellised peas.** One month before your last spring frost date, make a trellis in the Bed 1 planter by pushing six sticks into the planting mix around the edges of the container. Then bind the vertical sticks together at the top with string, tripod-style. Poke snap pea seeds into the soil 1 inch deep and 2 to 3 inches apart throughout the planter.

5 **Plant containers.** In the Bed 3 planter, scatter mesclun seeds atop the soil about 1 inch apart. Pat the seeds into place with your hand, barely covering them with soil. Slip one sweet alyssum seedling just inside the rim of the planter.

6 **Plant the sweet alyssum.** Plant two sweet alyssum seedlings at the front edge of Bed 3, and plant one in Bed 1.

7 **Finish bed prep.** Prepare Beds 1 and 3 for planting as described in Step 2.

8 **Add the parsley.** Plant parsley seeds (or set out seedlings) in Bed 3. Sow the seeds ¼ inch deep and ½ inch apart (fewer than half will germinate). Pat lightly to firm the soil over the seeds, then spritz with a light spray of water until thoroughly moist.

9 **Sow chard.** In Bed 1, sow a row of chard seeds, planting the seeds ½ inch deep and 2 inches apart. Plan to go back two weeks later to thin the seedlings (which emerge in pairs or clumps, see page 128).

10 **Plant onions and herbs.** In Beds 1 and 3, plant onions in groups of three, allowing 3 inches between plants. At the same time, set out purchased lemon thyme, garlic chive, and sage plants as shown in the plan on page 49.

11 **Sow lettuce.** In Bed 2, scatter the lettuce seeds over the soil's surface so that they are about 1 inch apart. Pat them into place with your hand, barely covering with soil.

LATE SPRING

12 **Plant tomatoes and more.** After the last frost passes, set out tomatoes, peppers, and basil. As you transplant tomatoes, bury the lower portion of the stem (as shown on page 27). Supplemental roots will sprout from the buried stem, which means your plants will grow faster and produce bigger, better crops. Install tomato cages soon after you set out the plants (see page 132).

13 **Sow bush beans.** Plant bush bean seeds 1 inch deep and 8 inches apart in Bed 3. Pull green onions as needed in the kitchen.

EARLY SUMMER

14 **Thin and enjoy your salad greens.** Pull lettuce and mesclun seedlings as you need them in the kitchen and to make more elbow room for the growing plants. Gather young garlic chive leaves for salads or soups.

MIDSUMMER

15 **Plant runner beans.** After you harvest most of the mesclun from the planter in Bed 3, fill the vacant space with scarlet runner beans, pushed 2 inches into the soil. Erect a trellis for the beans following the instructions in Step 4.

16 **Replace peas with sunflowers.** Harvest snap peas daily as they ripen, but wait until the pods plump up to get the best flavor. As the pea harvest ends, snip off the vines at the soil line and compost them; pull out the trellis. Plant six or so sunflower seeds in the planter, 1 inch deep and 6 inches apart. After the seeds germinate, pull out all but the three strongest plants.

Even in a container, scarlet runner beans turn a simple bamboo tripod into a pillar of color.

17 **Sow fall greens.** Pull up and compost tattered lettuce in Bed 2; harvest onions when the tops fall over. Scatter a dusting of organic fertilizer over the soil surface in the areas where you removed crops and lightly mix it in with a hand trowel. Then sow mustard seeds in Bed 1, cilantro in Bed 2, and arugula in Bed 3.

18 **Groom garlic chives.** Gather garlic chive blossoms to enjoy indoors as cut flowers, or you can snip them into salads. Prune off unharvested flower clusters as soon as the blossoms fade, because garlic chives (and regular chives) that are allowed to shed seed can become weedy.

FALL

19 **Put the garden to bed.** As fall turns to winter, protect your investment in plants by surrounding thyme and sage with a 6-inch-tall raised berm of mulch, which increases their tolerance of cold weather. Turn the planters on their sides so that the freezing and thawing of the soil inside won't cause breakage. Mulch exposed soil surfaces in the beds with shredded leaves or compost to insulate your beautiful bioactive soil from the ravages of winter.

A ring of mulch helps insulate the roots of perennial herbs from extreme winter cold.

YEAR TWO
GARDEN PLAN

With two new beds available for planting, year two of the Bountiful Border provides opportunities to get to know kale, scallions, and other easy cool-season edibles. And instead of putting the whole garden to bed when autumn arrives, this year you'll use your off-season to grow plump bulbs of garlic.

As the Bountiful Border expands in its second growing season, a trellis dripping with snow peas in early summer forms a dramatic visual backdrop that unifies the scene, with opposing back beds anchored by tall tomatoes. In summer, you can try your luck with eggplant, which often grows better in containers than it does in the ground.

Eggplants paired with mints in a container work well for two reasons. Mints grow and spread so vigorously that they quickly become an invasive nuisance when let loose in the garden. Yet they make great neighbors for eggplant. Underplanting eggplant with mint can reduce problems with flea beetles—irksome, tiny, black jumping beetles that riddle leaves with hundreds of tiny holes. Containers make this mutually beneficial partnership possible.

TELL ME MORE!
SYMMETRY AND BALANCE

Gardeners have been working with flower borders for several centuries, and major guidelines for border design are well established. To be most pleasing, the plantings should be balanced so that the "visual weight" of the opposing sides appears to be equal. Exact symmetry (planting the same plants on both sides of the border, like a mirror image) creates a very formal mood, but it also limits the choice of food crops you can grow.

As you tailor a garden plan to meet your needs, note that neat symmetry along this garden's front edge makes adjacent plantings appear more organized. Also do what you can to balance and beautify a garden's entry points. Growing mints, basils, and other aromatic herbs at the entrance to a garden has its special rewards, too. As you launch into a gardening session, swish your hands through the plants' foliage to release refreshing aromas.

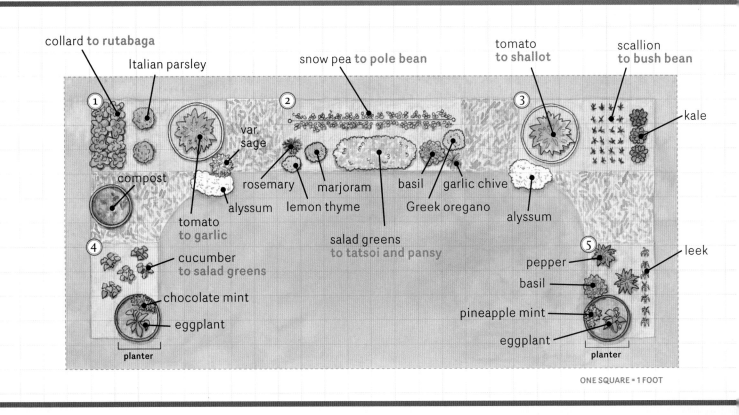

collard **to rutabaga**

Italian parsley

snow pea **to pole bean**

tomato **to shallot**

scallion **to bush bean**

kale

var. sage

compost

rosemary

marjoram

basil

garlic chive

alyssum

lemon thyme

Greek oregano

alyssum

tomato **to garlic**

salad greens **to tatsoi and pansy**

cucumber **to salad greens**

leek

pepper

basil

chocolate mint

pineapple mint

eggplant

eggplant

planter

planter

ONE SQUARE = 1 FOOT

NAME

A Bountiful Border: Year Two

FOOTPRINT

10 × 24 feet

SKILL LEVEL

Fine for first-timers

WHEN TO PLANT

Midspring: collards, Italian parsley, snow peas, salad greens, scallions, kale, leeks, and sweet alyssum

Late spring: basil, cucumbers, eggplant, mints, tomatoes, peppers, Greek oregano, garlic chives, marjoram, rosemary, and lemon thyme

Midsummer: bush snap beans, pole snap beans, and rutabaga

Late summer: more salad greens, tatsoi, and pansies

Fall: garlic and shallots

THE STUFF

FOR THE BEDS

○ Six 40-pound bags of composted manure

○ Seven 40-pound bags of yard-waste compost

○ Three 40-pound bags of hardwood or wood chip mulch

○ Two half-barrel planters at least 16 inches in diameter (from year one garden)

○ Newspaper or cardboard

FOR THE PEA AND POLE BEAN TRELLIS

○ Two 8-foot-long wood posts

○ Cotton string, jute or hemp, or polyester garden netting

TOOLS

○ Wheelbarrow, cart, or wagon for moving bags of soil amendments

○ Spade or shovel

○ Digging fork

○ Utility knife

○ Sledgehammer or hammer

○ Hand trowel

THE PLANTS

BED ①

- Collard or cabbage, 1 packet seeds
- Italian parsley, 2 seedlings
- Rutabaga, 1 packet seeds
- Sage (variegated), 1 plant
- Seed garlic, ¼ pound (about 3 large bulbs)
- Sweet alyssum, 2 seedlings (look for volunteers to transplant)
- Tomato, 1 seedling

BED ②

- Basil, 1 seedling
- Garlic chives, 1 plant
- Greek oregano, 1 plant
- Lemon thyme, 1 plant
- Marjoram, 1 plant
- Mesclun or mixed lettuce, 1 packet seeds
- Pansy, 6 seedlings
- Rosemary, 1 plant
- Snap bean (pole variety), 1 packet seeds
- Snow pea, 1 packet seeds
- Tatsoi, 1 packet seeds

BED ③

- Kale, 3 seedlings (or 1 packet seeds)
- Scallions (from the supermarket), 3 bunches
- Shallots, 25 plants
- Snap bean (bush variety), 1 packet seeds
- Sweet alyssum, 2 seedlings (look for volunteers to transplant)
- Tomato, 1 seedling

BED ④

- Chocolate mint, 1 plant
- Cucumber, 1 packet seeds
- Eggplant, 1 seedling
- Mesclun or mixed lettuce, partial seed packets leftover from spring (Bed 2)

BED ⑤

- Basil, 1 seedling
- Eggplant, 1 seedling
- Leek, 7–8 seedlings (or bulb onions)
- Pepper, 2 seedlings
- Pineapple mint (variegated), 1 plant

DIG THIS!

All tomatoes are pretty, but varieties that produce small yellow fruits (such as 'Sungold' or 'Yellow Pear') put on a great show and blend well with nearly all other colors.

YEAR TWO
PLANTING AND CARE

EARLY SPRING

❶ Enrich the end beds. Move planters and compost to their new locations as shown in the plan on page 54. Double-dig the newly exposed corners of Beds 1 and 3. Spread a bag of composted manure and a bag of compost over each bed along with a moderate dusting of organic fertilizer. Use the digging fork to mix in the soil amendments and the fertilizer.

❷ Double-dig new beds. Use the spade or shovel and digging fork to remove grass and weeds from the new beds (4 and 5). Toss them into the compost. Starting at the back edges, double-dig the new beds except for the space where the planters will be located. Lightly cultivate those corners and then set the planters in place. Apply a generous dusting of organic fertilizer to each bed, and spread one bag of composted manure evenly over each bed. Top the manure with a 2-inch layer of yard-waste compost (about one bag per bed). Without stepping in the bed, lightly turn the top 10 inches of soil once or twice to mix in the fertilizer and soil amendments. Water well.

❸ Distribute mulch. Use newspaper or cardboard and mulch to pave over the open spots between the new beds. Renew the mulch between the back beds as well.

❹ Refresh planters. Spread 1 inch of composted manure, 1 inch of yard-waste compost, and a moderate dusting of organic fertilizer over the surface of the planters. Use a hand trowel to stab, slice, and mix these amendments into the old potting soil.

❺ Enrich the center bed. Sprinkle on a generous dusting of organic fertilizer, and then spread two bags of composted manure and two bags of yard-waste compost over Bed 2. Lightly cultivate the top 10 inches of soil to mix in the soil amendments and fertilizer, and water well.

MIDSPRING

❻ Plant trellised peas. Make a trellis in Bed 2 by attaching netting or weaving strings between two posts that you've sunk at least 12 inches into the ground. (See page 132 for installing posts and page 25 for weaving a string trellis.) Poke snow pea seeds into the soil 1 inch deep and 2 to 3 inches apart in two rows, one on either side of the trellis.

❼ Keep on planting. In Bed 1, sow collard or cabbage seeds, about ¼ inch deep. Barely cover lettuce or mesclun seeds as you sow them in Bed 2. Set out scallions and kale, leek, and Italian parsley seedlings where shown in the plan on page 54.

LATE SPRING

❽ Plant sweet alyssum. As nighttime temperatures warm above 50°F (10°C), lift and move volunteer sweet alyssum seedlings to the center front corners of Beds 1 and 3, or set out purchased plants.

❾ Plant herbs. Transplant rosemary, lemon thyme, marjoram, garlic chives, and Greek oregano to Bed 2; plant variegated sage in Bed 1. Plant mints in the half-barrels, setting them about 3 inches in from the rim.

HAVE ONIONS ALL THE TIME

No matter where you live, you can probably manage to have an onion of some kind ready to harvest on any given day during the growing season. The trick is to grow different types, including onions such as scallions (also called green onions) and leeks that never form bulbs.

Scallions. Trim store-bought scallions to 6 inches long and plant them from early spring to late fall. Should forgotten scallions multiply into bunches, dig and divide them in early spring or early fall. Very high-quality varieties of Japanese gourmet scallions are also easy to grow from seed (see page 216).

Leeks. Slow to start from seed, leeks grow with little care once they are established in the garden. You need not wait until leeks grow large to start pulling, but if you have plants in the ground in fall, wait until the growing season's closing bell sounds to bring them in.

Garlic and shallots. These two crops are best grown from late fall to early summer, a time when there is a low demand for space for other garden crops. They also store beautifully, making them top crops for every low-maintenance kitchen garden. You can grow shallots from bulbs, and newer varieties do well when started from seed indoors in late winter.

Multiplying onions. These quirky yet productive plants are hardy to Zone 5, and they vary in their reproductive habits. Some form bulblets atop tall stems, and you can plant the bulblets to produce another crop. Others form a "nest" of small bulb onions; harvest most of these to eat, and replant a few for the next round. All multiplying onions are very easy to grow.

---

⑩ Plant tomatoes and more. After the last frost passes, set out tomatoes, peppers, eggplant, and basil as illustrated, and plant cucumber seeds 1 inch deep and 10 inches apart in Bed 4. As the seedlings grow, pull out all but the five strongest plants.

⑪ Pamper containers. To keep mint's aggressive roots from outcompeting the eggplant for water and nutrients, water the containers as often as needed to keep them from drying out. It is natural for eggplant leaves to droop slightly on hot, sunny days; if they have adequate moisture, they will perk up by late afternoon.

Broad eggplant leaves appear more refined in the company of pineapple mint.

MIDSUMMER

12 **Plant pole beans.** When old age and hot weather cause the snow peas in Bed 2 to fail, clip the plants at the soil line. Gather up as much vine growth as you can without mangling the trellis, and toss the material into your compost pile. It's okay if some stems and tendrils stay stuck in the trellis. Plant pole beans to replace the peas, pushing seeds into the soil 2 inches deep and 4 inches apart.

13 **Try bush beans, too.** Replace harvested scallions and summer-weary kale in Bed 3 with fast-growing bush beans. Sow rutabagas in the spot where you grew spring collards or cabbage in Bed 1. About three weeks after sowing, thin rutabaga seedlings to 12 inches apart.

LATE SUMMER

14 **Plant fall greens and pansies.** Sow tatsoi seeds in the spot vacated by spring lettuce or mesclun in Bed 2. After the seedlings appear, thin or transplant as needed to make the plants form a curve or other pattern. Set out pansies at regular intervals as neighbors to the tatsoi. (Northern gardeners, be sure to choose hardy pansy varieties that will overwinter in your area.) Compost the cucumber vines in Bed 4, and sow mesclun or other salad greens in their place.

LATE FALL

15 **Plant garlic.** Pull up tomatoes after they are damaged by frost. Replace the tomato in Bed 1 with garlic, planting cloves 6 inches apart and 4 inches deep with their pointed ends up. Use the same spacing as you replace the tomato in Bed 3 with shallots. Mulch over both plantings with at least 2 inches of grass clippings, weathered hay, or shredded leaves. By next summer, each garlic clove will mature into a big, new bulb; each shallot will multiply into three or more fat bulbs.

EARLY WINTER

16 **Put the garden to bed.** Mulch over the root zones of the hardy herbs with 3 inches of grass clippings, weathered hay, or shredded leaves. Compost the garden's debris, turn planters on their sides, and tuck in all beds with shredded leaves, pine straw, hay, or other biodegradable mulch.

YEAR THREE
GARDEN PLAN

As you expand your Bountiful Border in year three, the garden develops a gracefully curving front edge, while the crop list grows to 25 showy and delicious veggies and herbs. New plants on the list include kohlrabi, the most easygoing of the cabbage-family clan, and free-flowering dill, the simplest herb to grow from seed.

In designing the Bountiful Border, I borrowed several principles from landscape design to increase the garden's eye-candy quotient, including these four:

Increased vertical interest. A pillar of eye-catching scarlet runner beans flanked by feathery dill calls attention to one far corner. It is balanced on the other side of the garden by a vertical trellis of peas.

Rhythm and repetition. The appearance of bright calendulas and sweet alyssum at predictable points creates a feeling of unity.

Natural drifts. Instead of arranging everything in straight rows, the plan situates many plants in groups, which sharpens the contrast between varied textures, forms, and colors.

Manicured mulch. Open passageways between beds take on a handsome, polished look when covered with wood chip mulch. In a Bountiful Border, neatness counts!

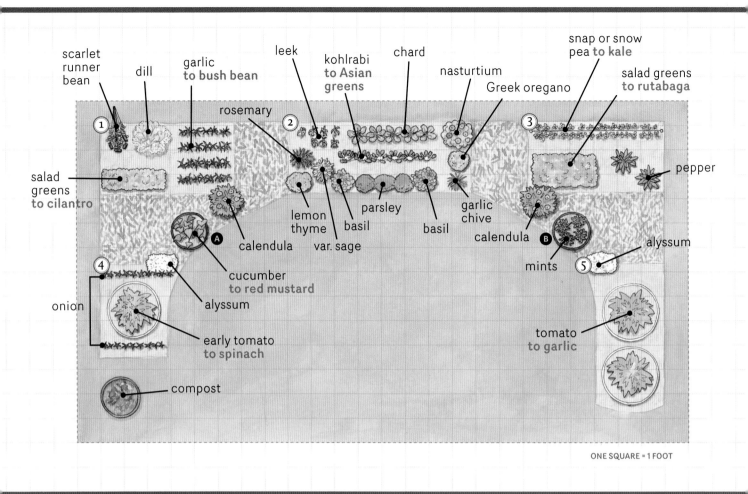

scarlet runner bean
dill
garlic to bush bean
rosemary
leek
kohlrabi to Asian greens
chard
nasturtium
Greek oregano
snap or snow pea to kale
salad greens to rutabaga

salad greens to cilantro

lemon thyme
basil
parsley
basil
garlic chive
calendula
mints

calendula
var. sage

pepper

cucumber to red mustard

alyssum

onion

early tomato to spinach

alyssum

tomato to garlic

compost

ONE SQUARE = 1 FOOT

NAME

A Bountiful Border:
   Year Three

FOOTPRINT

12 × 24 feet

SKILL LEVEL

Beyond beginner

WHEN TO PLANT

Early spring: mints

Midspring: onions, sweet alyssum, salad greens, dill, leeks, chard, kohlrabi, parsley, nasturtiums, snap or snow peas, and calendulas

Late spring: tomatoes, cucumber, scarlet runner bean, basil, and peppers

Midsummer: bush snap beans and rutabaga

Late summer: red mustard, cilantro, Asian greens, spinach, and kale

Fall: garlic

THE STUFF

FOR THE BEDS

- ⭕ Six 40-pound bags of composted manure
- ⭕ Nine 40-pound bags of yard-waste compost
- ⭕ Four 40-pound bags of hardwood or wood chip mulch
- ⭕ Two half-barrel planters at least 16 inches in diameter (from year one garden)

FOR THE BEAN PILLAR

- ⭕ One 6-foot-tall wood fence post
- ⭕ Cotton string or jute or hemp twine
- ⭕ Six bricks

FOR THE PEA TRELLIS

- ⭕ Two 6-foot-long wood posts
- ⭕ Cotton string, jute or hemp twine, or polyester garden netting

TOOLS

- ⭕ Spade or shovel
- ⭕ Digging fork
- ⭕ Wheelbarrow, cart, or wagon for moving bags of soil amendments
- ⭕ Sledgehammer or hammer
- ⭕ Utility knife
- ⭕ Hand trowel

THE PLANTS

BED ①

- ⭕ Calendula, 1 packet seeds or 2 seedlings
- ⭕ Cilantro, 1 packet seeds
- ⭕ Dill, 1 packet seeds
- ⭕ Mesclun or mixed lettuce, 1 packet seeds
- ⭕ Scarlet runner bean, 1 packet seeds
- ⭕ Snap bean (bush variety), 1 packet seeds

BED ②

- ⭕ Asian greens (bok choy, mizuna, many others), 1 packet seeds
- ⭕ Basil, 1 packet seeds or 2 seedlings
- ⭕ Chard, 1 packet seeds
- ⭕ Kohlrabi, 1 packet seeds or 6 seedlings
- ⭕ Leek, 7 seedlings
- ⭕ Nasturtium, 1 packet seeds or 2 seedlings
- ⭕ Parsley, 1 packet seeds or 3 seedlings
- ⭕ Replacement herbs as needed: rosemary, Greek oregano, variegated sage, lemon thyme, garlic chives

BED ③

- ⭕ Calendula, 1 packet seeds or 2 seedlings
- ⭕ Kale, 1 packet seeds or 6 seedlings
- ⭕ Mesclun or other mixed salad greens, 1 packet seeds

- ⭕ Pepper, 2 seedlings
- ⭕ Rutabaga, 1 packet seeds
- ⭕ Snap or snow pea, 1 packet seeds

BED ④

- ⭕ Onion, 20 seedlings or sets
- ⭕ Spinach, 1 packet seeds
- ⭕ Sweet alyssum, 1 seedling (purchased or transplanted volunteer)
- ⭕ Tomato, 1 seedling (early-maturing variety)

BED ⑤

- ⭕ Seed garlic, ¼ pound (about 3 bulbs)
- ⭕ Sweet alyssum, 1 seedling (purchased or transplanted volunteer)
- ⭕ Tomato, 2 seedlings

PLANTER A

- ⭕ Cucumber, 1 packet seeds or 3 seedlings
- ⭕ Red mustard, 1 packet seeds

PLANTER B

- ⭕ Mint, 4 or more plants (from prior year)

YEAR THREE
PLANTING AND CARE

EARLY SPRING

❶ Revive the garden. Move the planters and compost to their new locations. Double-dig the front corners of Beds 4 and 5, and extend Bed 5 by 2 feet as illustrated in the plan on page 60. Rake away winter mulch if you do not wish to turn it under. Except for the area planted with garlic last fall, spread one bag of manure and one bag of compost over each bed along with a moderate dusting of organic fertilizer. Use the digging fork to mix in the soil amendments and the fertilizer.

❷ Renew and extend mulch. Renew the mulch in the four open spots between the beds. Extend the mulch coverage to include the area around the planters, which will help to define the garden's front edge.

❸ Revive the planters. Use a sharp knife to cut crowns of mint from the containers. Set aside two of each type you want to keep and place the rest in the sun to thoroughly dry out. Because runaway mint is an invasive nuisance, be sure the plants are dead (including the roots) before you add them to your compost pile. Spread 1 inch of composted manure, 1 inch of yard-waste compost, and a moderate dusting of organic fertilizer over the surface of the planters. Use a hand trowel to stab, slice, and mix these amendments into the potting soil. Replant the mint in Planter B. Let Planter A rest until the weather warms (pull out any mint that sprouts in the container).

HOW LONG DO SEEDS LAST?

You may wonder whether the leftover chard, lettuce, and other seeds you purchased back when you started your Bountiful Border in year one are still good for planting in year three. When kept in a cool, dry place, most seeds will stay viable for at least three years, and sometimes much longer (see page 195). However, lettuce, onion, and parsnip seeds are notoriously short-lived, so buy a new supply each spring. Carrot and parsley seeds also punk out early, so replace them at least every other year.

To test whether seeds are still good, fold 10 or more into a very damp paper towel, enclose it in a sandwich bag, and put the bag in a warm place for a few days. (If you're testing more than one kind of seed, label each bag with the variety name.) If you see no signs of germination after five or six days, better get some new seeds! You often can find great deals on discounted packets in midsummer, about the time that many stores take down their seed displays. Look for seed racks that were kept in a climate-controlled place, because seeds exposed to humidity or hot sun may have lost their vitality.

MIDSPRING

❹ Plant trellised peas. One month before your last spring frost date, make a trellis in Bed 3 for snow or snap peas as described on page 25. Plant the bed with peas and spring salad greens, and look for sweet alyssum volunteers to move to the front of Beds 4 and 5.

❺ Sow cool-season crops. Set out onions in Bed 4 and leeks and kohlrabi in Bed 2. Sow parsley and calendulas where indicated, or set out seedlings. Sow nasturtiums in Bed 2, following instructions on the seed packet.

❻ Sow more salad. Two weeks after sowing the first salad greens, make a second sowing in Bed 1, and plant dill.

❼ Plant chard. As nighttime temperatures warm above 50°F (10°C), sow chard or set out seedlings in Bed 2.

LATE SPRING

❽ Plant tomatoes and more. After the last frost passes, set out tomatoes, peppers, and basil. Plant cucumber seeds or seedlings in Planter A. In Bed 2, replace herbs that performed poorly or died.

❾ Set up a bean pillar. Install a post for the scarlet runner beans in Bed 1. Tie lengths of string to the top of the post, and attach the ends of the string to bricks or other small weights, so that they angle outward from the post. The strings need not be taut, because the weight of the twining bean vines will soon pull them tight. Plant about six scarlet runner bean seeds 1 inch deep near each brick.

EARLY SUMMER

❿ Collect some scapes. Harvest the scapes from hardneck garlic varieties as soon as the stem makes a full curl (see What to Expect from Garlic, page 41).

As runner beans twine their way up a string trellis, their increasing weight will pull the strings taut. The result will be a tall pyramid of foliage, flowers, and pods.

MIDSUMMER

⓫ Dig the bulbs. About four weeks after the scape harvest, when one-third of the leaves have turned yellowish, dig or pull the garlic plants and set aside to cure. Cover the bed with a light dusting of organic fertilizer (about four handfuls) and a generous sprinkling of compost; then plant bush bean seeds.

⓬ Sow rutabaga. Sow rutabagas in the spot where you grew early-spring salad greens in Bed 3.

LATE SUMMER

⓭ Sow more fall crops. Sow cilantro seeds in the spot vacated by lettuce in Bed 1. Pull and compost the cucumber vines from Planter A and sow red mustard there. Plant Asian greens of your choice to fill the gap in Bed 2 left by kohlrabi. Plant spinach in Bed 4, and plan ahead to equip the bed with a winter cover (see page 186).

LATE FALL

⓮ Ponder next year's garden plan. Remove the tomato cages and pull up tomatoes after they have been killed by frost. Now you're ready to make your own plan for next season. If you want to grow garlic again, plant it now.

CHAPTER THREE

THE FRONT-YARD FOOD SUPPLY

Once you install a Front-Yard Food Supply garden, expect to get to know many more of your neighbors, because front-yard food gardens bring neighbors together. People who never bothered to nod at you before will stroll by to see how your tomatoes are doing or to have a look at your beautiful lettuce. You will discover nice, interesting people who live right in your neighborhood, and maybe, just maybe, they will go home and plant fresh vegetables and herbs in their yards, too.

If your backyard is too shady or cramped for food plants, grow them out front instead. You will have less lawn to mow, and you'll make use of a terrifically convenient place to grow salad greens, kitchen herbs, and a summer's worth of sun-sweetened tomatoes.

In this front-yard food garden, strategically placed flowers and colorful vegetables maximize the garden's attractiveness. In the garden's second year, you'll install a waist-high picket fence, which will add structure to the garden's front edge, provide constant color, and serve as a trellis for a spring crop of snap peas.

With the help of colorful edibles like stained-glass chard and snap beans with purple pods, this garden easily supplies as much visual appeal as would any flower garden. Even in winter, vibrant green cover crops make this garden a delight to behold.

The striking shades of red and purple in cabbage, chard, beets, and other vegetables are a beautiful disguise for anthocyanins— flavonoid compounds that are good for your joints and your heart.

YEAR-BY-YEAR OVERVIEW

YEAR ONE

A narrow mulched pathway separates two 30-inch-wide beds, which allows for a wide diversity of plants in a small space. A boundary bed defines the edge of the garden.

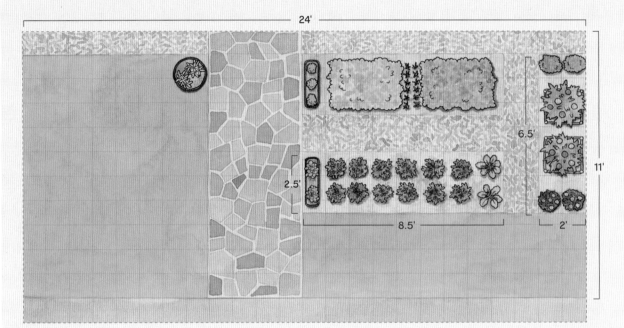

ONE SQUARE = 1 FOOT

YIELD

SPRING CROPS
- **lettuce:** 7 lbs.
- **scallions:** about 12
- **potatoes:** 25 lbs.

SUMMER CROPS
- **bush snap beans:** 10 lbs.
- **tomatoes:** 16–20 lbs.
- **chard:** 4 lbs.

FALL CROPS
- **arugula:** 3 lbs.
- **bok choy:** 3 lbs.
- **spinach:** 2 lbs.

HERBS
- **basil:** 10 bunches
- **parsley:** 10 bunches
- **sage and thyme:** a year's supply

The garden's foreground gets a facelift from a decorative fence, which doubles as support for snap pea vines. At the back of the garden, a trellis adds height while making use of vertical growing space.

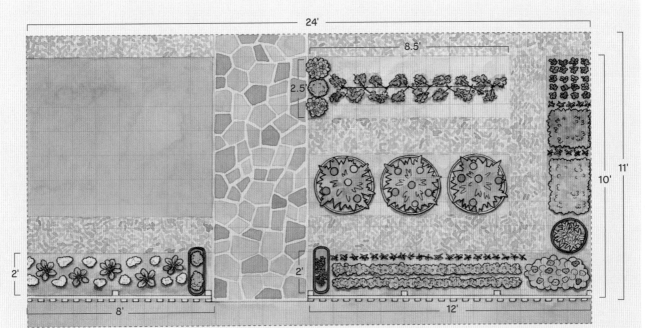

ONE SQUARE = 1 FOOT

YIELD

SPRING CROPS
- **lettuce:** 2–3 lbs.
- **snap peas:** 4 lbs.
- **spinach:** 1 lb.

SUMMER CROPS
- **pole snap beans:** 20 lbs.
- **tomatoes:** 50–60 lbs.
- **onions:** about 20
- **scallions:** about 15
- **beets:** 6 lbs.
- **chard:** 10 lbs.

FALL CROPS
- **stir-fry greens:** 2 lbs.
- **lettuce:** 3 lbs.
- **Chinese cabbage:** 6 lbs.

HERBS
- **basil:** 10 bunches
- **parsley:** 10 bunches
- **rosemary, sage, and thyme:** a year's supply

By year three, the garden has roughly tripled in size from about 55 square feet of planting space to 50 square feet. A balanced design and plenty of color make this easy-care garden as pretty as it is productive.

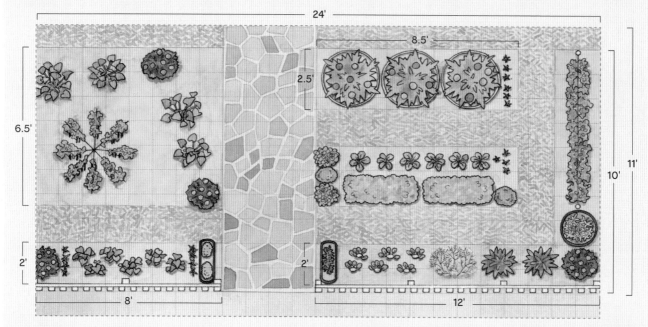

ONE SQUARE = 1 FOOT

YIELD

SPRING CROPS
- **lettuce:** 7 lbs.
- **snow peas:** 3–4 lbs.
- **onions:** about 25

SUMMER CROPS
- **pole snap beans:** 18 lbs.
- **tomatoes:** 50–60 lbs.
- **peppers:** 4–6 lbs.
- **chard:** 12 lbs.
- **kohlrabi:** 6 bulbs
- **cucumber:** 15 lbs.
- **summer squash:** 20 lbs.

FALL CROPS
- **lettuce:** 2 lbs.
- **arugula:** 2 lbs.
- **red mustard:** 4 lbs.
- **carrots:** 12 lbs.
- **turnips:** 10 lbs.
- **winter squash:** 10 lbs.
- **garlic:** about 20 bulbs (harvested the following season)

HERBS
- **basil:** 10 bunches
- **parsley:** 10 bunches
- **dill, rosemary, sage, and thyme:** a year's supply

YEAR ONE
GARDEN PLAN

Designed to make good use of limited space in a postage-stamp front yard, this little garden will be the talk of the neighborhood.

A patch of spring salad greens is as pretty as any flower bed. And as the weather warms and colorful chard stretches up and out, it will charm everyone who sees it.

In view of its prominent location, you'll take a few special steps to make your Front-Yard Food Supply garden as attractive and inviting as possible. Instead of using industrial-looking cages to provide discipline to naturally messy tomatoes, let front-yard formality come into play as you weave a trellis with hints of color provided by cloth ribbon—a trick that will heighten the visual unity between the garden and the house. Mulched pathways dress up the garden, too. If you have enough time and mulch, add a mulched pathway along the garden's front edge to further enhance a well-dressed look.

The traditional, tried-and-true soil-improvement method used in this garden consists of digging in a new supply of organic matter each time you plant a crop. Over time, any soil will gain better texture and drainage when regularly enriched with compost and supplemented from the top down with biodegradable mulches.

DIG THIS!
Expect exuberance— and lots of questions— to grow out of the front-row potatoes in this garden. Many people eat potatoes every day, but most folks have never seen live potatoes-in-process.

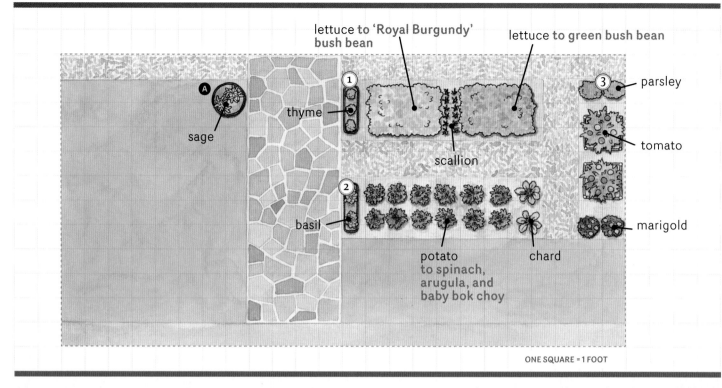

lettuce to 'Royal Burgundy' bush bean

lettuce to green bush bean

sage

thyme

scallion

parsley

tomato

basil

potato to spinach, arugula, and baby bok choy

chard

marigold

ONE SQUARE = 1 FOOT

NAME
The Front-Yard Food Supply: Year One

FOOTPRINT
6.5 × 12 feet

SKILL LEVEL
Fine for first-timers

WHEN TO PLANT
Midspring: potatoes, lettuce, parsley, chard, arugula, and scallions

Late spring: basil, thyme, sage, tomatoes, and marigolds

Midsummer: bush snap beans

Late summer: spinach, more arugula, and baby bok choy

THE STUFF

FOR THE BEDS
- Six 40-pound bags of compost or shrub planting mix, or about 4 wheelbarrow loads
- One 2-pound box of organic vegetable garden fertilizer
- One 2-foot-tall stack of newspapers
- Four 40-pound bags of hardwood or wood chip mulch, or about 3 wheelbarrow loads

- Two oblong planters, 8 inches wide by 28–30 inches long
- One round 14-inch-diameter planter
- One 40-pound bag potting soil

FOR THE TOMATO TRELLIS
- Ten 6-foot-long wood garden stakes
- 12 yards of cloth ribbon that matches the trim color of your house

TOOLS
- Spade or shovel
- Digging fork
- Lawnmower for cutting grass short
- Plastic tub for soaking newspaper
- Wheelbarrow, cart, or wagon for moving compost and mulch
- Trowel
- Sledgehammer or hammer
- Soil rake
- Clean, sharp knife (for cutting potatoes)

THE PLANTS

BED ①

- O Scallions, 1 bunch with roots attached, trimmed to 5 inches
- O Lettuce, 3 packets seeds in varying colors and textures, or 1 packet of a mixture
- O 'Royal Burgundy' snap bean (purple-podded bush), 1 packet seeds
- O Snap bean (green-podded bush), 1 packet seeds
- O Thyme, 3 plants

BED ②

- O Arugula, 1 packet seeds
- O Baby bok choy, 1 packet seeds
- O Basil, 1 packet seeds or 2 seedlings
- O Red or orange chard, 1 packet seeds or 2 seedlings
- O Seed potatoes, 3 pounds (about 6 small to medium potatoes)
- O Spinach, 1 packet seeds

BED ③

- O Dwarf French marigold, 1 packet seeds or 2 seedlings
- O Parsley, 1 packet seeds or 2 seedlings
- O Tomato, 2 seedlings

PLANTER A

- O Sage, 2 plants

CHOOSE AN ACCENT COLOR

In this planting plan, dwarf French marigolds are the anchor color plant, chosen because they are very easy to grow in a wide range of climates. Depending on variety, these marigolds can be orange, yellow, or mahogany. White sweet alyssum also works well as an anchor color plant (it's used that way in the Bountiful Border garden on page 60). But what if you want to gild your front-yard garden with some other color? Expand your color possibilities with these easy annual flowers that are widely available as bedding plants.

Pinks or purples. Petunias are powerful bloomers as long as they get a half day of sun. Pink petunias are especially heavy-flowering, and many new strains do an amazing job of adapting to extreme heat or cold.

Pastels. Zinnias come in pale yellow, pink, and even lime green, but you may need to mail-order seeds to obtain those special colors. Yellow or apricot calendulas or nasturtiums also bring a soft touch to the garden.

Blues. Blue is the garden's go-with-everything color, easily had in dwarf ageratum, a warm-natured annual that does well in humid heat. Where summers stay mild, consider solid-colored pansies that cover themselves with light blue or lilac blooms.

YEAR ONE
PLANTING AND CARE

ARE THERE HIDDEN RULES?

What if the neighbors don't like your out-of-the-ordinary front yard? Of course you should do everything you can to avoid conflict. Just in case you live near a person who loves to enforce random rules, check to see whether your municipality has ordinances that restrict front-yard gardening. It's possible that you might run into silly rules that limit the size of any garden to less than 30 to 40 percent of the landscape. But in most areas, your only challenge is to keep your front-yard garden from looking junky. This is easy to do with a simple design, attractive mulch, and eye-catching plants.

EARLY SPRING

1 **Prepare your site.** Select a site and use the spade or shovel and digging fork to remove grass and weeds from the beds. Evenly distribute the compost over the beds, and sprinkle on a generous dusting of organic fertilizer. Check soil moisture, and whenever the soil in your garden is dry enough to dig, use a spade or shovel and digging fork to mix the soil amendments and fertilizer into the top several inches of soil, and water well.

2 **Mulch the pathways.** Cut the grass in the pathways between beds as short as possible, and then use newspaper to pave over the pathways. To prevent the newspaper from blowing about, first dip sections in a tub of water before slapping them on the ground. Immediately cover the paper with 2 inches or more of hardwood or wood chip mulch.

MIDSPRING

3 **Plant potatoes.** One month before your last spring frost date, cut the potatoes in half and allow them to dry for a day before planting them in Bed 2. Plant each piece 2 inches deep, and allow 12 inches between pieces.

4 **Sow lettuce and parsley.** Sow the first patch of lettuce by scattering the seeds over the soil's surface so that they are about 1 inch apart. Pat them into place with your hand, barely covering with soil. Sow or transplant parsley in Bed 3.

5 **Plant more salad.** Two weeks later, plant the second patch of salad greens in Bed 1 and the chard in Bed 2. Plant scallions between the patches of greens—and anywhere else you find a place for them.

Using a green ribbon to weave tomato cages will create a nearly invisible trellis (left). Use broader, brightly colored ribbon to echo colors from your house or nearby flowers (right).

LATE SPRING

6 **Set out herbs.** After the last frost passes, plant thyme and basil in the oblong planters in Beds 1 and 2. Set the sage plants into Planter A.

7 **Plant tomatoes.** In Bed 3, dig planting holes for tomatoes 8 inches deep. As you transplant tomatoes, bury the lower portion of the stem as shown on page 27. Supplemental roots will grow from the buried section of stem. Pound four stakes into the ground at equal distances around each plant, forming two 18-inch squares. Tie the ribbon around the stakes in parallel tiers 12, 20, and 36 inches above soil level. Loop the ribbon around each stake to keep it from sagging too much. Trim the ends after tying them off in secure knots. As you work, protect the seedling from injury with a short stake, or cover it with a small pail or flowerpot.

8 **Start up some marigolds.** Sow marigold seeds in Bed 3, following instructions on the packet. If too many germinate, the extras are easy to move to other parts of your yard.

9 **Thin and weed.** As spring turns to summer, pull lettuce and scallions as you need them in the kitchen, and to make more elbow room for the growing plants. Check beds often for weeds, and pull them out when the soil is moist.

SUMMER

10 **Replace lettuce with beans.** Pull up and compost tattered lettuce from Bed 1. Soak bush bean seeds in water overnight before planting them as a replacement crop.

11 Dig potatoes, sow greens. Pull up potato plants from Bed 2 when the viney stems begin to lose their color and die back. Attached to each one—and hidden in nearby soil—you should find a cluster of four to seven potatoes to harvest. Scatter a dusting of organic fertilizer over the soil's surface and lightly mix in with a hand trowel. Rake soil to level the surface. Sow spinach, bok choy, and arugula seeds ¼ inch deep and 1 inch apart. Keep the soil moist until the seeds germinate. Gradually thin plants to 4 inches apart.

FALL

12 Put the garden to bed. A heavy frost will end the season for the snap beans, tomatoes, basil, and marigolds, but cold nights actually improve the flavor of leafy greens. Continue harvesting them as long as you can. As winter causes more and more vacancies, mulch the garden with shredded leaves or another mulch that looks attractive in winter.

COPING WITH URBAN GARDENING CONDITIONS

Urban spaces and old houses often have a long history that includes a variety of uses, some of which can be hazardous to your health if you're not careful. For example, use of lead-based house paint was common until the 1970s. In areas where painted buildings have stood for more than 50 years, you will need to have the soil tested for lead, which accumulates in soil over time as chips of lead-based paint flake off and land on the ground. In Massachusetts, data collected by an urban gardening group called The Food Project (http://thefoodproject.org) shows that lead concentrations tend to be highest in places where water drips from the roof. Since plants can absorb lead from the soil, you will need to garden in containers filled with purchased soil if tests show that your soil is contaminated. Your local Cooperative Extension office can tell you how to have your soil tested for lead or other contaminants.

Another common practice in times past was having a household trash heap on the property. Be sure to wear thick gloves the first few times you dig through your soil, and have a container ready for collecting bits of metal and broken glass. Many gardeners collect small bottles, lost toys, and other treasures they discover while digging.

Food plants in city gardens may need frequent showers, especially during periods of dry weather. Wash down plants with a fine spray of water to remove city grit before it builds up into a film that screens out the sunlight plants need to grow.

YEAR TWO
GARDEN PLAN

Exciting changes unfold as your Front-Yard Food Supply becomes a permanent part of the landscape. To start with, you'll install a decorative wood fence to protect the garden and define the front edge. As for the plants, a front-yard vegetable garden needs to look good year-round, and what could be prettier than a vibrant patch of green? You'll plant a small stand of wheat that you'll leave in place through winter.

I n year two, your Front-Yard Food Supply garden will remain a destination for neighbors out for an evening stroll. They're sure to admire your new fence, too, as long as you install it right. Keep these points in mind:

Wheat seedlings provide a welcome patch of green through winter.

- The benefits of a front-yard fence include the pretty and the practical, like supporting plants and deterring dog visitations, but do keep it low, at 2 to 3 feet. In most municipalities, the installation of a fence tall enough to restrict visibility requires a building permit.

- When selecting fencing materials, do not use pressure-treated wood. The chemicals used to preserve the wood can leach into the soil and be taken up by the plants you intend to eat. Opt for rot-resistant woods like cedar or redwood, or simply preserve the life of your fence with a waterproofing stain product or latex paint.

- In terms of fence design, an open picket pattern is best for plants because such fences allow fresh air to circulate and don't cast excessive shade. In a front-yard situation, see-through fences enhance safety and are considered fundamental to being a good neighbor, too.

- It's best to install a garden boundary fence after you have dug out weeds and turned the soil but before the bed is prepared for planting. To avoid accidentally causing a blackout or water or gas leak, find out where underground electric cables, water lines, and natural gas pipes are located before you dig postholes. Ask your local utility company to find and mark them for you.

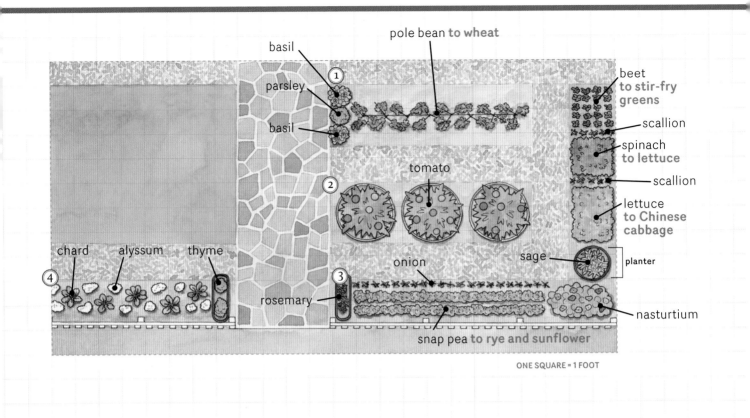

ONE SQUARE = 1 FOOT

NAME

The Front-Yard Food Supply: Year Two

FOOTPRINT

10 × 24 feet

SKILL LEVEL

Beyond beginner

WHEN TO PLANT

Midspring: snap peas, sweet alyssum, parsley, lettuce, spinach, beets, onions, scallions, nasturtiums, chard, and rosemary

Late spring: basil, tomatoes, and pole snap beans

Midsummer: sunflowers and rye or oats

Late summer: Chinese cabbage, more lettuce, and stir-fry greens

Fall: wheat

THE STUFF

FOR THE FENCE

- Seven 5-foot fence posts
- Five 3-foot preassembled panels of decorative wood fencing
- Medium-grade sandpaper
- Waterproofing stain or paint
- Bricks or logs (to help with fence assembly)
- Screws or other hardware for attaching fence to posts

FOR THE BEDS

- Ten 40-pound bags of compost, or about 7 wheelbarrow loads
- One 5- to 7-pound package of organic vegetable garden fertilizer

- One 10-inch stack of newspapers
- Three 40-pound bags of hardwood or wood chip mulch, or about 2 wheelbarrow loads
- Two oblong planters, 8 inches wide by 28–30 inches long (from year one garden)
- One round 14-inch-diameter planter (from year one garden)

FOR THE BEAN TRELLIS

- Twenty-four 8-foot-long bamboo poles or 1×2 pieces of lumber
- Cotton string or jute or hemp twine

FOR THE TOMATOES

- Three 5-foot-tall tomato cages
- Dark green or black rust-proofing paint

TOOLS

- Tape measure
- Posthole digger (a manual one will do the job)
- Carpenter's level
- 2 disposable paintbrushes
- Drill
- Screwdriver
- Wheelbarrow, cart, or wagon for moving bags of compost and mulch
- Spade or shovel
- Digging fork
- Hand trowel
- Scissors

THE PLANTS

BED ①

- Basil, 1 packet seeds or 2 seedlings
- Parsley, 1 packet seeds or 2 seedlings
- Snap bean (pole variety), 1 packet seeds
- Wheat, 1 packet seeds or 1 ounce wheat berries from the health food store

BED ②

- Tomato, 3 seedlings

BED ③

- Beet, 1 packet seeds
- Chinese cabbage, 1 packet seeds
- Lettuce mix, 2 packets seeds
- Nasturtium, 1 packet seeds
- Onion, 20 seedlings or sets
- Rosemary, 1 plant
- Rye or oat berries from the health food store, 1 ounce
- Sage, 1 plant (if needed as replacement)
- Scallions (with roots attached), 2 bunches, trimmed to 5 inches
- Snap pea (compact variety), 1 packet seeds
- Spinach, 1 packet seeds
- Stir-fry greens mix, 1 packet seeds
- Sunflower (dwarf variety), 1 packet seeds

BED ④

- Chard, mixed or single color, 1 packet seeds
- Thyme, 1 or 2 plants (if needed as replacements)
- White sweet alyssum, 1 packet seeds

YEAR TWO
PLANTING AND CARE

EARLY SPRING

1 Prepare the beds. About six weeks before your last frost, evenly distribute the compost over the old beds and sprinkle on a generous dusting of organic fertilizer. Dig through the beds to mix in the soil amendments and fertilizer. Renew hardwood or wood chip mulch in pathways.

2 Expand the footprint. As weather permits, dig and turn the soil in the new bed along the front edge of the garden, shaking out and composting chunks of grass or weeds. Install the fence (see Putting Up a Fence, page 80). Then work in 4 inches of compost.

3 Mulch the new pathways. Cut the grass in the new pathways as short as possible. Pave them over with wet newspaper covered with 2 inches or more of mulch or wood chips.

Dress up front-yard beds with easy bedding plants like blue ageratum.

MIDSPRING

4 Plant peas and friends. Three weeks before your last frost date, sow a double row of snap peas in the new section of Bed 3, and sow beets, spinach, and mixed lettuces as shown in the plan on page 76. Use scallions to mark divisions between plantings. Also plant onion seedlings or sets behind the peas in the new section of the bed and plant a few nasturtium seeds in the right front corner.

5 Mix up some chard and sweet alyssum. Plant chard seeds ½ inch deep and 4 inches apart in Bed 4. After the seeds germinate, thin them until the five prettiest plants remain. Scatter sweet alyssum seeds (about half a packet) between the chard; thin so that the thrifty flowers fill any open spaces between chard plants and dress up the edge of the bed.

6 **Update the herbs.** Move the sage container to Bed 3. Move the thyme and empty basil containers to the garden's entryway. Sprinkle 1 inch of compost into the containers of thyme and sage. As soon as plants become available, plant rosemary in the container used to grow basil the year before. Replace sage or thyme plants if the old ones succumbed to winter cold. Plant parsley in Bed 1.

LATE SPRING

7 **Plant tomatoes.** When the soil feels warm to your bare feet, set out tomato seedlings in Bed 2. Surround them with tomato cages that have been painted with dark green or black rust-retardant paint. Painting the cages helps them disappear into the background, which is a big plus in a front-yard setting.

8 **Plant trellised beans.** Make a tripod-style bean trellis in Bed 1, as described on page 33. Poke the bean seeds into the soil 1 inch deep and 4 inches apart around both sides of the trellis. Plant basil on both sides of the parsley.

MIDSUMMER

9 **Sow sunflowers and a cover crop.** Pull up the peas in Bed 3 and replace them with a mixed planting of cereal rye or oats and dwarf sunflowers. Broadcast the grain seeds so they are about 2 inches apart, and use your hands to cover them with soil. Sow sunflower seeds down the center of the row, planting them 1 inch deep and 6 inches apart. The grain will help improve the soil while serving as a lush green companion for upright sunflowers.

LATE SUMMER

10 **Sow fall greens.** Replace the spring crops in Bed 3 with stir-fry greens, more lettuce, and Chinese cabbage. Be sure to mix in a light application of compost and organic fertilizer before replanting the bed.

FALL

11 **Sow wheat.** When cold weather halts the growth of your pole beans, pull up the vines and take down the trellis. Store the poles in a dry place. Plant wheat seeds throughout the bed, ½ inch deep and about 2 inches apart. The wheat will grow throughout fall, but cold weather may kill it (and the rye) eventually. Even so, these crops are likely to stay green all winter.

PUTTING UP A FENCE

1 Outdoors or in a well-ventilated place, lightly sand the fence panels to remove splinters. Apply a water-proofing stain product or two coats of outdoor latex enamel; allow to dry.

2 Starting at the corners or ends of the fence, use the posthole digger to dig narrow 18-inch-deep holes for the fence posts, 4 feet apart. Use the tape measure to measure out the distance between posts carefully. Also use the tape measure to check the depth of each hole. Set the posts in place and backfill soil around them, packing it in firmly. Use the carpenter's level to make sure the posts are perfectly upright.

3 Attach the panels to the posts with wood screws or fence brackets (some panels come with their own hardware). Position the fence so that the bottom edge is 2 inches from the ground. Even with two people working together, it helps to place bricks, logs, or other spacers beneath the fence panels to hold them steady as you work. Have your helper hold the posts as you attach the fence panels, so you don't push posts loose in their holes.

YEAR THREE
GARDEN PLAN

Just when your neighbors think they have seen it all, your fabulously productive front-yard garden erupts with a tall tripod dripping with purple snap beans, flanked by supercharged summer squash.

More new crops will keep your gardening education on track, including enough cucumbers and dill to make a batch of pickles. Kohlrabi and carrots will bring crunch to your summer, followed by turnips in fall. You will have summer squash to enjoy with fresh tomatoes, and delicata squash (also called sweet potato squash) for roasting well into winter.

The Front-Yard Food Supply garden continues to borrow design tricks from flower gardening to make it worthy of front-and-center placement. Repeating a single type of flower (marigolds) and a veggie with a strong form and texture (onions) gives the planting a feeling of unity. A triangle of vertical elements (two trellised crops and a trio of caged tomatoes) create depth within a small space. A color parade led by chard adds to the excitement, but the Front-Yard Food Supply garden is about more than eye appeal. The vegetables here are famous for productivity, making it easy to grow more food than you ever imagined in a small front yard.

TELL ME MORE!
WHEN TO LET OLD CROPS GO

Keeping fall crops on schedule often means pulling up pea vines that are still holding a few blossoms, or summer squash plants that may yet produce a few more fruits. Put your nurturing instincts on the back burner, and resist the urge to continue tending crops that are past their prime. Remember that most vegetables are annual plants, so after they have produced a good crop of seed-bearing fruits, they figure their job is done. As you might expect, elderly plants are much more likely to develop pest and disease issues compared to vigorous young ones, so getting rid of aged plants at the first sign of trouble can go a long way toward keeping your garden healthy and productive. Failing plants detract from the appearance of a front-yard garden, too, so you are doing the right thing by pulling them up, digging in some compost, and planting something else.

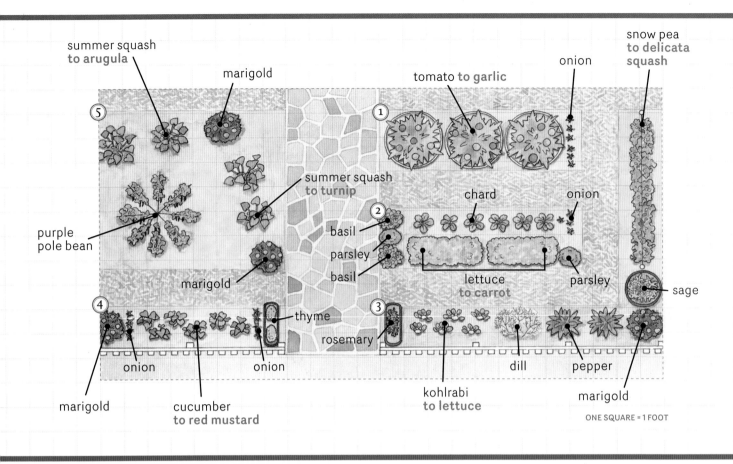

summer squash **to arugula**

marigold

tomato **to garlic**

onion

snow pea **to delicata squash**

⑤

summer squash **to turnip**

chard

onion

purple pole bean

basil

parsley

basil

②

lettuce **to carrot**

parsley

sage

marigold

④

thyme

rosemary

③

dill

pepper

onion

onion

kohlrabi **to lettuce**

marigold

marigold

cucumber **to red mustard**

ONE SQUARE = 1 FOOT

NAME

The Front-Yard Food Supply: Year Three

FOOTPRINT

10 × 24 feet

SKILL LEVEL

Beyond beginner

WHEN TO PLANT

Midspring: snow peas, parsley, lettuce, onions, kohlrabi, dill, and chard

Late spring: basil, tomatoes, peppers, pole snap beans, cucumbers, and summer squash

Midsummer: carrots and delicata squash

Late summer: more lettuce or other salad greens, turnips, arugula, and red mustard

Late fall: garlic

THE STUFF

FOR THE BEDS

- Twelve 40-pound bags of compost, or about 8 wheelbarrow loads
- One 5- to 7-pound package of organic vegetable garden fertilizer
- Two oblong planters, 8 inches wide by 28–30 inches long (from year one garden)
- One round 14-inch-diameter planter (from year one garden)

FOR THE PEA TRELLIS

- Two 6-foot-long wood or metal posts
- Cotton string, jute or hemp twine, or polyester garden netting

FOR THE TOMATOES

- Three 5-foot-tall painted tomato cages (see page 79)

FOR THE BEAN TRIPOD

- Eight 8-foot bamboo or slender wood stakes
- Cotton string or jute or hemp twine

TOOLS

- Wheelbarrow, cart, or wagon for moving compost
- Hand trowel
- Scissors
- Spade or shovel
- Digging fork
- Sledgehammer

THE PLANTS

BED ①

- Onion, 7 or 8 seedlings or sets
- Seed garlic, 2 to 3 bulbs (about ¼ pound)
- Tomato, 3 seedlings

BED ②

- Basil, 1 packet seeds or 2 seedlings
- Carrot, 1 packet seeds
- Chard, 1 packet seeds or 6 seedlings
- Lettuce, 3 packets seed, or 2 packets of a lettuce mix
- Onion, 4 or 5 plants or sets
- Parsley, 1 packet seeds or 2 seedlings

BED ③

- Delicata squash (also called sweet potato squash), 1 packet seeds
- Dill, 1 packet seeds or 3 seedlings
- Kohlrabi, 1 packet seeds or about 6 seedlings
- Lettuce or other salad greens, 1 packet seeds
- Marigold (dwarf variety), 3 seedlings
- Pepper (small-fruited variety), 2 seedlings
- Rosemary, 1 plant (if needed as replacement)
- Sage, 1 plant (if needed as replacement)
- Snow pea, 1 packet seeds

BED ④

- Cucumber, 1 packet seeds or 6 seedlings
- Onion, about 12 seedlings or sets
- Marigold, 1 seedling
- Red mustard, 1 packet seeds
- Thyme, 2 or 3 plants (if needed as replacements)

BED ⑤

- Arugula, 1 packet seeds
- Marigold (dwarf variety), 1 packet seeds or 2 seedlings
- Snap bean (purple-podded pole variety), 1 packet seeds
- Summer squash, 1 packet seeds or 4 seedlings
- Turnip, 1 packet seeds

YEAR THREE
PLANTING AND CARE

EARLY SPRING

1 Pull up cover crops. As soon as the soil dries out enough to work, pull up any remaining wheat or rye plants in Beds 1 and 3 (see page 79) and lay them atop the soil. After they have dried to death, they will make wonderful mulch.

2 Prepare for snow peas. During the first warm spell, dig 2 inches of compost into Bed 3 for the snow peas. Install a trellis for the peas between two posts, as described on page 25.

MIDSPRING

3 Start peas and planters. About four weeks before your last frost date, plant the peas. Prune back rosemary and thyme until you encounter live wood, which will show green at the center of the stem. Replace plants lost to winter cold, but rejuvenate the soil in the planters first: Spread 1 inch of composted manure, 1 inch of yard-waste compost, and a moderate dusting of organic fertilizer over the surface of the planters. Use a hand trowel to stab, slice, and mix these amendments into the potting soil. In containers with live plants, simply sprinkle 1 inch of compost over the surface of each container.

4 Plant lettuce and more. Dig 2 inches of compost and a light sprinkling of organic fertilizer into Bed 2. Plant lettuce or other salad greens, parsley, onions, and chard.

5 Finish spring planting. Two to three weeks later, set out kohlrabi and sow dill in Bed 3. Also sow more lettuce or salad greens mix in Bed 2.

6 Dig the new bed. Use the spade or shovel and digging fork to remove grass and weeds from Bed 5. Spread 3 inches of compost over the bed along with a generous dusting of organic fertilizer. Dig through the bed again to mix in the soil amendments and fertilizer.

7 **Plant tomatoes and more.** After the last frost passes, set out peppers and tomatoes and install tomato cages. Transplant basil into Bed 2. You can direct-sow basil if you live in a climate where the soil warms rapidly in late spring. Plant cucumber in Bed 4 and summer squash in Bed 5, or set out seedlings.

8 **Plant trellised beans.** In Bed 5, erect a 6- to 7-foot-tall tripod using the bamboo or wood poles, bound together near the top with string. Push the bases of the poles 2 inches into the ground before planting pole bean seeds all around the trellis.

ECHO KEY COLORS

Just because taste wins out over beauty in a food garden doesn't mean it can't be gorgeous. Adding flowers, keeping weeds under control, and using an attractive mulch are important, but you can also use the color of your food plants to create stunning visual pictures. One of the easiest techniques to use is color echoing—repeating similar colors provided by different plants. For example, you might grow bright orange 'Sweet Tangerine' tomatoes and orange chard, which becomes a three-way echo when they meet up with bright orange marigolds. Or play with purple by using purple basils, bush beans, and eggplant (which produces lovely lavender blossoms). In fall, red-to-bronze mustards and kales will quickly pump up the color in any garden—especially those dominated by arugula, collards, turnips, and other dark green leaves.

Crunchy kohlrabi matures quickly enough to make way for a fall planting of salad greens.

Closely spaced leafy greens shade out weeds when grown in blocks instead of rows.

MIDSUMMER

9 **Replace peas with squash.** When the peas in Bed 3 begin to fail, pull them up or cut the vines off at the surface, recondition the soil with compost and organic fertilizer, and plant seeds or seedlings of delicata squash. As the vines grow, help them climb by pushing new stem tips through the trellis netting.

10 **Swap in some fall crops.** Replace spring salad greens in Bed 2 with carrots. Fill space vacated by kohlrabi in Bed 3 with lettuce or other salad greens.

LATE SUMMER

11 **Sow leafy greens after vines.** Pull up and compost summer squash and cucumber plants as they begin to fail. This interrupts the life cycles of several pesky insects. Recondition the soil with compost and organic fertilizer before sowing arugula and turnip seeds in place of the squash and red mustard in place of the cucumbers. All of these leafy greens are easy to care for when grown in blocks. To create a block planting, broadcast the seeds, striving to have them land about an inch apart, and then walk over the planting to press the seeds into place. Provide water as needed to keep the soil moist until the seeds germinate. Gradually thin the plants to about 4 inches apart; eat the thinned ones.

12 **Harvest delicatas.** Cut delicata squash from the vine when the rinds become so hard that they cannot be easily pierced with your fingernail. When you cut one open, the seeds should appear plump and mature. Bring in all the squash before the first frost. The less-mature ones won't store well, but they are a nice fresh vegetable to roast, sauté, or add to stir-fry dishes. Just be sure to pare off the tough rinds first.

13 **Envision the future.** Remove the tomato cages and pull up tomatoes after they have been killed by frost. Now you're ready to make your own plan for next season, which will probably be a repeat of your previous years' successes along with a few new adventures. Just remember that if you want to grow garlic again, plant it in fall.

DOUBLE-CROP A TRELLIS

As long as you've gone to the trouble of putting up a trellis for your peas, why not get a bit more life out of it by following up with a crop of small-fruited winter squash? It can be done, but you'll need to use a couple of season-squeezing techniques to make it happen.

★ Choose a fast-maturing pea and get it started on time.

★ As soon as the peas start producing heavily, sow squash seeds in 4-inch pots, kept outdoors in filtered sun. Check the seedlings daily to make sure they don't dry out.

★ When the pea harvest slows to a trickle, use pruning shears to snip off the vines at the soil line. Clip off as much pea foliage as you can, but don't worry if there are still stems and tendrils stuck in the trellis.

★ Gently transplant the squash seedlings, disturbing the roots as little as possible. In sunny weather, cover the plants with shade covers for a few days to reduce transplant shock.

CHAPTER FOUR

FAMILY FOOD GARDENS

Worried about rising food prices and the quality of store-bought produce? You will save money and sleep better once you put a Family Food Garden to work in your backyard. This garden is designed to produce most of the vegetables a three- to four-person family can eat in a summer, plus a little extra to put by. Three climate-specific planting plans are tailored to fit short, medium, and long growing seasons.

If you've already done some vegetable gardening on your own or learned the ropes by installing one of the other gardens in this section of the book, you should be able to successfully implement a Family Food Garden. You can follow the planting plan suitable for your climate exactly as presented or modify the crop lists to better suit your personal tastes or your food preservation plans.

First, two comments. There is no sweet corn in any of these plans, mostly because it is such a space-hungry crop. Yet sweet corn offers up one of the finest tastes of summer, so by all means grow some if you like. Doing so will require adding more garden space or giving up other warm-season vegetables like tomatoes, peppers, and squash, which share the same weather preferences as sweet corn. The art of growing sweet corn is covered in Sweet Corn & Company on page 158.

Gardeners in cool climates will need to fill every square inch of garden with food crops in order to compensate for their short growing season. But gardeners in milder climates can devote some bed space to herbs and flowers as desired. Or you can install the complete Angel Wings Herb Garden garden plan that appears on page 96. Keep in mind that Part 3 discusses numerous options for varieties. Those pages will help you whether you're studying beautiful basils or looking for guidance on choosing varieties of lettuce or tomato. The more extreme your climate, the more likely you are to need specialized varieties.

SHORT, COOL SUMMERS GARDEN PLAN

From the Rocky Mountains to chilly New England hillsides, determined gardeners grow wonderfully productive food gardens like the one shown here. You have a fundamental choice: Work with what you have by emphasizing vegetables that grow well in cool weather, or push your luck to succeed with warm-natured crops. Here's some help thinking things through.

Hardy perennials. Two hardy perennial vegetables—asparagus and rhubarb—are foundation crops in cold climates. Their great asset is that they are well rooted and poised to grow as soon as the ground thaws in spring. Well-tended patches stay productive for years.

Onions, potatoes, cabbage, and cousins. The onion and cabbage families should be star players in cold-climate gardens, because they naturally grow well in cool conditions. Potatoes are usually easy-care crops, too.

Leafy greens. The same goes for leafy greens, so much so that it's easy to grow more than you can eat. Long-lived greens like kale and chard are often phenomenally productive when given water during dry spells. You need only a few plants.

Heat-loving crops. Want more than two tomatoes? Okay, but keep in mind that you'll need to stick with fast-maturing, cold-tolerant varieties (see page 220). Tomatoes need warmth, so unless you have a greenhouse, they will never be the strongest crops in a cold-climate garden. Think carefully before giving up a well-adapted crop like spinach or carrots in favor of comparatively risky tomatoes, peppers, or eggplant. A better idea is to grow these warm-natured veggies in black plastic pots kept on your deck or patio. The plants' roots will grow faster in the warm soil in the pots than they would in the ground, meaning more good food for you.

THE PLANTS

HARDY PERENNIALS: asparagus, rhubarb, thyme
When to plant: early to midspring, as soon as the ground thaws

EARLY COOL-SEASON ANNUALS OR BIENNIALS: potatoes, shallots, cabbage, peas, kale, lettuce, arugula, radishes, scallions, parsley
When to plant: starting four weeks before your last spring frost date

FROST-TOLERANT COOL-SEASON CROPS: onions, carrots, kohlrabi, chard, beets, leeks, spinach, dill, cilantro, Chinese cabbage, mustard
When to plant: one week before last spring frost date

WARM-SEASON CROPS: summer squash, winter squash, cucumbers, pole snap beans, tomatoes, basil
When to plant: one to three weeks after last spring frost

SUMMER-PLANTED COOL-SEASON CROPS: rutabaga, turnips
When to plant: as soon as space becomes available in summer

NAME
Family Food Garden for Short, Cool Summers

LENGTH OF GROWING SEASON
Less than 120 days between spring and fall frosts

FOOTPRINT
25 × 28 feet

SKILL LEVEL
Experience counts

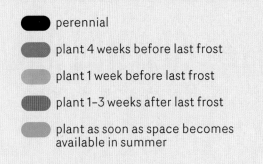

- perennial
- plant 4 weeks before last frost
- plant 1 week before last frost
- plant 1–3 weeks after last frost
- plant as soon as space becomes available in summer

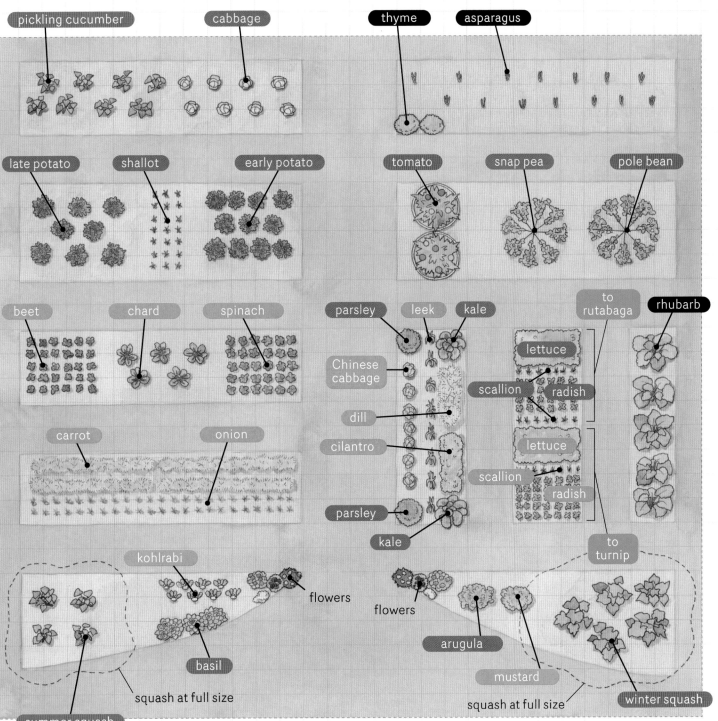

pickling cucumber · cabbage · thyme · asparagus

late potato · shallot · early potato · tomato · snap pea · pole bean

beet · chard · spinach · parsley · leek · kale · to rutabaga · rhubarb

Chinese cabbage · lettuce · scallion · radish

dill

cilantro · lettuce

scallion · radish

carrot · onion

parsley · kale · to turnip

kohlrabi · flowers

flowers · to turnip

arugula

basil · mustard

summer squash · squash at full size · squash at full size · winter squash

ONE SQUARE = 1 FOOT

FULL-SEASON SUMMERS GARDEN PLAN

From the mid-Atlantic states through the Midwest, gardeners have plenty of opportunities to grow a mix of superproductive crops like bush snap beans and easy-to-store winter squash, along with all the leafy greens you can eat. Where summer heat waves divide the growing season in half, strive to capture both cool seasons. Get an early start in spring, then gear up again in late summer for a second round of cool-season veggies.

FULL-SEASON SUMMER GARDEN TIPS

⭐ To make sure you have a continuous supply of salad greens, plant a few square feet every two to three weeks starting in early spring. In summer, use shade covers as described on page 114 to shield leafy greens from scorching sun.

⭐ Experiment to find the best spring planting dates for cabbage-family crops such as broccoli and kohlrabi. Expect a tight seven-day planting window: Try to set out four-week-old seedlings two to three weeks before your last frost date. Planting too early can backfire, because exposure to too much cold can trigger a flowering response.

⭐ Don't miss the chance to put winter to work by growing garlic, shallots, and other hardy perennial onions. If you're not familiar with all the onions and their cousins, see pages 203, 206, 207, 208, 210, 216, and 217.

THE PLANTS

EARLY COOL-SEASON CROPS: potatoes, cabbage, snap peas, first sowing of lettuce

When to plant: starting four to five weeks before your last spring frost date

CHILL-SENSITIVE COOL-SEASON CROPS: chard, kohlrabi, broccoli, beets, onions, scallions, first sowing of radishes, second sowing of lettuce

When to plant: three weeks before last spring frost date

WARM-SEASON CROPS: summer squash, winter squash, cucumbers, peppers, bush snap beans, tomatoes, last spring sowing of radishes and lettuce

When to plant: one to two weeks after last spring frost

SUMMER-PLANTED CROPS FOR FALL HARVEST: bush shell beans, carrots, parsnips, rutabaga, kale, arugula, mizuna, Asian greens, lettuce, spinach, turnips

When to plant: as soon as space becomes available from midsummer to early fall

HARDY ALLIUMS: garlic, shallots

When to plant: mid- to late fall, between the first frosts and the first hard freeze

Family Food Garden for Full-Season Summers

LENGTH OF GROWING SEASON
120–200 days between spring and fall frosts

FOOTPRINT
25 × 28 feet

SKILL LEVEL
Experience counts

plant 4–5 weeks before last frost

plant 3 weeks before last frost

plant 1–2 weeks after last frost

plant as soon as space becomes available in summer

plant in fall for overwintering

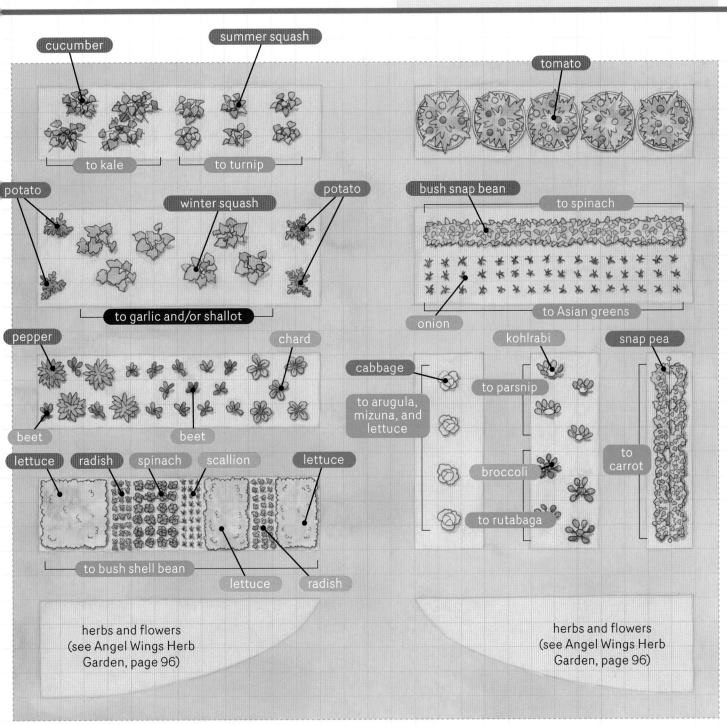

cucumber

summer squash

tomato

to kale

to turnip

potato

winter squash

potato

bush snap bean

to spinach

to garlic and/or shallot

onion

to Asian greens

pepper

chard

cabbage

kohlrabi

snap pea

to parsnip

to arugula, mizuna, and lettuce

beet

beet

broccoli

to carrot

lettuce radish spinach scallion lettuce

to rutabaga

to bush shell bean

lettuce radish

herbs and flowers
(see Angel Wings Herb
Garden, page 96)

herbs and flowers
(see Angel Wings Herb
Garden, page 96)

ONE SQUARE = 1 FOOT

LONG, HOT SUMMERS GARDEN PLAN

In most climates with hot summers and mild winters, you can keep your garden productive year-round.

True, only a few vegetables will actually offer good things to pick in winter, because short, dim winter days don't provide enough light to power most sun-loving vegetables. Yet numerous edibles will survive mild winters, making it possible to get your garden going very early in spring and keep it going well into fall.

The soil must work hard to support two or sometimes three crops planted back to back in the course of a growing season. So fall-to-spring cover crops of crimson clover, hairy vetch, and other soil-building plants are important players in long-season gardens. Managing relay plantings, crop rotations, and soil building can get complicated in a garden that never stops. Here are three ways to hold off chaos.

Plant in logical groups. Try to keep plant families grouped together as much as you can. For example, plant squash and cucumbers in the same row. When that's not practical, look for crops that grow on the same schedule, such as potatoes and onions (spring) or sweet potatoes and okra (summer).

Rely on diversity. Diversify to grow a wider assortment of crops and confuse pests. It's the best way to minimize losses due to insects, disease, or bad weather.

Take good care of "idle" soil. Keep soil microbes well fed by adding compost between plantings, using biodegradable mulches, and planting cover crops when soil will not be needed for more than a month.

THE PLANTS

EARLY COOL-SEASON ANNUALS OR BIENNIALS: peas, potatoes, onions, lettuce and other salad greens
When to plant: starting four to six weeks before last spring frost date

CHILL-SENSITIVE COOL-SEASON CROPS: chard, kohlrabi, radishes, beets, carrots
When to plant: three weeks before last spring frost date

WARM-SEASON CROPS: summer squash, cucumbers, pole snap beans, tomatoes, eggplant, peppers
When to plant: one to two weeks after last spring frost

HEAT-TOLERANT WARM-SEASON CROPS: okra, sweet potatoes, southern peas, buckwheat (cover crop), bush snap beans, edamame
When to plant: as soon as space becomes available in summer

COOL-SEASON FALL CROPS: collards, kale, salad greens (arugula, mesclun, lettuce, spinach), broccoli, turnips
When to plant: in late summer, as nighttime temperatures become cooler

HARDY CROPS TO GROW FROM FALL TO SPRING: shallots, spinach, garlic, hardy cover crops (including hairy vetch, winter peas, wheat, and other cereal grains)
When to plant: midfall, at around the time of first frost

NAME
Family Food Garden for Long, Hot Summers

LENGTH OF GROWING SEASON
More than 210 days between spring and fall frosts

FOOTPRINT
25 × 28 feet

SKILL LEVEL
Experience counts

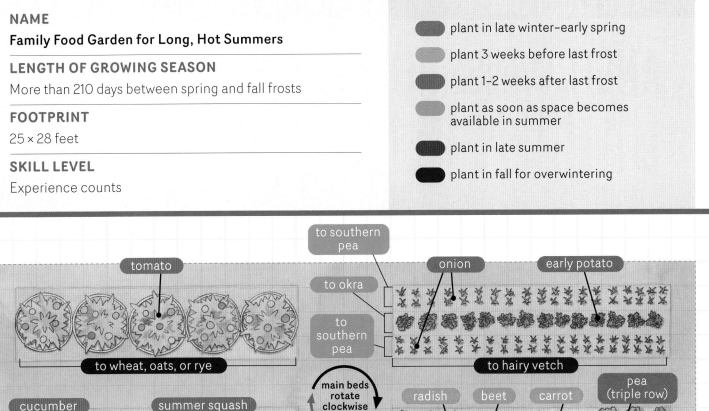

- plant in late winter–early spring
- plant 3 weeks before last frost
- plant 1–2 weeks after last frost
- plant as soon as space becomes available in summer
- plant in late summer
- plant in fall for overwintering

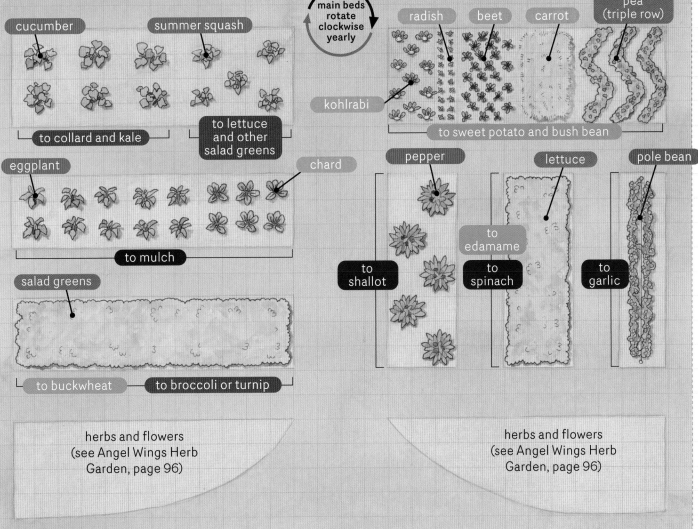

tomato

to southern pea

to okra

to southern pea

onion

early potato

to wheat, oats, or rye

to hairy vetch

main beds rotate clockwise yearly

cucumber

summer squash

radish

beet

carrot

pea (triple row)

kohlrabi

to collard and kale

to lettuce and other salad greens

to sweet potato and bush bean

eggplant

chard

pepper

lettuce

pole bean

to mulch

to edamame

salad greens

to shallot

to spinach

to garlic

to buckwheat

to broccoli or turnip

herbs and flowers
(see Angel Wings Herb
Garden, page 96)

herbs and flowers
(see Angel Wings Herb
Garden, page 96)

ONE SQUARE = 1 FOOT

ANGEL WINGS HERB GARDEN
GARDEN PLAN

A food garden without culinary herbs is missing its most important part. From basil to peppermint, herbs valued for their flavors and aromas deserve a place in your garden. Ideally, that place should be close to your kitchen door, because in terms of frequency of picking, no crop will outdo herbs. In summer, you may find it impossible to cook a meal without running out to pick fresh herbs at least once.

Herbs are often touted as requiring only poor soil, but most perform much better if the soil is improved with at least a 2-inch layer of compost or other rich organic matter as the beds are prepared. Excellent drainage is important, so this is one area of the garden where raising the beds a bit is a good idea. Framing the beds is optional; mere mounding of improved soil about 4 inches high will do.

Plenty of sun brings out the best flavors of culinary herbs, so take care to locate tall herbs such as dill and big-framed varieties of basil where they won't shade their neighbors. As you play with your own designs, look for ways to add contrasting colors and textures. The gray leaf tones of sage and rosemary impart a natural glow that flatters neighboring plants with darker leaves. And though they are not used here, frilly lettuces and dwarf chards such as 'Pot of Gold' are great for adding color and gloss to a small herb garden. All of the smallish herbs—chives, parsley, marjoram, thyme, and winter savory—make great plants for softening the edges of the beds.

MIDSPRING

1 **Plant hardy herbs.** About four weeks before your last frost date, direct-sow parsley and cilantro seeds. Set out purchased chive, garlic chive, tarragon, and creeping thyme plants. You also can set out container-grown lavender, oregano, sage, parsley, peppermint, winter savory, and English thyme while nights remain cool.

THE PLANTS

HARDY PERENNIALS: winter savory, sage (variegated and plain), oregano, garlic chives, peppermint, thyme (creeping and English or upright), chives, tarragon, lavender
When to plant: early spring to early summer

COOL-SEASON ANNUALS OR BIENNIALS: parsley (Italian and curled), cilantro, dill
When to plant: midspring and early fall

HALF-HARDY PERENNIALS: rosemary (creeping and upright), marjoram
When to plant: midspring; overwinter indoors or with protection

WARM-SEASON ANNUAL: basil (all types)
When to plant: late spring, after frost date has passed; direct-sow more in midsummer

NAME
Angel Wings Herb Garden

FOOTPRINT
4 × 28 feet

WHEN TO PLANT
Spring: for the main garden
Summer: a few additional plantings

SKILL LEVEL
Experience counts

⬤ plant in early spring–early summer
⬤ plant midspring and early fall
⬤ plant midspring
⬤ plant in late spring, after frost has passed

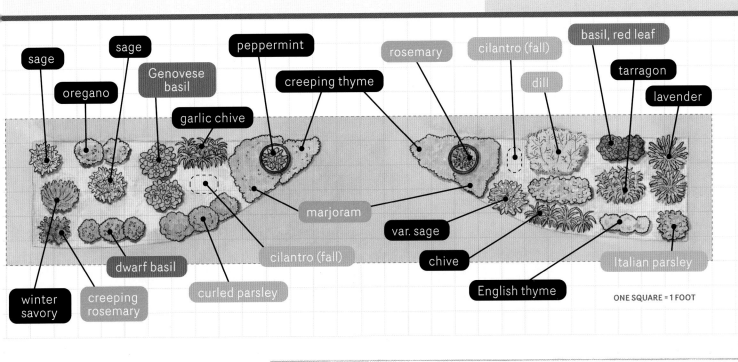

sage
sage
peppermint
rosemary
cilantro (fall)
basil, red leaf
oregano
Genovese basil
creeping thyme
dill
tarragon
lavender
garlic chive
marjoram
var. sage
dwarf basil
cilantro (fall)
chive
Italian parsley
winter savory
creeping rosemary
curled parsley
English thyme
ONE SQUARE = 1 FOOT

LATE SPRING

❷ **Plant basil and more.** As your last frost date passes, plant dill and basil seeds and set out purchased marjoram and rosemary plants.

FALL

❸ **Sow more cilantro.** After harvesting or trimming the plants, sow cilantro to fill gaps with color and flavor.

WILL THEY COME BACK?

Planting an herb garden can be a big investment of time and money, but many hardy perennial herbs will come back year after year, even in cold climates. Chives, mints, and tarragon are hardy to Zone 3; lavender and oregano survive winter in Zone 5; sage, winter savory, parsley, and a few types of rosemary are hardy to Zone 6. Wherever you garden, you can improve the winter survival of your hardy herbs by mulching them with 4 inches of shredded leaves or other lightweight material in fall. In addition, wait until spring to prune back the dead tops from the plants. Through winter, the old stems will help shelter the plants' crowns from drying winds and other dangers of the season.

If you'd rather be safe than sorry, pot up your rosemary and other marginally hardy herbs in late summer. Leave them outdoors until the first hard freeze comes. Trim back the plants, then move them to a cool place like an unheated garage where they can wait out winter. Replant soon after the ground thaws in spring.

ESSENTIAL TECHNIQUES
AND MORE PLANTING PLANS

A good garden must be grown from the ground up, its soil coaxed toward fertility with heaping helpings of organic matter, but a gardener's art is not only about building soil and picking produce. Gaining a working knowledge of the mini-seasons in which vegetables and herbs grow best is basic, and in the process you will match your plants' preferences with the weather trends in your garden.

PURPOSEFUL PLANTING PLANS

The garden plans in this part of the book are designed to help you understand how crops, climate, and specialized methods work together to make a food garden healthy, beautiful, and productive. Each chapter includes charts and other information related to issues like weeding and watering, and among these I've sprinkled dozens of practical tips I learned the hard way.

These 11 planting plans give new gardeners and those with some experience a chance to try out or refine gardening skills, such as starting seeds indoors in containers or using special hoses called soaker hoses to water more efficiently. Some of the plans also demonstrate how to design a garden around a culinary theme (think homemade marinara sauce). To keep things simpler still, most of the layouts match footprints of the garden plans in Part 1. So once you've created a garden based on Part 1, you'll find it easy to try out a plan from Part 2 in your existing framework of garden beds.

The instructions in this section will help you take on gardening challenges as they come, which they surely will. Each season there will be new insects to identify (many more friends than foes), and you will develop a new appreciation for grass clippings and shredded leaves as your need for mulch increases. My goal here is to get you started using sound techniques and good gardening habits that will serve you well for the rest of your life.

CHAPTER FIVE

DECIDING WHAT TO GROW

Any experienced vegetable gardener will tell you that the key to success is finding vegetables that like your garden as much as you like them. While engaged in this quest, be prepared to try some new tastes. Your garden's best crops may turn out to be a little different from those you're accustomed to buying at the store. Keep an open mind and an open kitchen, and your garden will gradually transform your diet into one based upon the freshest, most nutritious foods on earth—vegetables you've grown yourself.

IT'S ALL IN THE TIMING

Most of the garden plans in this book use vegetables that will grow just about anywhere as long as you plant them at the right time. Exact planting dates for a particular crop vary wildly from one region of the United States to another, but in general veggies are planted in seasonal phases, in the following groups (note that some crops fall into more than one group):

Group 1: Cold-tolerant plants. These crops can be set out or planted before the last frost, while the soil is still cool. They often benefit from row covers, cloches, or plastic tunnels, which raise and moderate temperatures while shielding plants from cold winds. Crops in this group include arugula, bok choy, broccoli, cabbage, collards, garlic, kale, lettuce (and mesclun mixes), mizuna and other Asian greens, mustard, onion, peas (snap, snow, and shelling), radish, shallot, spinach, and turnip. Several perennial vegetables and herbs fall into this category as well: asparagus, chives, garlic chives, mints, and rhubarb.

Group 2: Semi-hardy plants. This group prefers cool to moderate growing temperatures but may be damaged by hard freezes or cold winds. They often benefit from row covers, cloches, or plastic tunnels, or you can use old blankets for overnight protection from cold. Crops in this group include beet, carrot, cauliflower, celery, chard, Chinese cabbage, cilantro, dill, endive, kohlrabi, leek, lettuce (and mesclun mixes), parsley, parsnip, potato, radish, and rutabaga. Four favorite perennial herbs belong in this category, too: oregano, rosemary, sage, and

HIGH-YIELD INVESTMENT PLANTING

Which food crops give the best return in dollars and cents? Salad greens and fresh herbs rank high, along with very seasonal veggies like delicate peas in early summer. Your preferences also play a part, so you may want to try this experiment. During a season when your garden is not producing, save all of your grocery store receipts and take a close look at where your produce department money is going. Fine-tune your planting plans to include expensive veggies you would like to eat more often if they didn't cost so much—but only if they are a good fit for your climate.

thyme. Rosemary is the least tough, needing protection in areas colder than Zone 7, while the other three can survive Zone 4 winters once established. (For an explanation of hardiness zones, see the box on the facing page).

Group 3: Warm-natured plants. In this group you'll find crops that are unable to tolerate frost; they grow best when soil temperatures are warm. This group includes basil, beans, corn, cucumber, edamame, eggplant, marjoram, melons, okra, pepper, pumpkin, squash (all types), sweet potato, tomato, and watermelon.

Group 4: Plants for fall. These crops grow well when planted from late summer to fall. Very hardy species like garlic and spinach can be grown through winter. Use row cover or plastic tunnels to stretch the harvest season for the following veggies into early winter: arugula, beet, bok choy, broccoli, cabbage, cauliflower, Chinese cabbage, cilantro, collards, garlic, kale, leek, lettuce, mesclun, mizuna, mustard, parsley, parsnip, radish, rutabaga, scallion, shallot, spinach, and turnip.

VEGETABLES AND CLIMATE

Depending on the climate in your area, one of the seasonal veggie groups may perform much better than another. Here are some general guidelines to

keep in mind as you study the planting plans in this book and fine-tune them to fit your tastes and your garden's special quirks.

Cool Summers and Cold Winters

Frost-tolerant root crops like broccoli, cabbage, carrot, onion, and beet are safe, sure bets, as are all types of peas. Develop a taste for spinach, chard, arugula, and other leafy greens, and celebrate your brief summer with cucumbers, squash, and bush snap beans. These veggies grow quickly anyway, and using fast-maturing varieties will bring them in even sooner. Use large, dark-colored containers to provide warm roots for prolific cherry tomatoes. In cold climates, even vegetables like garlic and shallots that are planted in fall for harvest the following summer do well when they are protected from winter cold by a thick layer of mulch. Hardy perennial vegetables like asparagus and rhubarb have a unique advantage, in that they are already well rooted and ready to grow first thing in spring.

Warm Summers and Cold Winters

Use spring, fall, or both cool seasons to juggle quick crops of lettuce, spinach, and other leafy greens. Move quickly in spring to grow a good crop of peas and potatoes before hot weather comes. Tomatoes, peppers, and most beans love summer's heat, but you'll need to keep them mulched to stop soil moisture from cooking away. You'll have to experiment to find the best planting times for broccoli and other cabbage-family crops. If cabbage cousins don't do well when planted in spring because cool nights don't last long enough, try growing them from late summer to fall.

Hot Summers and Mild Winters

Garlic grown from fall to spring is amazingly productive because you can grow special types that are not winter hardy in northern areas. The type of garlic best for braiding (called softneck types), as well as juicy, sweet, short-day onions (like those grown in Georgia and Texas), must have mild winters to do their best. Peppers, eggplant, and sweet potatoes love hot, humid summers, and you may find that tomatoes and summer squash grow almost too well. Fall is often a dream season in mild-winter climates, ideal for growing broccoli, collards, and a long list of leafy greens from every corner of the world.

HARDINESS ZONES AND FROST DATES

USDA Hardiness Zone Map

The United States Department of Agriculture (USDA) created the hardiness zone map based on minimum winter temperatures, and knowing your zone helps you predict the length of your growing season. Type in your zip code at www.garden.org/zipzone to find your hardiness zone. Keep in mind that climate factors like high elevation or extreme wind can push you into a colder zone. Gardeners sometimes add an "a" or "b" to their zone number, with "a" being colder than "b." So gardeners in central Missouri may say they are in Zone 5b, while Iowans might regard themselves as being in Zone 5a.

First and Last Frost Dates

Vegetable plants grow on set schedules, and it's up to you to find the best planting dates for them based on the average dates of your first and last frosts. You can get these dates from your local Cooperative Extension office, or look them up on the internet. Victory Seeds (www.victoryseeds.com) hosts a simple first and last frost finder for the United States and Canada, as do many other online resources.

You should commit your garden's average first and last frost dates to memory (or write them on your calendar), but keep in mind that they are merely averages. In some years, spring will come early, and in others it may run as much as a month late, and the same thing can happen in fall. However, using your average frost dates as a guide is still smart, because they reflect seasonal changes in soil temperatures, which is often of crucial importance to your garden plants.

CHAPTER SIX

DESIGNING BEAUTIFUL FOOD GARDENS

In addition to growing gardens of my own, as a writer I have been able to get behind-the-fence looks at hundreds of great food gardens over the last 30 years. Anyone who thinks food gardens aren't pretty hasn't looked lately, because organic gardens are getting more beautiful all the time—and for purely practical reasons. A good organic garden needs flowers, which attract crucial pollinators and legions of other beneficial insects. And here's something I've noticed in my years of garden snooping: Ornamental gardens with a few edibles thrown in often look tacky, but edible gardens with an artful smattering of flowers are usually nothing short of stunning.

FROM FLOWERS TO FOOD

Are you transitioning into edibles after spending many seasons working primarily with flowers? Or perhaps you feel torn between growing beautiful ornamental plants and good things to eat. You really can have it all by adapting several standard design tricks used in flower gardens to beautify your edible beds. As you study the design guidelines shown on the next few pages, spend some time imagining how they might play out in your one-of-a-kind garden.

If you're actually replacing ornamentals with edibles, keep in mind that many chemicals used to maintain flowers and lawns are not legal (or safe) for edible plants. Don't grow edibles in sites where pesticides have been heavily used in the past, such as an exhibition rose garden. Several vegetables, including spinach, chard, and beets, easily absorb funky chemical residues from tainted soil. In addition, some herbicides used on lawns can damage tomatoes, beans, and other sensitive crops.

You can't go wrong by planting colorful flowers along your garden's main point of entry, as is done here with dark-leafed coleus and spiky celosia.

Exploit the Edges

Dwarf curled parsley is a perfect plant to weave into low edgings, where it combines easily with compact marigolds, upright clumps of chives, or mounds of lemon thyme. Colorful leafy greens, including lettuce, beet greens, and red-leafed spinach, make great edging plants, too. I once saw an edging at a famous public arboretum composed of pansies and tatsoi, a beautifully symmetrical Asian green.

Look for Fine Neutrals and Blues

White, gray, and blue go with everything, so puddles of white sweet ageratum or upright spikes of blue-green leeks look great anywhere. The sage family is a rich source of blue flowers, and you can eat the flowers and leaves of most species. The gray foliage of culinary sage is also a great neutral choice for a mixed bed.

Anchor the Ends

When a manageable-size planting won't quite fill a bed, use the ends of the beds for flowers or herbs. This approach puts kitchen herbs in accessible spots while increasing the plant diversity within the bed—two fundamental goals of any successful planting plan.

Above: It's easy to bring light and color to the edges of veggie beds by planting pansies and other easy annuals. When you are working mostly with the color green, you can still create visual drama by combining plants with different textures, as is done here with herbs, leafy greens, and kale.

Right: Lavender, cabbage, and eggplant work together to echo the color purple.

Pole beans form a curtain of green behind a riot of red cabbage.

Stack Plants by Size

Placing tall plants behind shorter ones creates visual depth while ensuring that all plants get plenty of sun. And just as an ornamental border often needs a vibrant green backdrop, edible gardens may benefit from the addition of dramatic backdrop plants like sunflowers and sweet corn or tall trellises dripping with pole beans, asparagus beans, or cucumbers.

Group Like Plants Together

It's much easier to tend to plants' special needs when they grow side by side, but group work in the vegetable garden has another benefit. Keeping plant families together makes it simple to rotate or move plantings from year to year, so you don't plant the same (or similar) plants in the same place over and over. Rotating from one plant family to another (for example, tomatoes to squash, or garlic to beans) prevents numerous problems with diseases and insects that live in the soil. The planting plans in Part 1 show many examples of well-chosen plant groupings and basic rotation principles in action.

TEMPTING TEXTURES

In garden design, plants with big, floppy leaves such as tomatoes and chard are said to have a coarse texture, while plants with small or intricately cut leaves (carrots, bulb fennel) have a fine texture. Contrasting textures often please the human eye. Unfortunately, most vegetables are on the coarse side, texture-wise, so you will need to combine them with nonveggie, fine-textured plants to make the most of this design trick. Culinary herbs such as parsley, oregano, rosemary, and thyme are great fine-textured plants, and the ferny fronds of dill will lighten the look of any bed. With their frothy flowers, sweet alyssum, ageratum, and portulaca (moss rose) are easy-to-grow annuals that fall into the fine-textured category.

CHAPTER SEVEN

WORKING WITH SEEDS AND SEEDLINGS

Except for asparagus, rhubarb, and hardy perennial herbs, most of the food plants you will grow are annuals. Botanically speaking, annual plants need only one year to go from seed to seed in a complete life cycle. So a food gardener is always starting seeds of something, whether it's indoors under lights or outdoors in the garden. These days, you also have the option of starting your entire garden from purchased seedlings, which gets the season off to a very fast start.

The three garden plans in this chapter cover the three main ways to plant your garden—from purchased seedlings, from seeds sown directly in the garden, or from seeds started indoors. You should learn all three skills, because each has its place in your garden.

- You can learn the fundamentals of how plants grow and receive fast rewards by working with purchased lettuce, tomato, and cucumber seedlings in the Overnight Success garden plan (page 110). This is a great way to get over beginner jitters or to save time if you're off to a late start.

- Several vegetables grow best when the seeds are sown right where they are to grow. The Strictly from Seed garden plan (page 118) shows you how to coax direct-sown seeds to life at different times during the growing season.

- Starting your own seedlings indoors under lights is fun and rewarding, because it enables you to try interesting varieties and control their planting dates, and it can save you money. The Paintbrush Beds garden plan (page 126) provides a small sample of the excitement ahead for gardeners who learn to grow their own seedlings.

Most experienced gardeners use all three methods every year, relying on a few purchased seedlings for convenience, direct-seeding easy crops like beans, and starting a few special seedlings indoors. With a little practice, you will be able to get your garden growing—and keep it going—by using all of these planting techniques.

Thinning to one plant per pot helps seedlings grow fast and strong.

OVERNIGHT SUCCESS
GARDEN PLAN

If you're among the many gardeners who like the idea of an instant organic garden grown from plants picked up at your local garden center, this plan is for you. It will take you only a few hours to prepare the soil in this compact garden, and even less time to plant it.

On a pleasant spring day, you'll love taking an hour or so to plant cool-season parsley and lettuce, along with an eye-pleasing combo of frothy sweet alyssum and upright blue-green broccoli. As the soil warms, a second planting session of under an hour will get your peppers, tomatoes, squash, and cucumbers into the ground.

This is a great little garden for a beginner, because patience is one of the hardest lessons new gardeners must learn. Several of the plants here are famous for their vigorous growth, which gets faster as the weather becomes warmer. In a few short weeks, the exuberant squash and cucumbers will turn the front of the garden into a sea of foliage. To make it easier to harvest your squash and cucumbers without stepping on the vines, place small boards in several strategic spots for use as temporary stepping-stones.

The garden itself is simple enough, but the lessons you learn from it in the course of one short growing season will be huge. You will have grown six vegetables, three yummy kitchen herbs, and a fragrant flower, and you will be eager to try more varieties in your quest for the best.

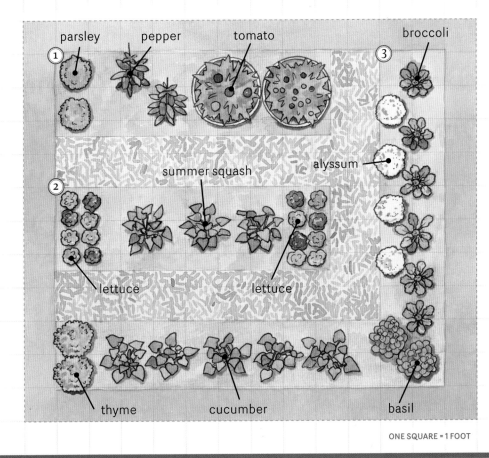

parsley pepper tomato broccoli
summer squash
alyssum
lettuce lettuce
thyme cucumber basil

ONE SQUARE = 1 FOOT

NAME
Overnight Success

FOOTPRINT
10 × 12 feet

SKILL LEVEL
Fine for first-timers

WHEN TO PLANT
Midspring: parsley, lettuce, thyme, sweet alyssum, and broccoli
Late spring: peppers, tomatoes, squash, cucumbers, and basil

THE STUFF

FOR THE BEDS
- Ten 40-pound bags of compost, or about 7 wheelbarrow loads
- One 5- to 7-pound package of organic vegetable garden fertilizer
- 12-inch stack of newspapers or cardboard
- Three 40-pound bags of hardwood or wood chip mulch
- Small boards or flat stones for stepping-stones

FOR THE TOMATOES
- Two 5-foot-tall tomato cages

FOR THE PEPPERS
- Two 3-foot-long wood stakes
- Strips of soft cloth about 1 inch wide and 10 inches long

FOR THE BROCCOLI
- Six 3 × 6-inch strips of aluminum foil

TOOLS
- Wheelbarrow, cart, or wagon for moving compost and mulch
- Spade or shovel
- Digging fork
- Hand trowel
- Scissors (for compost bags and cloth strips)

THE PLANTS

BED 1
- Parsley, 2 seedlings
- Pepper (small-fruited varieties), 2 seedlings
- Tomato, 2 seedlings, including 1 cherry type

BED 2
- Lettuce (varying colors and leaf textures), 16 seedlings
- Summer squash, 3 seedlings

BED 3
- Basil, 2 seedlings
- Broccoli, 6 seedlings
- Cucumber, 5 seedlings
- Sweet alyssum, 4 seedlings
- Thyme, 2 plants

OVERNIGHT SUCCESS
PLANTING AND CARE

EARLY SPRING

1 **Prepare the beds.** About six weeks before your last frost, prepare the beds. If starting from scratch, use a spade or shovel and digging fork to remove grass and weeds from the bed. Evenly distribute the compost over the beds, and sprinkle on a generous dusting of organic fertilizer. Check soil moisture, and whenever the soil in your garden is dry enough to crumble easily when dug, use your preferred digging tool to mix the compost and fertilizer into the top 10 inches of soil.

2 **Mulch the pathways.** Cover pathways with damp newspaper or cardboard, topped with 2 inches of hardwood or wood chip mulch (see page 148).

MIDSPRING

3 **Pamper your seedlings.** As soon as you bring seedlings home from the garden center, water them thoroughly and keep them in a bright place, protected from wind. If roots are growing out through the drainage holes in the containers, transplant the seedlings to slightly larger pots if it's too early to plant them outdoors. Fertilize plants weekly with a mix-with-water organic fertilizer. For more tips on caring for seedlings, see Guaranteed Seedling Success on page 114.

DIG THIS!

When shopping for veggie and herb seedlings, keep in mind that smaller is usually better. Young plants that have not suffered the stress of cramped roots will grow faster and better than older plants that have sat around too long in small pots. If you end up with extra plants, repot them in roomy containers and keep them in a sunny but protected spot outdoors. That way, you will have a ready replacement should you lose a plant in your garden to accidental damage, hungry critters, or disease.

HOW DEEP TO PLANT?

The default setting is to transplant a seedling at the same depth it grew in its container, but this rule does not apply with several popular home garden vegetables.

✱ Tomatoes eagerly form new roots on sections of buried stem. Plant them deep, so that only the top four to six leaves show at the soil line. (See page 27 for more on planting tomatoes.)

✱ Planting peppers slightly deeper than they grew in their containers—up to the nubby seedling leaves—helps insulate the roots from heat and drought.

✱ Leafy greens and some members of the cabbage family often show a short length of stem at the surface that connects the roots to the growing crown, or point from which new leaves emerge. In this situation, set the plants so that the growing crown sits right at the soil line. To do this, place seedlings a little deeper than they were in their containers, and then mound up loose soil over the exposed section of stem.

4 Set out cool-season crops. Three weeks before your last frost date, watch the forecast for a period of calm weather, because harsh winds can easily damage tender seedlings. Set out lettuce, parsley, sweet alyssum, thyme, and broccoli, taking time to water the plants well before you begin. To remove seedlings from plastic containers, hold the containers sideways, and push and then squeeze the bottom to pop out the rootball. It is often easiest to cut or tear away containers made of paper, peat, or other biodegradable materials. Handle plants by the rootball, and avoid touching the main stem.

5 Make cutworm collars. Gently encase the base of each broccoli seedling with a loose armor of aluminum foil. Mound a little soil around the foil "collar" to hold it in place. These collars prevent cutworms from munching on seedling stems. These soil-dwelling caterpillars often cause heavy casualties to seedlings set out in spring, but they can't get through the foil collars.

A foil collar protects a newly transplanted broccoli seedling from night-feeding cutworms.

LATE SPRING

6 Plant tomatoes and more. One to two weeks after the last frost has passed, set out peppers, tomatoes, squash, cucumber, and basil seedlings. Push a stake firmly into the ground beside each pepper plant, but wait until the plants grow to 12 inches tall before tying them to the stake with soft strips of cloth. Install tomato cages as soon as the plants are set out, as shown on page 132.

GUARANTEED SEEDLING SUCCESS

Whether they're store-bought or homegrown, healthy seedlings save you weeks of growing time, and robust seedlings have a huge advantage over weeds. Many vegetables grow as well—or better—from transplanted seedlings as from direct-sown seeds, while others have well-deserved reputations for being difficult to transplant. But in my experience, you can transplant just about anything once you develop good instincts for the task. Practice makes perfect.

Most of the "starts" you buy will be true seedlings (juvenile plants grown from seed), but perennial herbs are often grown from rooted cuttings. Plants grown from cuttings are generally a bit tougher than newborns, so they are good plants to work with if your thumb is just starting to turn green.

Have you killed adopted seedlings in the past? Ensure your success with everything you transplant by following these four guidelines.

Give your seedlings daily attention. Make sure their roots stay lightly moist by dribbling small amounts of room-temperature water into the containers every two to three days. Every other time you water, use a dilute organic plant food (such as a fish/kelp product). Mix with water at half the strength recommended on the label. If you're growing your plants from seed, begin fertilizing the seedlings two to three weeks after the seeds sprout.

Give them room to grow. If you can see roots growing out of the bottom of a container, gently replant the seedling into a slightly larger container. When potting, try to handle the plant by the rootball, which will come out of the container best if it's quite wet and you give it a good shove from the bottom. Avoid touching the main stem, which can cause invisible bruises.

Gradually introduce them to the outdoors. Even the youngest veggie seedlings crave sunshine, so give them all you can, but not too much all at once. Start exposing them to increasing levels of sunlight by placing them in a sunny window. Then, about two weeks before you plan to plant out the seedlings in garden beds, begin the process called hardening off by carrying the trays of containers outdoors on calm, sunny days. If the weather turns windy, either bring them in or place them in a protected frame or plastic-covered tunnel (described on pages 186 and 187). In the last two to three days before transplant day, leave the seedlings outside all day and all night.

Create good conditions for your transplants. To help your little plants start stretching their roots into surrounding soil the day they go into the ground, thoroughly water the bed the day before you transplant. Water the plants again after they have been settled into place. Immediately cover the plants with roomy shade covers such as upturned flowerpots or bushel baskets, cardboard boxes, or a piece of cloth held aloft with hoops or stakes. Remove the covers after two days, but keep them handy. Should the weather turn very windy or cold, pop the covers back on until conditions improve. *Warning:* Failure to spoil seedlings rotten during the first few days after transplanting may spoil your success.

HOW LONG DO THEY GROW?

This chart groups vegetable crops by the length of time it takes from sowing seeds in containers until the seedlings are ready to plant outside in a garden bed. Use this table to decide which crops to grow yourself and which ones to buy prestarted. Much of the value of purchased seedlings lies in time you didn't have to spend growing them yourself, so seedlings in the 10- to-12-week group are usually good buys.

Indoor Growing Time	Crops	Seedling-Growing Tips
10–12 weeks	Celery, leek, onion, most hardy herbs	These are naturally slow-growing plants. With onions, trim back tops to 4 inches every 2 weeks to promote stocky growth. Hardened-off plants tolerate cold but don't really like it. Exposure to too much cold can trigger premature bolting.
5–8 weeks	Broccoli, cabbage, cauliflower, eggplant, lettuce and other leafy greens, pepper, tomato, basil, cilantro, dill	These seedlings need plenty of light, so plants grown in greenhouses are usually very stocky and strong. Tomato-family crops cannot be transplanted until the soil is warm, but it's fine to plant cabbage-family crops under cool conditions.
3–4 weeks	Cucumber, muskmelon (cantaloupe), squash, sweet corn, watermelon	Use roomy 4-inch plastic pots for cucumber-family crops. Deep, narrow containers are best for sweet corn. These are high-sun plants, so it's important to get them into the garden promptly.

DIRECT-SEEDING IN YOUR GARDEN

Many of us carry a scene of pastoral perfection in our heads, in which we tuck seeds into fluffy brown soil and return the next day to find every seed exploding with Jack-and-the-Beanstalk exuberance. Hold on to that dream as you learn to sow seeds directly in garden beds, but give it more than a day—or a week—to come true. Six weeks after you sow a food garden from seed, you will definitely be surrounded by homegrown abundance everywhere you look, with much more in store for later in summer.

Direct-sowing saves time and trouble. Direct-sown plants are spared the trauma of transplanting, so they tend to grow fast and strong. You can also save money by direct-sowing crops that are also available as seedlings. Take cucumbers, for example. A single packet of cucumber seeds costs about as much as one seedling, but the packet will provide most gardeners with cucumbers for three years when direct-sown. Store, swap, or use up leftover seeds within three years of purchase, and you will always have a secure supply with which to start your garden.

It's important to commit to two tasks when you start your garden from direct-sown seeds: weeding and thinning. Both are essential to ensure sturdy plants that produce well. It's easy to learn these skills when you direct-seed crops that sprout fast and don't look anything like weeds.

TELL ME MORE!
FROM SEED TO SPROUT

A seed is a plant in the ultimate stage of dormancy. Moisture, temperature, and contact with soil trigger a seed to break dormancy and germinate (sprout). Some seeds need more germination time than others, for various reasons. Moisture moves slowly through the hard seed coats of beans, peas, and okra, but once the seeds plump up with water, germination proceeds quickly. To speed sprouting, soak large seeds in room-temperature water overnight before planting them. Other seeds like parsley and carrot sprout slowly in part because they enter dormancy with underdeveloped embryos; a natural delay occurs as numerous new cells grow before the seed sprouts, so keep the seedbed moist and be patient. Then there are the speedy sprouters, which include mustard, turnips, and rustic salad greens like arugula. Under good germination conditions, these seeds may be up and growing in only three days.

When thinned gradually, leafy greens like spinach and lettuce will quickly fill in any open spaces between plants.

Choosing Strong Candidates

Crops that have large seeds (beans, peas, squash, and cucumber) quickly produce big, easy-to-recognize seedlings, so they are the easiest food crops for beginners to grow from seed. But there is a catch, which is that you have to plant when soil temperatures are warm enough to support strong germination. The Best Temperatures for Sprouting chart on the facing page tells you which plants like what temperatures.

Direct-Sowing Tips

- Read the packet. Most offer instructions on seed spacing and depth.

- Sow seeds thickly (at close spacing) when germination temperatures are less than ideal, to ensure a margin for casualties.

- Instead of planting a whole packet of seeds at once, hold back a few. A week or two later, check for gaps in your rows of seedlings and pop in more seeds to fill the spaces.

- Cover newly planted seeds with an old blanket, boards, or thick folds of damp newspaper for the first three to four days after sowing. The covers will help maintain moisture while protecting the germinating seeds from the drying effect of sunlight and from curious dogs and cats.

- Learn to recognize natural signs that coincide with the major planting "windows" in your climate. For example, you might sow cold-tolerant seeds such as arugula and peas when forsythias bloom; move on to crops with moderate temperaments when lilacs and apples are in flower; and wait until the dogwood petals start to fall to plant seeds that need still warmer temperatures.

- Soak large, hard seeds like peas, beans, and okra overnight in room-temperature water just before you plant them. These big seeds germinate quickly when given a chance to plump up with water.

- Pick up any seeds you spill, because they could attract the unwanted attention of sharp-eyed crows or sharp-nosed mice. These critters will dig up the planted seeds if they want more after they have consumed all the spilled ones.

- As direct-seeded crops grow, thin them gradually to the spacing recommended on the packet. You can eat your thinnings of herbs and leafy greens, but most other pulled seedlings should be composted. If you want to move a seedling, use a tablespoon to lift the little wanderer without breaking up the attached ball of soil and roots. Quickly slip it into better digs, water it gently, and cover with a flowerpot or other shade cover for a couple of days.

BEST TEMPERATURES FOR SPROUTING

Seeds sown when the soil is too cold or too hot often fail to make a good stand. Soil temperatures at the surface vary widely between morning and night, but you can feel the difference between the three soil temperature gradients described below by digging down 4 inches and placing your palm on the soil. Remember that the less time seeds spend sitting in the soil waiting for good germination temperatures, the less likely they are to rot or be eaten by a hungry mouse.

Soil Temperature	Willing Sprouters	Tips
Cool (45–60°F/7–15°C) Typical of early to midspring and late fall	Arugula, beet, cabbage, carrot, chard, lettuce, onion, parsley, pea, radish, spinach	Cloches, cold frames, or tunnels often warm the soil enough to push planting dates up by a month (see page 186).
Moderate (60–70°F/15–21°C) Typical of midspring to early summer and late summer to early fall	All of the above plants that germinate under cool conditions, plus celery, corn, cucumber, lettuce, pepper, and tomato	Try direct-seeding broccoli and kin in a nursery bed in early summer; transplant the seedlings for your fall crop.
Warm (70–85°F/21–30°C) Typical of summer to early fall	Most plants with tropical temperaments, including tomato, bean, and cucumber-family crops	Use black plastic mulch to warm soil in cold climates; elsewhere, be patient and the heat will come.

STRICTLY FROM SEED
GARDEN PLAN

Working strictly from a handful of seed packets purchased at any garden center, you can create miracles. This tasty little garden will produce more than two months of fresh salad greens, a summer's supply of basil, and plenty of carrots and beets for several meals. Late summer brings snap beans and cucumbers, followed by a radical revival of leafy greens in fall.

Soil temperature is controlled by the weather, so timing is everything with this seeds-only garden plan. It is also designed to acquaint you with how direct-sowing works in cool, moderate, and warm soil—and with a cross section of seed types. Special techniques that address common direct-sowing challenges—for example, covering the seeded bed with a blanket to retain moisture—are included in the step-by-step directions.

You will need to provide two special services for all of your direct-sown crops: thinning and weeding. Seedlings seldom sprout at exactly the right spacing, and in some situations you may have to thin out twice as many seedlings as you leave behind. Still, it's a good idea for beginners to seed generously, because you will need a thick stand of seedlings to help you distinguish your crop plants from weeds. First, identify the seedlings of the crop you planted, which will probably sprout in a straight row or another distinct pattern. Next, pull out all weeds, and then thin the seedlings at least until the leaves of neighboring plants do not overlap. Weed and thin again a week later, this time thinning to each plant's preferred spacing (usually listed on the seed packet), and your veggies will be well on their way to a productive season. After the soil warms in late spring, you can use mulches to seriously suppress weeds between your thinned plants. See page 146 for more information on using mulches in your garden.

NAME
Strictly from Seed

FOOTPRINT
6 × 12 feet

SKILL LEVEL
Fine for first-timers

WHEN TO PLANT
Early spring: lettuce, parsley, radishes, and snap peas

Midspring: carrots and beets

Late spring: bush snap beans and basil

Midsummer: cucumber

Late summer to early fall: spinach, Asian greens, and more radishes and lettuce

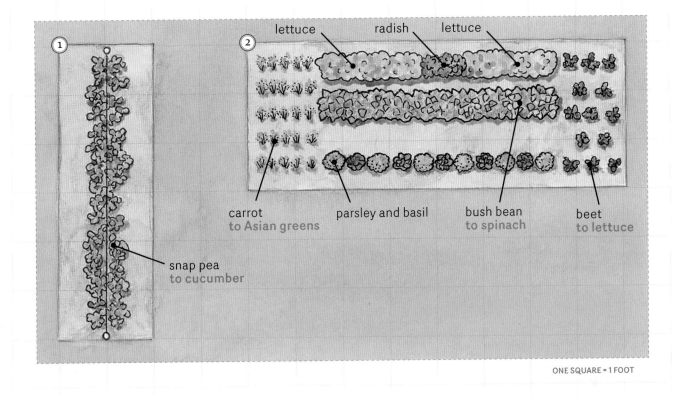

lettuce   radish   lettuce

snap pea
to cucumber

carrot
to Asian greens

parsley and basil

bush bean
to spinach

beet
to lettuce

ONE SQUARE = 1 FOOT

THE STUFF

FOR THE BEDS
- Three 40-pound bags of compost, or about 2 wheelbarrow loads
- One 3- to 4-pound package of balanced organic fertilizer, enough for 40 square feet
- Old blankets (or row cover)

FOR THE PEA TRELLIS
- Two 6-foot-long stakes or posts
- Cotton string, jute or hemp twine, or polyester garden netting

TOOLS
- Wheelbarrow, cart, or wagon for moving compost
- Spade or shovel
- Digging fork
- Sledgehammer or hammer
- Scissors

THE PLANTS

BED ①
- Cucumber, 1 packet seeds
- Snap pea (early-maturing, compact variety), 1 packet seeds

BED ②
- Asian mustard or mizuna, 1 packet seeds
- Basil, 1 packet seeds
- Beet, 1 packet seeds
- Carrot (Nantes type), 1 packet seeds
- Lettuce (different types), 3 packets seeds
- Parsley (curled), 1 packet seeds
- Radish, 1 packet seeds
- Snap bean (bush variety), 1 packet seeds
- Spinach, 1 packet seeds

STRICTLY FROM SEED
PLANTING AND CARE

EARLY SPRING

❶ Prepare the beds. About six weeks before your last frost date, prepare the beds. If starting from scratch, use a spade or shovel and digging fork to remove grass and weeds from the bed. Spread the compost over the beds and cover with a moderate sprinkling of organic fertilizer. Check soil moisture, and whenever the soil in your garden is dry enough to crumble easily when dug, use your preferred digging tool to thoroughly mix in the amendments.

❷ Erect the trellis. Install the pea trellis in Bed 1 as described on page 25. If you are weaving string, position the lowest string no more than 6 inches from the ground, with the top string 4 feet higher.

MIDSPRING

❸ Plant the pea seeds. One month before your last spring frost date, plant a row of pea seeds on each side of the trellis. Use your finger to poke the seeds into the soil 1 inch deep and 2 to 3 inches apart, or dig a furrow.

❹ Sow cool-weather crops. In the foreground of Bed 2, sow about 25 parsley seeds ¼ inch deep and 2 inches apart (their germination rate is usually low). Scatter lettuce seeds atop the soil in one of the rear blocks of the bed, about 1 inch apart. Pat the seeds into place with your hand, barely covering with soil. Plant 6 to 8 radish seeds ¼ inch deep to mark the end of this first planting.

❺ Plant beets and carrots. As nighttime temperatures warm above 50°F (10°C), sow beets, carrots, and more lettuce in Bed 2. Soak carrot and beet seeds overnight in water before planting them ½ inch deep and 2 inches apart. If the weather is sunny, cover the seeded beds with old blankets during the day to keep the soil's surface from drying out. Remove the covers when you see sprouts or after six days, whichever comes first.

SPRINKLE SEEDS SOFTLY

When it comes to watering newly planted seeds, repeated light surface watering is best. Use a fine spray of water from your hose, or a gentle sprinkle from a watering can, to keep the soil constantly moist until seeds germinate. Heavy watering often washes small seeds out of place. Be prepared to gently water newly planted beds daily in hot weather.

LATE SPRING

6 Sow summer crops. After the last frost has passed, plant bush beans and basil. Large bean seeds can be pushed into the ground with your finger, 1 inch deep and 4 inches apart. Plant the basil in gaps within the parsley row; cover seeds with ¼ inch of loose soil and pat into place with your hand. Thin parsley seedlings to 6 inches apart. If you have extras, lift and transplant them to containers or other parts of your garden, or pop into a salad.

7 Thin beets and carrots. Use scissors if necessary to thin the beets to 6 inches apart; thin carrots by pulling seedlings until the strongest ones are 3 inches apart. Keep both crops carefully weeded. Beets and carrots grow slowly at first and then suddenly gain size.

MIDSUMMER

8 Replace peas with cucumbers. Pull up and compost peas in Bed 1 as soon as production wanes. Snip large sections of vine from the trellis, but don't worry about getting it completely clean. Sow about 12 cucumber seeds on each side of the trellis, planting the seeds ½ inch deep. Scatter a light dusting of organic fertilizer over the planted bed. In cold climates, choose small or quick-maturing varieties to make sure there is time for a decent crop.

LATE SUMMER

9 Sow fall crops. Pull up and compost tattered lettuce and bush beans left from spring planting. Scatter a dusting of organic fertilizer over the soil's surface, and lightly mix it in. Sow Asian greens (mustard, mizuna, or a mix), spinach, and a fall crop of lettuce, though not necessarily all on the same day.

STARTING SEEDS INDOORS

Why should you go to the trouble of growing your own seedlings instead of buying them at the store or planting seeds right in your garden? Here are five good reasons.

1. **Save money.** Even the most costly mail-ordered seeds don't come close to matching the expense of buying most or all of your plants as purchased seedlings.

2. **Unique varieties.** Starting your own seeds may be the only way to grow and taste samples of the hundreds of delicious gourmet varieties available.

3. **Precise timing.** You have seedlings exactly when you need them. Once the spring planting season has passed, many garden centers have very few healthy veggie seedlings to sell.

4. **Constructive fun.** Starting seeds indoors is fun, and it keeps you busy in early spring, when it can be very difficult to wait for the soil to dry out and warm up. In areas where winters are long, starting seeds is the perfect antidote to late-lingering snow outside.

5. **Pest protection.** In any season, starting seeds indoors is often safer than direct-sowing, because you can control temperature and moisture. In addition, indoor-grown seedlings are safe from hungry summer insects.

The four essentials for starting seeds indoors are seeds, containers, soil mix, and a well-lit place where the seeds can sprout and grow. For containers, one easy choice is small paper cups, which you'll enclose in a plastic bag after planting. It's a primitive yet infinitely practical method that works every time.

Any good-quality potting soil will work for most seeds, but disease problems can develop in soil that has been stored moist. Damp potting soil can host active communities of many microorganisms, including some that damage plants. Seed-starting mix is a specialty soil blended with disease suppression in mind, so it's unlikely to host soilborne diseases. The choice is yours, but do be sure to start with a fresh bag.

Ready to get started? Most vegetable seeds are handled the same way, so you can follow the step-by-step instructions on the following pages with any crop that needs a head start indoors under lights.

SPECIAL LIGHTS FOR SEEDLINGS

Once you discover the fun of growing your own seedlings, you will probably want to invest in a fluorescent or LED light fixture dedicated to your gardening projects. You can buy lights made for plants or make your own from an inexpensive shop-light fixture that holds two bulbs. For example, a 24-inch-long utility strip with two bulbs can be mounted on a board, which can then be suspended from the ceiling. Or you can hold it above seedlings by placing supports under the ends of the boards. As the seedlings grow, adjust the height of the light so that it is no more than 2 inches above the topmost leaves.

Whether you make your own plant light or buy one, plug it into a timer set to turn it on automatically for about 12 hours a day. You can set the lights for 16 hours a day if you want to push your seedlings to grow a little faster. Longer light periods can be especially beneficial to tomatoes, peppers, and other plants that need a long, warm growing season. However, when growing leafy greens and onion seedlings indoors, limit light time to 12 hours daily. Too much time under lights can cause these veggies to bolt (produce flowers and seeds) while they are still very young.

STARTING SEEDS
STEP-BY-STEP

THE STUFF

- One small bag of fresh seed-starting mix or potting soil
- One package of small disposable paper cups (4- or 6-ounce "bathroom" cups are perfect)
- Two 8-inch-diameter square or round baking pans
- ½ × 2-inch strips of rigid plastic (cut from discarded food container)
- Seeds for planting
- One large clear or translucent produce bag
- One desk lamp with 75-watt-equivalent fluorescent bulb

TOOLS

- Large bowl or small pail
- Large measuring cup
- Large long-handled spoon
- Sharp pencil
- Waterproof marker
- Pump spray bottle
- Tweezers or small scissors

1 **Moisten the mix.** Place about 4 cups of seed-starting mix or potting soil in a bowl or pail and sprinkle generously with lukewarm water. If the seed-starting mix is very dry, you will need to add 2 cups or more of water to make it evenly moist; already-moist potting soil will require much less, perhaps only a few tablespoons. Use the spoon to stir the water into the potting mix. Allow the moistened planting medium to rest while you prepare the cups and labels.

2 **Poke holes.** Use the pencil to poke about five small drainage holes in the bottom of each planting cup.

3 **Prepare labels.** Select the seeds you want to plant. Make labels by using the marker to write the plant or variety name and the date on a plastic strip. You'll need one label for each cup. When the seedlings are set out in the garden, the labels can go with them.

FREEBIE CONTAINERS

Disposable plastic food containers with clear domed tops are great for starting seeds (fast-food restaurants and supermarket delis are easy sources). The domes retain extra humidity, which helps the seeds germinate quickly.

❹ Fill containers. Stir the potting mix again, and add more water (or dry potting mix) until it is light and fluffy yet thoroughly moist. Fill the cups to the rim with moist planting mix. Tamp several times to eliminate air pockets. Fill as many cups as the number of plants you want to grow.

❺ Sow and label. Sow two or three seeds per cup by using the pencil tip to poke holes about three times as deep as the diameter of the seeds. With very tiny seeds like lettuce, place them on the surface, barely cover them with more moist potting mix, and press them in place with your finger. Plant larger seeds like chard and pepper about ¼ inch deep. As you plant, insert the labels inside the edges of the cups.

❻ Bag 'em up. Place the planted cups in the baking pan and thoroughly moisten with several sprays of water. Enclose the pan and cups loosely in the plastic bag. You can close the bag with a twist tie, or simply tuck under the edges. Set the enclosed planted cups in a warm place that gets some natural light.

❼ Check for sprouting. After three days or so, open the bag and check for signs of germination. Remove any cups that show sprouting activity and place them in the second pan or some other small waterproof container that will keep them from tipping over. Position them beneath the light, using a stack of old newspapers, magazines, or an old phone book to raise the level of the seedlings to within 2 inches of the light.

❽ Thin as needed. Use tweezers or small scissors to thin the seedlings in the cups until each cup contains no more than two seedlings.

❾ Monitor needs. As the seedlings grow, mist them daily if the indoor air is very dry, but do most of your watering from the bottom by flooding the pan with ½ inch of lukewarm water every few days. Also adjust their height as needed to keep the topmost leaves 1 to 2 inches from the light.

Review the discussion on working with seedlings on page 114 as you prepare your seedlings for their transition to the garden. You'll find additional tips on handling your seedlings in the Paintbrush Beds garden plan, which begins on page 126.

❼

It is often easier to adjust the position of your seedlings by using props (such as books) than to change the height of your bright light fixture. Try to keep the topmost leaves about 2 inches from the light source.

PAINTBRUSH BEDS
GARDEN PLAN

This little garden will richly reward you for the small trouble of starting seeds indoors by producing a summer's worth of breathtakingly beautiful veggies. The size and shape of veggie seeds differ, which is part of what makes seed starting so interesting. Purple kohlrabi and fast-sprouting bok choy will introduce you to the smooth-seeded cabbage clan. By comparison, chard seeds look and feel like little nuts, and sliver-small lettuce seeds will scatter if you sneeze.

This garden plan is designed to help you learn how different seeds grow, so you will never again be intimidated when it comes to growing your own seedlings. One of the privileges you earn by becoming a seed starter is unlimited access to distinctive varieties, which are well represented in the Paintbrush Beds by two open-pollinated tomatoes famous for flavor, chocolate-red 'Pruden's Purple' and green-and-yellow-striped 'Green Zebra'. I have also specified many other remarkable varieties, or you can choose varieties yourself. Don't worry about ending up with leftover seeds. If you fall in love with certain varieties this season, you can plant them again next year for free using your partial packets.

Expect to be successful, but do grow a few more seedlings than you intend to plant in your garden. Keep the extras until a week after their brethren have been set out, because you may lose a few to wind, animals, or insect pests. If you end up not needing replacement plants, share your special babies with friends.

TELL ME MORE!
PURPLE TOMATOES?

When asked about their favorite nonred tomatoes, many gardeners name varieties that ripen to shades of purple. But 'Pruden's Purple', 'Cherokee Purple', and several other popular purple-fruited varieties that produce big tomatoes may not ripen quickly enough in cool climates. Where summers are short, try 'Black Cherry' or 'Purple Plum' instead.

NAME
Paintbrush Beds

FOOTPRINT
4 × 4 feet

SKILL LEVEL
Beyond beginner

WHEN TO PLANT
Early spring: kohlrabi, lettuce, chard, peppers, eggplant, marjoram, sweet alyssum, and tomato (all indoors)

Midspring: sweet alyssum, kohlrabi, lettuce, chard, marjoram (outdoors)

Midsummer: Chinese cabbage

Late summer: bok choy

'Pruden's Purple' tomato
'Green Zebra' tomato
'Kolibri' purple kohlrabi to 'Mei Qing' white-stemmed bok choy
'Patio Baby' eggplant
marjoram
'Patio Baby' eggplant
alyssum
chard
'Lipstick' pepper
lettuce to Chinese cabbage

ONE SQUARE = 1 FOOT

THE STUFF

FOR THE BEDS
- ⚪ Two 40-pound bags of compost, or about 1½ wheelbarrow loads
- ⚪ One 4- to 5-pound package of organic fertilizer, or enough for 50 square feet
- ⚪ Two 5- to 6-foot-tall tomato cages
- ⚪ Two 16-inch-diameter half-barrel or plastic planters
- ⚪ Enough organic potting soil to fill the planters (about two 20-pound bags)

TOOLS
- ⚪ Seed-starting equipment (see page 124)
- ⚪ Wheelbarrow, cart, or wagon for moving compost
- ⚪ Spade or shovel
- ⚪ Digging fork
- ⚪ Cuticle scissors and/or tweezers
- ⚪ Hand trowel

THE PLANTS

BED ①
- ⚪ 'Green Zebra' tomato, 1 packet seeds
- ⚪ 'Kolibri' or other purple kohlrabi, 1 packet seeds
- ⚪ 'Mei Qing' or other baby bok choy, 1 packet seeds
- ⚪ 'Pruden's Purple' tomato, 1 packet seeds

BED ②
- ⚪ Chinese cabbage (any variety), 1 packet seeds
- ⚪ Lettuce seed mixture of different varieties, 1 packet seeds
- ⚪ 'Lipstick' pepper, 1 packet seeds
- ⚪ 'Ruby Red' or other red-stemmed chard, 1 packet seeds
- ⚪ 'Buttercrunch' or other green lettuce, 1 packet seeds

PLANTERS A AND B
- ⚪ 'Patio Baby' eggplant, 1 packet seeds
- ⚪ Marjoram, 1 packet seeds
- ⚪ Sweet alyssum, 1 packet seeds

PAINTBRUSH BEDS
PLANTING AND CARE

EARLY SPRING

❶ Sow seeds in containers. About eight weeks before your last frost, start two containers each of marjoram and sweet alyssum and six containers of lettuce, following the instructions on pages 124–25. Two weeks later, start six containers of kohlrabi, three containers of peppers, three containers of eggplant, four containers of chard, and two containers of each type of tomato. If you have space under your lights, you can start a few more lettuce seedlings indoors, too.

❷ Dig and enrich beds. About six weeks before your last frost, prepare the beds. If starting from scratch, use a spade or shovel and digging fork to remove grass and weeds from the bed. Evenly distribute a 2-inch blanket of compost over the beds, and sprinkle on a moderate dusting of organic fertilizer. Check soil moisture, and whenever the soil in your garden is dry enough to crumble easily when dug, use your preferred digging tool to mix the compost and fertilizer into the top 10 inches of soil.

❸ Thin your seedlings. After the seeds in your containers have germinated, use tweezers to pull out any extra seedlings, gradually thinning to one per container. The best time to thin is before the seedlings show their third leaf, which is usually their first "true" leaf (seedling leaves often have plainer shapes). Bumpy chard seeds are actually capsules that contain two or more seeds (this is true of beet seeds also). If more than one germinates, use cuticle scissors to snip off all but one at the soil line. Scissors are always a good tool for thinning very closely spaced seedlings.

❹ Prepare to transplant. Gradually "harden off" your seedlings as described on page 114.

MIDSPRING

❺ Transplant lettuce and more. About three weeks before your last frost date, set out the sweet alyssum near the rim of Planter A, kohlrabi in Bed 1, and lettuce (if you started seedlings) in Bed 2. Thoroughly water seedlings before you begin. To remove a seedling from its cup, push upward from the bottom of the cup and lay the seedling on its side. Tear or cut away the cup, and roll the rootball into your hand. If you encounter a tight spiral of roots at the bottom of the cup, gently tease them apart with your fingers before slipping the seedling into its hole. Try to handle the seedling by its lowest leaves or rootball. Avoid holding or pinching the main stem, which can cause a serious bruise.

❻ Sow more lettuce. Even if you started a few plants indoors, sow lettuce directly in Bed 2. Scatter lettuce seeds atop the soil, about 1 inch apart. Use the flat of your hand to pat the seeds into place, barely covering them with soil.

❼ Transplant some more. One to two weeks later, set out chard and marjoram, planting the latter just inside the rim of Planter B.

8 Set out heat lovers. One to two weeks after your last frost, set out tomatoes, peppers, and eggplant. Install tomato cages after setting out tomatoes, as described on page 132.

MIDSUMMER

9 Start Chinese cabbage. When the lettuce is on its last leg, start five containers of Chinese cabbage indoors. Seedlings will be ready to transplant about three weeks after sowing. Set them in a zigzag row in Bed 2, with plants 12 inches apart. As long as you premoisten the soil in the bed and cover the transplanted seedlings with shade covers as shown on page 187 for a few days after setting them out, you should not lose a single seedling.

5

Remove seedlings from containers by pushing up through the bottom.

10 Start bok choy. Start bok choy seedlings indoors, and set them out in Bed 1 when they are about three weeks old. Plant them in a zigzag pattern, with plants 6 inches apart.

DIG THIS!

Instead of using a plastic bag, try covering seeded containers with a cake cover made of glass or clear plastic.

TELL ME MORE!
SEED-STARTING KITS

Most garden centers sell seed-starting kits in spring, or you can buy them by mail order year-round. Look for kits that include a sturdy tray that can stand up to thorough washing and a clear dome that fits over it. I do not recommend peat pots or pellets because plants do not like them very much; they would much rather stretch their roots in seed-starting mix or potting soil.

CHAPTER EIGHT

SUPPORTING YOUR PLANTS

Several of the most popular crops in home gardens—tomatoes, peas, and pole beans—grow so tall and lanky that they must have appropriate support. Taking the time to install a trellis for these and other veggies brings many benefits, including better sun exposure, easier access to the plants for monitoring pests and picking fruits, and more efficient use of space. Crops that grow upward rather than outward typically give big returns per square foot of planting space compared to low-growing, bushy plants.

SHADY SOLUTION

Using trellised vegetables as backdrops in a garden creates a lush look, but think carefully about what to plant in the shade cast by tall vine-covered trellises. Leafy greens such as lettuce and spinach are the best choices to grow in the shadows of a trellis.

TYPES OF SUPPORT

Plant supports may be as simple as a single stake or as elaborate as a tall tripod. Simple stakes will do for peppers and eggplant, which tend to topple over as they become heavy with fruit. Slender, 4-foot-long pieces of wood or bamboo work well when a single stake is needed, or you can use a long, straight stick. Push the stake into the ground about 4 inches from the base of the plant that needs support, and use 1-inch-wide strips of soft cloth to tie plants to their stakes.

The next level of support is to combine stakes with string or long pieces of cloth wrapped around stakes. This is a good way to support short-season tomatoes, which need to be held up above the ground but often do not grow tall enough to benefit from a tomato cage. Another option is to install stakes on the outside of the planting and between every other plant, and weave jute or hemp twine, or even ribbon between the plants and stakes. Start 6 inches above the soil line, and tie horizontal tiers of twine at 8-inch intervals.

The most productive, best-tasting tomato varieties are vigorous indeterminate plants, and their exuberant growth requires a sturdy

cage or thoughtful trellis. Most gardeners try standard store-bought cages, which are adequate when well-behaved tomatoes are grown in cool climates. However, they will not contain the spirited growth of tomatoes in warm summer climates, where cages made of 6-inch mesh concrete-reinforcing wire give better support. To consider your options, see How to Cage a Tomato on page 132.

Peas (left) wrap tendrils tightly around a light trellis, as do many cucumber-family crops (center). Bean vines (right) twine around poles or other supports.

Tendrils vs. Twining

True vining crops such as peas and beans use different methods to hold on to a trellis, so it's important to provide support that works well with the plants' equipment. Peas, for example, cling to a trellis with threadlike curling tendrils, so a net trellis serves them well. Do be sure to check the seed packet to make sure your trellis is the right height for the pea variety you plan to grow. Depending on variety, peas may grow to only 2 feet high or they can grow taller than you.

Cucumber-family crops latch onto support structures with curling tendrils, too, but they are not very nimble climbers. You can easily encourage cucumbers and small-fruited pumpkins, squash, or melons to cover a trellis by gently guiding the vines' growing tips upward through the trellis once a week until the plants begin to bloom.

Beans twine their way up support structures, and they do their best twining on slender poles. Beans will twine up a string trellis, but because the plants are much heavier than peas, there is a risk that a lightweight string trellis will collapse from their weight. A pole trellis with a tripod design, on the other hand, actually becomes more stable as the season progresses, because the weight of the plants will anchor it more firmly. Several garden plans in this book (including High-Value Verticals on page 134) use tripods to support vigorous twining crops.

One of the oldest trellising methods of all is to simply let plants support other plants, as is done in the Sweet Corn & Company garden plan on page 158. In addition, you can use an existing fence to support plants as long as the fence does not block too much light.

HOW TO POUND A POST

Use a small board as an aid when using a hammer to pound in posts.

The best way to install sturdy end posts for a trellis is to pound them into moist ground. Dry soil makes your work harder (when it is dry, clay subsoil can be brick hard). The posts must be made of a strong material like wood, metal, or PVC pipe. Each should have a pointed end. To avoid splinters, wear gloves when working with wood posts.

Measure and mark the location of your posts. If your soil contains lots of large rocks or other underground obstructions, pound an iron (rebar) stake several inches into the ground first, then wiggle it a bit before pulling it out with both hands. In addition to revealing hidden obstacles, the rebar stake will create a guide hole in which to insert your post.

Push a post into the ground or guide hole as far as it will go. Stand on a ladder or other sturdy support, if necessary, to put your weight behind the task of soundly pounding on the end of the stake. If the best tool you have available is an ordinary hammer, place a small piece of scrap wood over the top of the post and hammer on the wood. Better yet, use a sledgehammer, the preferred tool for pounding posts. Sledgehammers have extraheavy heads, and they come in a range of sizes.

When the post begins to feel firm, pause to make sure it is going in straight. Adjust as needed, and continue pounding until the post feels very firm in the soil. Don't worry if the tops of trellis posts are not precisely even. Once the trellis is covered with vines, no one will notice.

HOW TO CAGE A TOMATO

The fastest way to set up support for tomatoes is to use wire cages, of which two styles are worth considering. At garden centers, look for tall prewelded circular tomato cages that have five horizontal rings and four legs. (The three-ring, three-legged version is inadequate for all but the shortest of the determinate types; they work better for peppers or eggplant.) You can also buy tomato cages made from 6-inch mesh concrete-reinforcing wire or make your own. These are the best choice in warm-summer climates, where tomato plants tend to grow quite large. Either type of cage may topple when the tomatoes become top heavy in late summer, so plan to add stakes as needed to keep your cages upright.

Protect the plant first. Plant a tomato in a prepared planting hole or bed (see page 27). Place a large flowerpot, box, or bucket over the plant so it will not be injured as you install the cage. Lightly mulch the area around the plant.

Option 1: Install a welded cage. If you are using a circular welded cage, position it around the plant and push the legs into the soil. Move around the cage, pushing downward on the lowest ring, to work the cage into the soil as deep as it will go. If a leg hits an obstruction, pull up the cage, rotate it a few inches, and try again. When the cage feels sturdy, remove the pot, box, or bucket and add more mulch around the base of the plant.

Option 2: Install a heavy-duty cage. Cages made from concrete-reinforcing wire have no legs that anchor them to the ground, so after you position one of these cages around a plant, you will need to secure it to stakes pounded into the ground. You can tie the lowest section of the cage to several short wood stakes or use two longer stakes positioned on opposite sides of the cage.

Prune and train as needed. As the tomato plants grow, poke branches back inside the cages whenever you see them. Don't be reluctant to trim off tomato branches that are growing in the wrong direction or that won't stay up off the ground. Healthy plants will quickly grow new ones.

After transplanting, cover the tomato seedling with a pot to protect it from injury.

Push the cage into the ground, using your feet to apply pressure to the lowest ring.

As the plants grow, prune off branches that protrude into garden pathways.

HIGH-VALUE VERTICALS
GARDEN PLAN

How many fresh veggies can you grow in a small garden? You may be surprised! By making use of vertical space with a net trellis for peas and tripods for beans, this planting plan can deliver enough snap and snow peas to eat fresh and freeze and up to 15 pounds of pole beans—all at easy-to-pick eye level. But before the High-Value Vertical crops start reaching for the sky, there is time enough for fast spring crops of lettuce, onions, and radishes. Through summer, the sheltered nook between two tall tripods is filled with basil and parsley—the two indispensable herbs in any kitchen garden.

You may recognize the woven-net pea trellis and the tripod-style bean trellis included in this garden because they appear in several other planting plans in this book. The installation of tomato cages may sound familiar, too, because staking or caging is a routine step in growing big crops of great-tasting tomatoes. The new type of trellis introduced here is a low tripod that gives cucumbers a small mountain to climb. The added vertical growing space increases the leaf area of the plants, which in turn helps them churn out bumper crops of cool, crisp cucumbers.

As you accumulate materials for building trellises, keep in mind that most wood or bamboo posts and stakes will last for two seasons (or more) if you gather them up and store them in a dry place through winter. Bring along a pair of old scissors when you take down trellises made with cotton string or hemp or jute twine, and snip the strings into small pieces. When tossed into your compost, short pieces of string will decompose faster—and will be less likely to get tangled in the tines of your digging fork—than longer pieces.

THE STUFF

FOR THE BEDS
- Eight 40-pound bags of compost, or about 5 wheelbarrow loads
- One 5- to 7-pound package of organic vegetable garden fertilizer

FOR THE PEA TRELLIS
- Three 6-foot-long stakes or posts
- Cotton string, jute or hemp twine, or polyester garden netting

FOR THE TOMATOES
- Three 5-foot-tall tomato cages

FOR THE PEPPERS
- Two 4-foot-long wood stakes

NAME
High-Value Verticals

FOOTPRINT
14 × 12 feet

SKILL LEVEL
Beyond beginner

WHEN TO PLANT
Midspring: parsley, lettuce, peas, onions, radishes, and chard

Late spring: pole snap beans, yard-long beans, peppers, tomatoes, cucumbers, and basil

Midsummer: miniature pumpkins

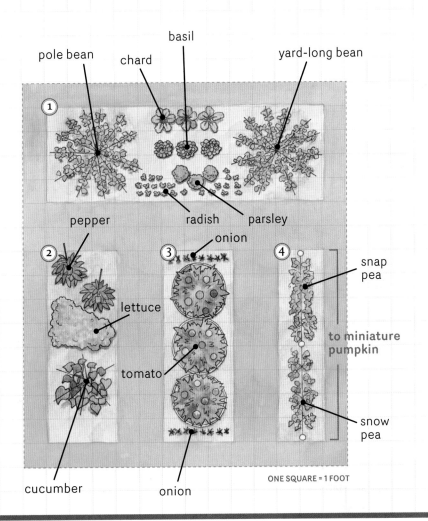

ONE SQUARE = 1 FOOT

FOR THE BEAN TRIPODS
- O Twenty-four 8-foot-long bamboo poles
- O Cotton string or jute or hemp twine

FOR THE CUCUMBER TRIPOD
- O Six 4-foot-long bamboo poles
- O Cotton string or jute or hemp twine

TOOLS
- O Wheelbarrow, cart, or wagon for moving compost
- O Scissors
- O Hand trowel
- O Spade or shovel
- O Digging fork

THE PLANTS

BED ①
- O Basil, 3 seedlings
- O Chard, 1 packet seeds or 3 seedlings
- O Parsley, 1 packet seeds or 3 seedlings
- O Radish, 1 packet seeds
- O Snap bean (pole variety), 1 packet seeds
- O Yard-long beans, 1 packet seeds

BED ②
- O Cucumber, 1 packet seeds or 4 seedlings
- O Lettuce, 1 packet seeds
- O Pepper, 2 seedlings

BED ③
- O Onion, 20 seedlings or sets
- O Tomato, 3 seedlings

BED ④
- O Pumpkins (miniature variety), 1 packet seeds; or salad greens or spinach, 1 packet seeds
- O Snap peas, 1 packet seeds
- O Snow peas, 1 packet seeds

HIGH-VALUE VERTICALS
PLANTING AND CARE

DIG THIS!

Trellises and other vertical structures like trellises often attract bug-eating birds, which perch on the posts to scout for food.

EARLY SPRING

❶ Prepare the beds. About six weeks before your last frost, prepare the beds. If starting from scratch, use a spade or shovel and digging fork to remove grass and weeds from the beds. Evenly distribute the compost over the beds, and sprinkle on a moderate dusting of organic fertilizer. Check soil moisture, and whenever the soil in your garden is dry enough to crumble easily when dug, use your preferred digging tool to mix the compost and fertilizer into the top 10 inches of soil.

❷ Erect the pea trellis. Install the pea trellis in Bed 4 as described on page 25. If you are weaving string, have the lowest string no more than 6 inches from the ground, with the top string near the tops of the posts.

MIDSPRING

❸ Sow peas. One month before your last spring frost date, plant snap pea seeds at the base of half of the trellis, one row on each side of the trellis. Plant snow peas along each side of the other half of the trellis.

❹ Sow lots more. Set out onions along the ends of Bed 3, and sow lettuce in Bed 2 as shown. While the weather is still cool, sow radishes and sow or set out parsley and chard in Bed 1.

LATE SPRING

❺ Plant peppers and tomatoes. After the last frost has passed, set out peppers in Bed 2 and tomatoes in Bed 3. Push a stake firmly into the ground beside each pepper plant, but wait until the plants grow to 12 inches tall before tying them to the stake with soft strips of cloth. Install tomato cages as soon as the plants are set out (see page 132).

6 **Plant basil and trellised beans.** Set out basil in the center of Bed 1. Near the ends of the bed, erect two 40-inch-diameter tripods using 12 or more bamboo poles for each one. Bind the poles together near the top with string. Push the bases of the poles 2 inches into the ground before planting pole bean seeds all around the left tripod. Plant yard-long beans around the right tripod.

7 **Plant trellised cucumbers.** In Bed 2, erect a 24-inch-diameter tripod using the 4-foot bamboo poles. Transplant cucumbers at even spacing around the base of the tripod, or sow cucumber seeds 1 inch deep and 3 inches apart. Thin to the strongest four plants.

8 **Train and groom plants.** As the cucumber vines grow, gently guide them to scramble over the trellis. Clip back flowering spikes on your basil plants to encourage the production of leafy side shoots.

7

This small bamboo tripod is ready to plant with cucumber seeds or seedlings.

MIDSUMMER

9 **Replace peas.** Pull up and compost peas as soon as production wanes. Snip large sections of vine from the trellis, but don't worry about getting it completely clean. Sow about 12 pumpkin seeds on each side of the trellis. Scatter a light dusting of organic fertilizer over the planted bed. In cold climates where there may not be time to grow pumpkins after peas, substitute cool-natured leafy greens such as lettuce or spinach for the miniature pumpkins.

10 **Store trellises.** When the first freeze comes, gather up withered plants and compost their remains. Disassemble trellises and lay the pieces on the ground. Use bits of string or twine to bind together bundles of matching stakes. Nest together tomato cages, like stacking chairs. Store your trellis materials in a dry place through winter to extend their useful life in your garden.

CHAPTER NINE

WATER: MAKE EVERY DROP COUNT

Vegetables thrive when rain comes twice a week, with each shower dropping about a half inch of rain. Arranging for such precise precipitation is beyond your control, so you must often step in to make sure your plants never run short of water.

The most direct way to water plants is to use a hose with an adjustable nozzle, and this is an enjoyable way to water small plantings. But as your garden grows, you will want to spend more time planting, weeding, and picking and less time holding a hose. This is when you should look to the greatest reincarnation ever of old automobile tires—the humble soaker hose. Soaker hoses are porous along their full length, so they slowly "weep" out water when the faucet is turned on at very low pressure. Using soaker hoses is fabulously efficient in terms of both water and time. The Marinara Medley garden on page 142 and the Sweet Corn & Company garden on page 158 are examples of garden setups that rely solely on soaker hoses to provide water. And for tips on using soaker hoses successfully, knowing when to water, and which watering gadgets will help you save even more time on watering chores, see pages 140 and 141.

Special Watering Needs

Providing water to plants grown in containers requires special considerations. Roots in pots have nowhere to go to find moisture, and small containers may dry out within hours of watering. Use large containers, which dry out slowly and retain water well. Move container-grown plants to shade during heat waves to ease your watering chores. You may find it easier to use a watering can or hose.

A watering can or hose also works better than a soaker hose when direct-sown seeds are germinating in outdoor beds, and just after seedlings are set out in the garden.

Overhead watering cleans leaves of lettuce and kale in preparation for picking.

TELL ME MORE!
SIMPLE WATER-SAVING HARDWARE

Use these simple gadgets to save hours of watering time, season after season.

Shutoff valves make it easy to switch a hose from one job to another without turning off the faucet.

Splitters make it possible to attach two or more hoses to one faucet, which is essential if you want to keep a soaker hose hooked up all the time. Most have built-in shutoff valves.

Spray nozzles come in a range of styles, so you might want to try a few. Brightly colored nozzles are harder to lose in the garden.

Timers take the worry out of remembering to turn off a sprinkler or soaker hose.

KNOWING WHEN TO WATER

Sandy soils tend to lose soil moisture quickly, while heavier clay soils retain water for a long time, especially if they have been enriched with plenty of organic matter. Plants also vary in how much water they use, depending on how well equipped their roots are to find soil moisture. Lettuce, for example, has fibrous, shallow roots, so it often needs supplemental watering. In comparison, the roots of an established tomato plant often stretch out several feet, so they can cover much more territory as they forage for water.

Experience will teach you many lessons about how your soil and plants interact, which will make you a wiser user of garden water. For example, gardens often appear to need water in the middle of a hot summer day, because plants actually defend themselves from the stress of intense sunlight by wilting on purpose. However, by evening, squash that looked limp at two o'clock will regain its normal appearance if the plants have ample moisture. Plants that show drooping leaves first thing in the morning are usually seriously short of water. If a deep watering does not perk them up, however, they may have been hit with a root injury caused by an insect or disease.

Some crops suffer heartbreaking damage when soil moisture fluctuates between wet and dry. Tomatoes often split when dry conditions give way to a soaking rain, and potatoes stop making tubers when the soil becomes warm and dry. Mulches combined with soaker hoses are the easiest way to keep soil consistently moist, especially in hot summer weather. In addition to blocking surface evaporation, biodegradable mulches like leaves and grass clippings suppress weeds and make important contributions to the soil's organic matter supply.

TIPS FOR WISE WATERING

★ Station a watering can near plantings of lettuce or other salad greens, and give plants a quick splash each time you pick.

★ Use mulches to minimize fluctuating soil moisture levels. Dry conditions followed by heavy rain can cause tomatoes to split and root crops to crack, so consistency is especially important as vegetables approach maturity. See page 146 to learn more about mulch.

★ Sprinklers are great in emergencies, but they can lose up to half the water that runs through them when handled too casually. When you use a sprinkler, make sure it covers only the area that needs water. Running a sprinkler in several 20-minute spurts, with 10-minute soak-in periods in between, is the best way to achieve deep watering when using a sprinkler.

SUCCESS WITH SOAKER HOSES

★ Soaker hoses come in various lengths, with either 10 or 25 feet the best lengths to work with in a home garden. Short hoses tend to deliver water more evenly than longer ones. Use an ordinary garden hose long enough to reach from the faucet to the end of a row or bed; attach the soaker hose to the garden end of this hose.

★ At first, allow three minutes for the hose to fill with water, then experiment with your faucet to set the right pressure. Adjust the flow up or down until drops of water steadily weep along the entire length of the hose.

★ When working with seedlings, arrange the soaker hose over the bed and turn it on *before* you set out the plants. Observe the moisture pattern made by the hose, and plant your seedlings where you know they will get plenty of water.

★ When adding a soaker hose to an existing planting, either snake it between the plants, using small stakes as hose guides if necessary, or run the hose around the planting's outer edges.

★ Soaker hoses are stiff and hard to manage when they're cold. Stretch the hose out in a sunny spot and allow it to heat up to make it easier to bend to your will.

★ Once a soaker hose is in place, covering it with mulch will slow the loss of water to evaporation and make the hose last longer by protecting it from the sun.

MARINARA MEDLEY GARDEN PLAN

When your purpose in gardening is to grow great things to eat, why not begin with a delicious end in mind, like homemade tomato sauce or the toppings for a dozen pizzas, all from your garden? You can have fun pursuing your culinary dreams with this little garden, which can easily be watered by snaking a soaker hose among the plants.

This **Marinara Medley garden** is historical as well as remarkably tasty and nutritious. About 400 years ago, when the strange new fruit called the tomato was making its way into European gardens, the wives and mothers of Italian sailors were among the first to appreciate the tomato's flavor and nutrition. As seafaring men of Naples, Italy, returned to port, they were served a robust tomato sauce with their pasta. It worked such miracles among the malnourished men that it became known as mariner's, or sailor's, sauce. Decades later, an English physician discovered that scurvy, the illness that had plagued sailors for centuries, is caused by a vitamin C deficiency. Vine-ripened tomatoes are bursting with vitamin C, so the restorative powers of marinara sauce should never be in doubt.

The simplicity of this garden plan, and the smart use of a soaker hose, make this a great little garden for people who think they don't have time to garden. Even a weekend-only gardener/cook can keep up with the needs of the Marinara Medley, at least until late summer. When your basil, tomatoes, and peppers start to ripen, you will need to pick them every two or three days. If you like, save them up for a weekend cooking extravaganza (see the recipe on page 145). A bunch of cut basil stems will stay fresh for several days if you place it in a jar or vase of water kept in a cool, shaded place indoors, as you would cut flowers. Store tomatoes on your kitchen counter, because refrigeration ruins their flavor. Do refrigerate peppers after you pick them, unless they are in the process of changing colors. Peppers that are actively ripening from green to red, yellow, or orange will continue to ripen for a day or two when kept at average room temperatures.

THE STUFF

FOR THE BEDS

- Two 40-pound bags of compost, or about 1½ wheelbarrow loads
- One 4- to 5-pound package of organic fertilizer, or enough for 50 square feet
- Two 5- to 6-foot-tall tomato cages
- 1 bale of hay or straw, or 1 to 2 wheelbarrow loads of shredded leaves to use as mulch
- One 25-foot-long soaker hose

TOOLS

- Wheelbarrow, cart, or wagon for moving compost
- Spade or shovel
- Digging fork

NAME
Marinara Medley

FOOTPRINT
8 × 8 feet

SKILL LEVEL
Fine for first-timers

WHEN TO PLANT
Midspring: onions, Greek oregano, and parsley

Late spring: tomatoes, peppers, and basil

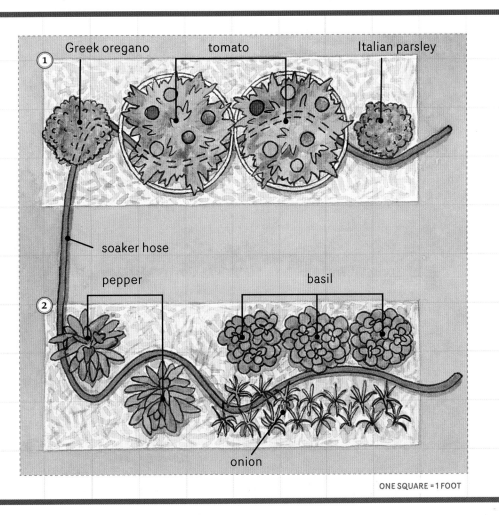

ONE SQUARE = 1 FOOT

THE PLANTS

BED ①
- ○ Greek oregano, 1 plant
- ○ Italian parsley, 1 packet seeds or 1 seedling
- ○ Paste tomato, 2 seedlings

BED ②
- ○ Basil (varying colors and textures), 3 seedlings or 2 to 3 packets of seed
- ○ Onion, 20 to 25 seedlings
- ○ Pepper, 2 seedlings

GET A GOOD DRIP

Fluctuations in soil moisture contribute to several physiological disorders that cause blemished fruits in tomatoes and peppers, and watering beds with a soaker hose is the easiest way to keep the soil lightly moist at all times. Turn the water supply on at very low pressure, wait a few minutes, and then adjust the flow up or down, until the farthest end of the hose barely drips. Leaving it on overnight can be ideal, but if you can't do that, be sure to run it until the soil is moist at least 6 inches below the surface (usually at least two hours). If you're running off to work in the morning, install a timer to shut off the hose so you won't drown your plants.

MARINARA MEDLEY
PLANTING AND CARE

Think of soaker hoses as drought insurance for your garden.

MIDSPRING

❶ Prepare the beds. About one month before your last frost, prepare the beds. If starting from scratch, use a spade or shovel and digging fork to remove grass and weeds from the beds. Evenly distribute the compost over the beds, and sprinkle on a moderate dusting of organic fertilizer. Check soil moisture, and whenever the soil in your garden is dry enough to crumble easily when dug, use your preferred digging tool to mix the compost and fertilizer into the top 10 inches of soil.

❷ Plant onions and herbs. Set out onions in a grid pattern in Bed 2 and plant parsley and Greek oregano in Bed 1.

LATE SPRING

❸ Install the soaker hose. After the last frost passes, on a warm, sunny day, stretch out the soaker hose and allow it to heat up in the sun, which makes the stiff rubber more pliable. Position the hose as shown in the plan on page 143, so that it weaves in and out between where the peppers and tomatoes will be planted.

❹ Plant tomatoes and more. Set out the tomatoes, peppers, and basil, rearranging the soaker hose as needed to get good coverage. Turn on the faucet at very low pressure to make sure water is released in the expected pattern. Install the tomato cages (see page 132), being careful not to accidentally poke a hole into the soaker hose.

5 **Mulch everything.** Weed the entire garden and then cover all exposed surfaces with 2 to 3 inches of mulch. After that, your garden should need minimal weeding. Check soil moisture weekly, and run the soaker hose as needed.

ALL SUMMER LONG

6 **Harvest often.** Pinch or clip the flowering tops from basil every two weeks to encourage the growth of new leafy branches. You can dry or freeze extra parsley and oregano to use through the winter months. All of the culinary elements in this garden come together in late summer when the onions bulb up, the basils grow into lush bushes, and the tomatoes ripen to red.

6

SAUCY MARINARA METHODS

In its pure form, marinara (mariner's) sauce consists of peeled and chopped tomatoes, garlic, olive oil, and basil. These ingredients are simmered together for an hour or so until enough moisture cooks away to form a thick sauce, but methods vary. Many modern recipes call for partial puréeing of the sauce before it is cooked, which saves a little time and produces a more cohesive sauce. Roasting the ingredients in an open pan before mashing them into a pulp has many fans, too, and it's a handy way to make large batches when you're knee-deep in tomatoes. Whether you use your stovetop or oven, the proportions remain the same:

¼ cup olive oil
1 onion, chopped
2–3 cloves garlic, minced
8 cups peeled, chopped tomato (paste types are best)
¼ cup *each* fresh oregano, parsley, and basil, chopped
½ teaspoon salt
½ teaspoon sugar
½ teaspoon freshly ground black pepper

Enjoy your homegrown marinara sauce on pasta, pizza, or as a dip for freshly baked bread. Double the ingredients for enough to freeze in 1-cup containers for pizza, or in larger amounts for pasta recipes. This is a great reuse for plastic food containers.

CHAPTER TEN

THE MAGIC OF MULCH

Covering exposed soil with mulch brings a long list of benefits to the garden, from fewer weeds to much less moisture lost to evaporation. Biodegradable mulches also make your soil a much cushier habitat for plant-friendly soil bacteria and fungi. Applying mulches is a fantastic passive soil-improvement method that saves you time, keeps roots comfortably cool and moist, and helps increase the amount of organic matter held by your soil.

Whenever you can mulch, do. Mulches are especially beneficial to root crops like potatoes and carrots, which suffer when strong sunlight reaches shallow spuds or carrot "shoulders" that are pushing up out of the soil as they mature. (They often do that.) Madly mulch your tomatoes, too, because it's the best way to keep the soil constantly moist. This is key to preventing cracked fruits as well as blossom-end rot, the nutritional disorder that causes black patches to form on the bottoms of fruits.

Now for the bad news. Slugs love mulch, as do their close cousins, snails. In many climates, continuous mulching leads to big populations of these slimy pests. Should this happen, rake up your mulches in spring and pile them into a compost pile. Then leave the soil uncovered, so that the top 2 inches dry out between rains. Just before the weather turns hot, start anew, with fresh mulch material. Slug populations should drop, but if they don't, you can use iron phosphate–based slug baits (see page 166) to bring them down to normal levels.

Choose mulch materials based on availability, price, and appearance. Use natural materials that have not been dyed or treated with chemicals.

WHEN LOOKS COUNT

If you're growing veggies in your front yard or you simply love the look of a perfectly groomed garden, there's nothing wrong with choosing mulch materials based on looks.

Straw-textured mulches like hay, wheat straw, or pine straw will radically reduce weeds while enhancing the growth of most plants. With tomatoes, a 4-inch-deep straw mulch can increase yields by more than 40 percent. Wet bales of any type of mulch quickly become moldy, and they weigh a ton, so keep bales in a dry place or cover with a waterproof tarp until you're ready to use them.

Wood mulches like shredded hardwood, bark, or wood chip mulch create a tailored look that lasts all season. For enhanced weed deterrence, cover the soil with wet newspaper before spreading wood chip mulches 2 inches deep. It is actually good for the soil to turn under well-weathered chunks, or you can rake them aside into pathways. If you're watching expenses, you often can get fresh wood chips for free from tree-trimming crews. Allow fresh chips to weather for a few months before applying them as mulch. Woody mulch materials purchased in bags or bulk can be used in the garden immediately.

HOMEGROWN GARDEN MULCHES

Just about any plant material that rots—including sawdust, wood chips, and the weeds you pull from your garden—can be used as mulch. Start by making use of materials generated right in your yard: grass clippings, leaves, and rough compost.

Material	Attributes	Handling Tips
Grass clippings	Degrade quickly, enriching soil with organic matter and nutrients. Ideal for nutrient-hungry veggies like cabbage-family crops.	Apply in thin, ½-inch layers every 2–3 weeks. Thicker layers become slimy mats that block rain. Do not use treated grass.
Leaves (chopped or shredded)	Degrade slowly, suppress weeds, and cool the soil. Leaching may interfere with growth of cabbage-family crops but not tomato-family vegetables.	Stockpile in a shady place where the leaves will stay moist, or keep inside garbage bags. Very handy for mulching vacant beds in winter.
Rough compost	Degrades quickly, enriching soil with organic matter and nutrients. Ideal for all crops except leafy greens, which easily pick up dirt and grit.	Chop to break up big pieces before spreading over the surface 2 inches deep. Dig in residue at the end of the season.

WHAT ABOUT BLACK PLASTIC?

Commercial vegetable growers routinely use black plastic as their primary mulch, because it raises soil temperature and warms plants while providing near-total weed suppression. Black plastic is most useful in cold climates, where supplemental soil warming in spring is essential for success with warm-natured crops. On the down side, tattered scraps require end-of-season collection and disposal, and black plastic contributes nothing to the soil in terms of organic matter. After removing black plastic, immediately pile on plenty of rough compost or biodegradable mulch to help get your microbes in the mood to mambo again.

MANAGED MULCH GARDEN PLAN

The Managed Mulch garden is specially designed to resolve the potential problems of using mulch so you and your garden reap the many benefits of mulch without its few disadvantages.

A thick layer of biodegradable mulch is a dream come true for potatoes, tomatoes, and crops such as chard that appreciate a cool, moist root zone. Mulch also adds organic matter to the soil. Unfortunately, mulch can become a haven for plant-eating slugs and snails. Also, many gardeners who have tried keeping their gardens under a thick mulch continuously (as was done by Ruth Stout, author of several classic books on this "no-work" gardening method) have found that mice, moles, and voles often become a problem after the second growing season.

In this garden plan, crops are separated based on their need for mulch and their susceptibility to slugs. Young bush beans, dill, and lettuce are much beloved by slugs, so they are located as far as possible from deeply mulched tomatoes and potatoes. Very fast-growing crops like snap beans and lettuce can be grown without mulch, and summer squash leaves are so large that they do a good job of shading out weeds.

Separating the garden into mulched and unmulched areas also makes it simple to flip-flop them from one year to the next. Thus, you will be building soil organic matter, but you'll also be altering habitat conditions from year to year, and that will prevent small four-footed critters from establishing permanent territory in your garden.

In this garden, a soldier-straight row of leeks shares bed space with potatoes, two great crops to grow beneath a thick mulch. When deprived of light, the bases of leeks grow into long, tender shanks, and deeply mulched potatoes are easy to harvest, because they tend to cluster close to the surface. In the adjacent bed, tomatoes benefit from a broad skirt of mulch—the best way to nurture the muscular lateral roots that tomatoes send out into surrounding soil.

THE STUFF

FOR THE BEDS

○ Five 40-pound bags of compost, or about 3 wheelbarrow loads

○ One 5-pound package of organic vegetable garden fertilizer

○ Two bales of dry straw or hay

FOR THE TOMATOES

○ Three 5-foot-tall tomato cages

TOOLS

○ Seed-starting equipment (see page 124)

○ Wheelbarrow, cart, or wagon for moving compost

○ Hand trowel

○ Spade or shovel

○ Digging fork

○ Clean, sharp knife (for cutting potatoes)

NAME

Managed Mulch

FOOTPRINT

9 × 28 feet

SKILL LEVEL

Fine for first-timers

WHEN TO PLANT

Early spring: leeks

Midspring: potatoes, lettuce, dill, and chard

Late spring: tomatoes, bush snap beans, cucumbers, summer squash, and basil

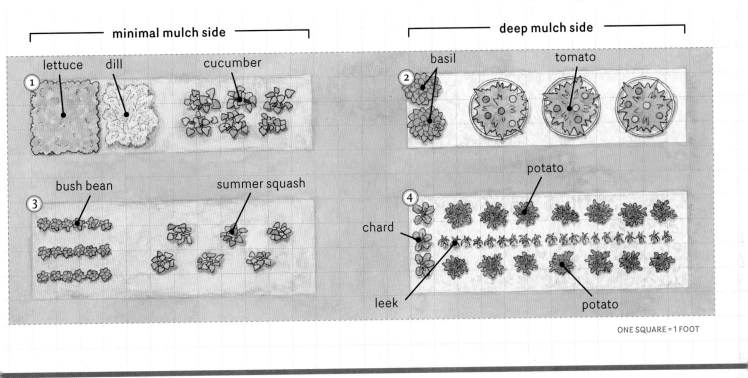

THE PLANTS

BED ①

- O Cucumber, 1 packet seeds or 6 seedlings
- O Dill, 1 packet seeds
- O Lettuce, 1 packet seeds

BED ②

- O Basil, 1 packet seeds or 2 seedlings
- O Tomato, 3 seedlings

BED ③

- O Snap bean (bush variety), 1 packet seeds
- O Summer squash, 1 packet seeds or 6 seedlings

BED ④

- O Chard, 1 packet seeds or 3 seedlings
- O Leek, 1 packet seeds or 20 seedlings
- O 5 to 7 small to medium seed potatoes

DIG THIS!

Both mulched beds serve as prime habitat for earthworms, the soil-building workhorses in most gardens.

MANAGED MULCH
PLANTING AND CARE

EARLY SPRING

① **Start seeds indoors.** Six to eight weeks before your last frost date, start leek seeds indoors under lights (see page 123). If you are growing your own seedlings, start chard and basil seeds indoors about two weeks later.

② **Prepare the bed.** About six weeks before your last frost, prepare the beds. If starting from scratch, use a spade or shovel and digging fork to remove grass and weeds from the beds. Evenly distribute the compost over the beds, and sprinkle on a moderate dusting of organic fertilizer. Check soil moisture, and whenever the soil in your garden is dry enough to crumble easily when dug, use your preferred digging tool to mix the compost and fertilizer into the top 10 inches of soil.

PREPARING POTATOES FOR PLANTING

Potatoes grow from the sprouting puckered "eyes" on each tuber. You can grow wonderful crops by saving and planting some of the potatoes you buy for eating in late winter. Potatoes naturally break dormancy in late winter, so it's a great time to buy a few pricey gourmet potatoes and plant them in your garden. You can also plant potatoes that sprouted in your kitchen pantry as long as they are not the big baking types, which require a long, cool growing season. For larger plantings, simply buy "seed" potatoes by the pound at local garden supply stores or from mail-order companies. Potatoes sold as seed have been inspected and certified to make sure they are free of several common potato diseases. As soon as you get them, place seed potatoes in a sunny spot indoors where they can turn green.

One to two days before you plant them, cut each potato into two or more pieces, with each piece having at least three puckered eyes. Allow the pieces to dry at room temperature. They will shrivel and may blacken, but don't worry. The dry, cut surfaces will help keep the potato pieces from rotting until after the sprouts have grown into new potato plants. Small seed potatoes can be planted whole.

❸ Plant lettuce and more. Three weeks before your last frost date, watch the forecast for a period of calm weather and then plant lettuce and dill in Bed 1. Cut potatoes in half and let them dry in a warm, sunny place for a day or two before planting. Set them 3 inches deep and at least 12 to 14 inches apart in Bed 4.

❹ Set out leeks and chard. As the soil warms, set out leeks and chard (or sow chard seeds) in Bed 4.

LATE SPRING

❺ Plant caged tomatoes. One to two weeks after the last frost has passed, set out tomato seedlings. Move the bales of hay to the right side of the garden. Nestle mulch around the tomato plants about 3 inches deep before installing tomato cages. Once cages are in place, add more mulch around the bases of the cages. Spread mulch 5 inches deep around the potato plants.

❻ Plant summer crops. Sow bush beans in Bed 3, and set out basil seedlings in Bed 2. Either direct-seed or transplant cucumbers in Bed 1 and summer squash in Bed 3.

WHY POTATOES LOVE MULCH

In addition to keeping the soil cool and moist, hay or straw mulch helps potatoes grow better in two more ways: It blocks sunlight that would otherwise turn shallow tubers green; and it makes it difficult for Colorado potato beetles to make their way to your potato plants, because they often stumble into the numerous openings in the mulch— home of natural predators like ground beetles and toads.

DIG THIS!

One of the easiest ways to build better soil is to mulch heavily during your garden's resting season. Make a habit of mulching vacant beds with shredded leaves in fall.

EARLY SUMMER

7 Add more mulch. As the tomatoes and potatoes gain size, add more mulch to keep it 3 inches deep around the tomatoes and 4 to 5 inches deep around the potatoes.

MIDSUMMER

8 Mulch even more. When your potato plants begin to die back, keep a close eye on them and toss mulch over the middles of the plants if it looks like sun can penetrate the plants' withering crowns. Once the weather turns hot, you cannot mulch tomatoes too deeply.

LATE SUMMER

9 Harvest potatoes. Harvest potatoes by raking back the mulch and pulling up the dying plants. Pushing the mulch toward the leeks will help blanch them. Gather the visible potato tubers, and then use your fingers to find more tubers in nearby soil. Deep mulch keeps the soil so soft that it is seldom necessary to actually dig to harvest potatoes. Be sure to cover potatoes as soon as you collect them to protect them from sunlight. The skins of garden-fresh potatoes are fragile, so wait until just before you eat them to scrub your tubers clean. Until then, keep them in a cool, dark, dry place.

10 Manage mulch. After the potatoes have been harvested, begin pulling leeks as you need them in the kitchen. You can let the bed rest beneath its mulch until fall and plant it with garlic or move the rotting mulch to the other side of the garden.

When mulched heavily after planting in fall, garlic survives winter and grows vigorously in spring.

WHEN MULCH MAKES A DIFFERENCE

In addition to potatoes and tomatoes, several other veggies respond dramatically to the right mulch applied at the right time.

★ Fall-planted garlic and shallots are less likely to be damaged by freezing and thawing of the soil if they are insulated by 3 inches of mulch in the south, or 4 to 6 inches in cold winter climates.

★ Spinach has an easier time obtaining soilborne nutrients when mulch keeps microbes active. Mulch also reduces the amount of dirt that gets splashed up onto the plants' crinkled leaves.

★ Leeks will often stretch taller if you surround them with a deep mulch just as they start to gain size, yielding bigger, longer shanks at harvesttime.

CHAPTER ELEVEN

FERTILIZING YOUR GARDEN

When it comes to your plants' food supply, an organic garden is an elegantly simple system. You withdraw stored energy from the system when you harvest crops. When you enrich the soil with compost and organic plant food before you plant the next crop, you are replacing the energy you took.

Throughout this book, I prescribe this simple procedure for feeding plants: Before you plant anything, dig in some compost and organic fertilizer. This practice slowly increases the soil's organic matter content while keeping plants well fed. Plenty of organic matter improves the soil's ability to retain nutrients and improves its physical properties, too.

Is it really that easy? Most of the time, it is. The compost feeds the soil, the fertilizer provides a standby source of nutrients that plants can claim if they need to, and mulches gone crumbly provide great digs for beneficial soil microcreatures, including many that form mutually beneficial relationships with plant roots.

Do not underestimate the power of this plan. Over time, you can probably reduce the amount of fertilizer you use, but most crops (in most soils) will need a little fertilizer.

THE SOIL FOOD PYRAMID

Plenty of bulky stuff is the base of the soil food pyramid. You will need smaller amounts of rich compost and only light applications of actual fertilizers.

Organic fertilizers and mineral amendments

Compost, rotted manure, and other sources of nutrient-rich organic matter

Biodegradable mulches, including grass clippings, shredded leaves, wood chips, straw, crop residue, and other dead plants

Plenty of compost and mulch are key to building fertile soil.

WEIGHING YOUR OPTIONS

Most backyard gardeners need only two or three fertilizer products to satisfy all of their plant-feeding needs. Here's what's in my fertilizer cupboard:

- A bag of blended organic garden fertilizer, which may be made from a dozen or more selected ingredients. These products balance fast-release nitrogen sources such as fish, alfalfa, or cottonseed meal with other minerals and micronutrients.

- A package of powdered or liquid mix-with-water organic plant food. Most of these products are based on fish (or seaweed). Seedlings started indoors often benefit from light feeding starting two to three weeks after the seeds sprout. Out-

side, if a slow-growing plant perks up after being drenched with a liquid fertilizer, you'll know why it was lagging behind.

- A small package of a high-nitrogen plant meal such as cottonseed, soybean, or canola meal to use as a fast-release nitrogen source in warm weather. Be sure to mix high-nitrogen meals into the soil, or make very light applications when using them as booster feedings, tucked beneath mulch on the soil's surface. When handled carelessly, a heavy application of cottonseed meal or other plant meal can burn plant roots.

The Sweet Corn & Company garden on page 158 is a good example of how to provide extra nutrition for a crop of sweet corn. And on pages 162 and 163, you'll find tips for fertilizing other types of crops, plus advice on avoiding overfertilizing and on regulating soil pH.

SWEET CORN & COMPANY
GARDEN PLAN

People who love sweet corn don't begrudge its space-hog personality. They will happily set aside a 15-foot square in return for six weeks of fresh sweet corn. This planting plan makes sweet corn work for its space. Stalks of the early crop serve as a trellis for half-runner snap beans, while the later plantings provide dappled shade—and plenty of running space—for pest-resistant butternut squash.

The tightly timed planting of three varieties of sweet corn in this garden should produce well over 100 ears of delicious corn to eat fresh or stash in the freezer, with plenty of choices between beautiful bicolors, classic yellows, or pristine late-season white varieties. The important thing is to team up three varieties that mature at different times (see page 204). And because sweet corn is pollinated by wind rather than insects, this planting plan calls for closely spaced double or triple rows of corn plants rather than long single rows.

Organic fertilizers are a great match for corn because they become more abundantly available to roots as soil temperatures rise. Research at Michigan State University showed that corn uses only 6 percent of its total nitrogen in its first month, 25 percent as it grows from knee-high to tassel, 25 percent during the pollination period, and a whopping 39 percent as the ears are developing. Obviously, this is one crop for which a midseason booster feeding is worthwhile.

TELL ME MORE!
BEANS IN THE CORN?

Many Indigenous people of North America grew corn, beans, and squash together in their village gardens, and the combination still works well today. Site beans on the sunniest side of your corn patch. Planting them on the outer edge or at row ends ensures a generous supply of sun. Corn seems to enjoy having its roots shaded by rampant squash vines, which also suppress weeds. No wonder this planting plan has been repeated with various twists for more than a thousand years.

THE STUFF

FOR THE BEDS

- Eight 40-pound bags of compost, or about 5 wheelbarrow loads
- One 10-pound package of balanced organic vegetable garden fertilizer
- Grass clippings, shredded leaves, or other mulch material
- Three 25-foot-long soaker hoses

TOOLS

- Seed-starting equipment (see page 124)
- Wheelbarrow, cart, or wagon for moving compost
- Spade or shovel
- Digging fork
- Sharp hoe

NAME

Sweet Corn & Company

FOOTPRINT

14 × 12 feet

SKILL LEVEL

Fine for first-timers

WHEN TO PLANT

Midspring: early sweet corn

Late spring: half-runner snap beans, butternut squash, and mid- and late-season sweet corn

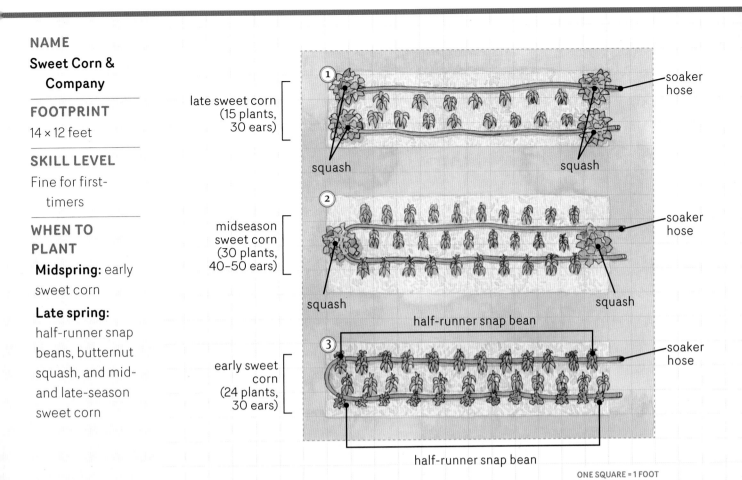

late sweet corn (15 plants, 30 ears)

squash

squash

soaker hose

midseason sweet corn (30 plants, 40–50 ears)

squash

squash

soaker hose

half-runner snap bean

early sweet corn (24 plants, 30 ears)

soaker hose

half-runner snap bean

ONE SQUARE = 1 FOOT

THE PLANTS

BED 1

○ Butternut squash, 1 partial packet seeds

○ 'Silver Queen' or other late-maturing sweet corn, 1 packet seeds

BED 2

○ Butternut squash, 1 partial packet seeds

○ Sweet corn (midseason type), 1 to 2 packets seeds

BED 3

○ Snap bean (half-runner type), 1 packet seeds

○ Sweet corn (early-maturing type), 1 packet seeds

GATHERING THE GOODS

When ears feel firm and hard when you squeeze them, harvest a sample ear and taste it. Sweet corn tastes almost as good raw as it does cooked! Perfect kernels will look glossy and plump, and they spurt a milky juice when pierced. Harvest sweet corn in the cool of the morning when you can, and immediately put it in the fridge.

Harvest green snap beans when the pods are young and tender. Pods that are not harvested "green" will plump up with delicious white beans in early fall.

Butternut squash are ripe when their rinds are hard and uniformly buff brown. Let them ripen as long as you can, but bring them in before your first fall frost.

SWEET CORN & COMPANY
PLANTING AND CARE

MIDSPRING

❶ **Fertilize the beds.** About two weeks before your last frost date, prepare the beds. If starting from scratch, use a spade or shovel and digging fork to remove grass and weeds from the beds. Evenly distribute the compost over the beds, and sprinkle on a heavy dusting of organic fertilizer. Check soil moisture, and whenever the soil in your garden is dry enough to crumble easily when dug, use your preferred digging tool to mix the compost and fertilizer into the top few inches of soil.

❷ **Start early corn.** Indoors, start about 24 sweet corn seeds in individual 2-inch paper cups or pots, using an early, cold-tolerant variety. Begin hardening off the seedlings when they are 3 inches tall.

LIME ENLIGHTENMENT

Chemically speaking, soil can be alkaline, neutral, or acidic. Most garden plants grow best in neutral or slightly acidic soil. In soil science lingo, the measurement of where soil falls on the acid-to-alkaline scale is called its pH. In some areas, the soil's pH is so extreme that plants have trouble taking up the nutrients they need. The pH tends to nudge toward neutral when organic matter is added regularly, but this takes many years. You can adjust the pH of acidic soil much more quickly by working a little lime (pulverized limestone) into your soil. Do spend ten bucks and five minutes doing a simple soil test before breaking out the lime, because you may need organic matter more than you need lime. Alkaline soil is harder to fix than acidic soil, but can be made neutral by adding soil sulfur and more organic matter.

You can buy inexpensive soil pH test kits at many garden centers, or you can order them by mail. However, if you want precise information about your soil's chemistry, you should have a soil test made. Most states make soil testing available for less than $20 and provide sample kits with instructions for collecting the sample and mailing it in.

3 **Plant the first patch.** Set out the hardened-off seedlings in Bed 3 when they are about two weeks old. Sow a few more seeds between the seedlings to make sure you get a good stand. Arrange the soaker hose on the planted bed.

LATE SPRING

4 **Sow the rest.** About two weeks after your last frost, when the soil feels warm to your bare feet, sow a triple row of midseason corn in Bed 2, planting the seeds 1 inch deep and 3 inches apart. Sow a double row of late-maturing corn in Bed 1. Arrange the soaker hoses on both of these beds.

5 **Sow butternuts.** Plant three or four butternut squash seeds 1 inch deep at each corner of Bed 1, close to the soaker hose. Plant three or four butternut seeds at the ends of Bed 2.

6 **Thin corn and squash.** As the corn plants grow, thin them to stand 12 to 14 inches apart. If needed, fill in wide gaps with more seeds; the little plants will quickly catch up. Thin squash to the four strongest plants in Bed 1. Thin to the two strongest plants in Bed 2.

EARLY SUMMER

7 **Sow beans.** In Bed 3, plant half-runner beans just outside the early sweet corn when the corn is almost 2 feet tall. Beans planted 12 inches apart will not need thinning.

Pole beans planted at the end of the row can use early sweet corn as a trellis.

ALL SUMMER LONG

8 **Feed and weed.** As soon as tassels emerge from the tops of the corn plants, scatter a light dusting of fertilizer over the plants' roots. With a hoe, lightly cultivate the surface to mix in the fertilizer and simultaneously slice down weeds. Water thoroughly, then mulch. Expect the squash vines to run where they like, including the space between the beds. Avoid stepping on the vines as you check on your corn. The beans will twine up and around the corn plants without assistance.

LATE SUMMER

9 **Gather the harvest.** Pick tender bean pods weekly from late summer to frost. Young butternuts can be eaten like summer squash, or you can let them mature until the rinds are hard.

CAN YOU USE TOO MUCH?

Working with organic fertilizers can be confusing, because they release nutrients slowly in cold soil. So in the spring, plants may grow slowly even in soil that's had organic fertilizer added, and the lack of response makes gardeners think their plants need more fertilizer. Then, when warming soil makes many more nutrients available, you find that you have overfed your plants. Should this happen, plants will grow to monstrous size, but they may set only a few bland-flavored fruits.

Don't let this happen to you! Never exceed the application rates given on a fertilizer package. Instead, be patient. If you suspect that a plant is starving, see whether it responds well to a drench with a fast-acting liquid plant food before adding additional fertilizer into the soil. It is also crucial to thoroughly mix organic fertilizers into the soil, which helps them work their best and reduces the chance that they might burn plant roots.

Be sure to store organic fertilizers in a dry place. You can keep a small supply handy in the garden by pouring it into a waterproof plastic jug, such as those used to package laundry detergent, plucked from the recycling bin. To avoid confusion, be sure to label the jug as fertilizer!

SATISFYING BIG APPETITES

Some vegetable crops need more nutrients than others.

Cabbage-family crops and spinach need abundant nitrogen at all stages of growth, which can be a problem when soil temperatures are low. (The biological processes that cause nutrient release slow down when it gets cold.) A liquid plant food can help satisfy the big appetite of these plants, especially in cool spring weather.

Tomatoes, peppers, and other crops that must grow all summer before producing a harvest may exhaust the soil's nutrient supply just when they need it most. When the plants load up with fruit, mix a light application of fertilizer into the top inch of soil over the plants' roots, and tuck it in with an organic mulch.

Onions, garlic, and other alliums respond well to "banding" fertilizer in a 6- to 8-inch-deep furrow before planting. Apply fertilizer, then partially refill the furrow and set seedlings or sow seeds on top of the buried cache of nutrients.

Sweet corn has been bred to be grown with more nitrogen than is present in most soils. It has a peculiar need for well-timed snacks, which you can satisfy by following the care instructions on the facing page.

CHAPTER TWELVE

YOUR INSECT FRIENDS AND FOES

When you're out in your garden on a warm summer morning, you will have plenty of insect company. Most of these guys are helpful garden allies that pollinate crops or sabotage troublemakers. Or they may be neither garden helpers nor foes, but they're still part of the overall food supply for general bug predators like spiders and toads.

A garden that's abuzz with insects is usually a good thing. But it's also wise to learn to recognize the most common pest species and manage them in ways that don't involve killing off your garden's secret police force. Many at-risk vegetables can be covered with a row cover or homemade bug barrier to keep pests away (see page 40).

In some situations you may opt to spray problem insects. The emergency organic pest control products described in this chapter will deter, cripple, or kill pest insects and their offspring, but preventive measures should always come first. Also keep in mind that an insect outbreak usually triggers the interest of natural predators, so it can pay to be patient. Studies have shown that light insect damage that removes less than 30 percent of a plant's leaves has little effect on its long-term yield.

Most gardeners tolerate the presence of a few parsleyworms, which eat their fill of parsley and closely related plants, and later hatch into beautiful black swallowtail butterflies.

TELL ME MORE!

TOP TEN INSECT PESTS

Sooner or later, most gardeners will see these plant-eating insects. The controls and remedies are listed in order of effectiveness.

Pest	Crops Affected	Preventive Measures	Organic Remedies
Aphids	Numerous species feed on vegetables, including tomato- and cabbage-family crops; several transmit viruses	Beneficial insects, including lady beetles, lacewings, and syrphid flies; row covers; reflective mulches; clipping off severely infested leaves or growing tips	Insecticidal soap, diatomaceous earth, horticultural oil
Cabbageworm	Cabbage, broccoli, kale, Brussels sprouts, cauliflower, occasionally turnips and kohlrabi	Row covers, handpicking, predation by birds and numerous types of wasps	Spinosad or Bt
Colorado potato beetle	Potato, bean, tomato	Straw mulch, row covers, resistant varieties, handpicking, crop rotation	Spinosad
Cucumber beetle	Cucumber, squash, pumpkin, melons	Row covers, handpicking, vacuuming, trapping in yellow pails filled with water; trapping with yellow sticky traps	Kaolin clay
Flea beetle	Various species feed on eggplant, potato, radish, arugula, spinach, and other leafy greens	Row covers, reflective mulch, intercropping with mints or other pungent herbs	Spinosad
Japanese beetle	Edamame, bean, tomato, grape, rose, and hundreds of ornamental plants	Row covers, handpicking, parasitic wasps	Beneficial nematodes, milky spore
Mexican bean beetle	Bean, tomato, occasionally squash	Scout twice weekly and handpick adults, eggs, and larvae; release beneficial *Pediobius* wasps	Neem, Spinosad
Slugs and snails	Most garden crops (these are not insects, but mollusks)	No evening watering, clean cultivation, handpicking, trapping, ground beetles and other natural predators, reduced mulching	Iron phosphate baits, diatomaceous earth, copper barriers
Squash bugs	Squash, melons, cucumber	Row covers, handpicking adults and egg masses, trapping under boards at night, growing nonpreferred varieties, prompt composting of debris	Neem
Tomato hornworm	Tomato, pepper, tobacco	Scout and handpick twice weekly starting in early summer	Spinosad or Bt

ORGANIC REMEDIES THAT REALLY WORK

Organic pest control has come a long way in recent years. Here are the basic remedies organic gardeners turn to in times of trouble:

- **Spinosad** is a fermented brew of two naturally occurring bacteria, and it slowly paralyzes insects after they eat it. Spinosad is widely used in fire ant baits, and it is also useful for controlling leaf-eating beetles such as Mexican bean beetles and Colorado potato beetles. It will control leaf-eating caterpillars, too.

- **Bt** (*Bacillus thuringiensis* ssp. *kurstaki*), a trusted, old biological pesticide, remains a good remedy for leaf-eating caterpillars. When caterpillars eat leaves that have been sprayed with Bt, these naturally occurring bacteria cause the caterpillars' intestines to rupture.

- **Diatomaceous earth (DE)** feels as soft as talcum powder in your hand, but each particle is a waffle of sharp edges. When enough of this powdery dust gets wedged into the head and joints of soft-bodied insects, they dry up and die. DE deters slug feeding, too, but it can also harm beneficial insects. Place it only where slugs, snails, and other soft-bodied pests are present.

- **Insecticidal soap** contains fatty acids that cause aphids and other insects to die through dessication. The leaves of some plants are burned by soap, so check the product's label for precautions. Avoid using soap in hot, sunny weather.

- **Neem** is one of several horticultural oils that clog up insects' sensory and breathing apparatuses. It may suppress fungal diseases, too. In addition to its smothering action, neem's active ingredient slows feeding and radically reduces reproduction.

- **Kaolin clay** is made up of tiny particles that form a thin paintlike mixture when mixed with water. Many common pests won't eat leaves covered with the stuff, and those that do partake end up eating a dirty dinner.

- **Disposable gloves** are not a spray-on remedy, but they make gathering bugs by hand less icky. Take a small pail of soapy water with you when you go on bug-gathering missions. Insects dropped into soapy water quickly drown.

BENEFICIAL BORDER
GARDEN PLAN

Many new gardeners fear insects as garden enemies, but in truth, insects do your garden more good than harm—especially if you go out of your way to attract hard-working beneficial species. This is easy to do if you love growing plenty of oregano for pizzas and pasta and don't mind tiptoeing among flowers as you gather summer tomatoes. Cultivating some blooming herbs and pretty flowers among your veggies is a no-fail way to capture the attention of insects that are on your side.

At first glance this planting plan may look like just another vegetable garden, but there is more going on here than meets the eye. In this mixed planting of vegetables, herbs, and flowers, tiny braconid wasps attracted to the nectar-bearing blossoms of the sweet alyssum are likely to become parasites of any tomato hornworms that dare to hatch, and hoverflies drawn in by blooming dill or cilantro will quickly bring aphid outbreaks under control. The garden sets up favorable battle lines on the ground, too, by using deep mulch and a core grouping of long-lived perennial herbs. This combo is preferred habitat for important night-shift predators including ground beetles, spiders, and garden toads.

When you encounter a new insect, assume it is harmless unless you catch it in the act of chomping on a plant. When you do nab an unknown evildoer, place it in a glass jar along with some of the vegetation it has been eating. Borrow an insect identification guide from your local library, and study up to figure out the identity and habits of the bug. The more you learn about the insects that inhabit your garden, the better job you can do creating happy habitats for your six-legged friends.

THE STUFF

FOR THE BEDS
- Four 40-pound bags of compost, or about 3 wheelbarrow loads
- One 5-pound package of organic vegetable garden fertilizer
- Grass clippings, shredded leaves, or other freely available biodegradable mulch material

FOR THE TOMATOES
- Two 5-foot-tall tomato cages

FOR THE HERBS
- Two 12-inch-diameter containers
- One 20-pound bag of potting soil

TOOLS
- Wheelbarrow, cart, or wagon for moving compost
- Hand trowel
- Spade or shovel
- Digging fork

NAME
Beneficial Border

FOOTPRINT
3 × 24 feet

SKILL LEVEL
Beyond beginner

WHEN TO PLANT

Midspring: parsley, cilantro, lettuce, sweet alyssum, mint, onions, Greek oregano, sage, garlic chives, and dill or fennel

Late spring: tomatoes, basil, bush snap beans, Dwarf French marigolds, and more lettuce

Late summer: more lettuce and cilantro

Early fall: spinach

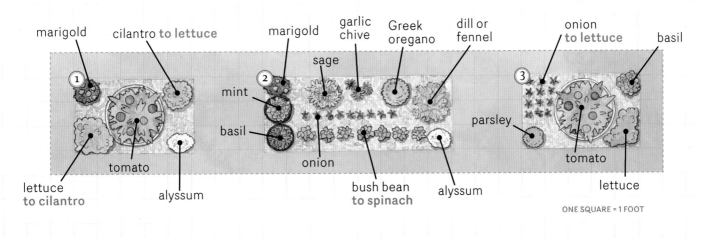

ONE SQUARE = 1 FOOT

THE PLANTS

BED ①
- Cilantro, 1 packet seeds
- Dwarf French marigold, 1 partial packet seeds
- Lettuce (mixed types), 1 packet seeds or 6 seedlings
- Sweet alyssum, 1 partial packet seeds or about 3 seedlings
- Tomato, 1 seedling

BED ②
- Basil, 1 packet seeds or 2 seedlings
- Dill or fennel, 1 packet seeds
- Dwarf French marigold, 1 partial packet seeds or 1 seedling
- Garlic chives, 3 small plants or one 4-inch-wide clump
- Greek oregano, 1 plant

- Onion, 12 to 15 seedlings or sets
- Peppermint or spearmint, 2 or 3 rooted cuttings
- Sage, 1 plant
- Snap bean (bush variety), 1 packet seeds
- Spinach, 1 packet seeds
- Sweet alyssum, 1 partial packet seeds or about 3 seedlings

BED ③
- Basil, 1 seedling
- Lettuce mix, 1 packet seeds or 6 seedlings
- Onion, 10 to 12 seedlings or sets
- Parsley, 2 seedlings or 1 packet seeds
- Tomato, 1 seedling

WHAT NOT TO WEAR

Bees, wasps, and thousands of species of other flying insects easily mistake brightly colored clothing for flowers, so it's best to wear neutral colors in the garden. Expect to get buzzed if you dare to wear red, bright blue, or hot pink on a warm summer day.

BENEFICIAL BORDER
PLANTING AND CARE

EARLY SPRING

1 **Dig and enrich beds.** About six weeks before your last frost, prepare the beds. If starting from scratch, use a spade or shovel and digging fork to remove grass and weeds from the beds. Evenly distribute the compost over the beds, and sprinkle on a light dusting of organic fertilizer. Check soil moisture, and whenever the soil in your garden is dry enough to crumble easily when dug, use your preferred digging tool to mix the compost and fertilizer into the top few inches of soil.

MIDSPRING

2 **Plant lettuce and more.** Three weeks before your last frost date, plant lettuce, sweet alyssum, and cilantro in Bed 1.

3 **Plant herbs and onions.** In Bed 2, plant mint in one of the containers; set out sage, garlic chives, and Greek oregano. Then plant a 6-foot row of onions down the middle of the bed. Sow dill (or fennel) and sweet alyssum seeds.

4 **Keep planting more.** Plant onions, 3 inches apart, in an 18-inch square in the corner of Bed 3. Also sow lettuce and parsley in Bed 3.

5 **Weed, thin, mulch.** As the seedlings grow, weed often and thin the dill to three plants. (Eat the thinnings.) Thin sweet alyssum to three plants in each position, and thin parsley to two plants. Mulch after thinning to reduce your future weeding chores.

LATE SPRING

6 **Plant and cage tomatoes.** One to two weeks after the last frost has passed, set out tomato seedlings in Beds 1 and 3. Nestle mulch around the plants about 3 inches deep before installing tomato cages (see page 132). Then add more mulch around the bases of the cages.

7 **Plant basil and more.** Sow or set out basil in Beds 2 and 3, and plant bush beans down the front of Bed 2. Sow marigolds in Beds 1 and 2.

8 Monitor bloom boom. As your plants grow, clip off the first basil blooms as they appear, but otherwise allow your herbs to flower freely. Watch for wild buzzing activity as each herb comes into bloom. Just as the garlic chive blossoms begin to fade in late summer (they bloom surprisingly late), cut and compost them to keep them from shedding seeds. Especially in cold climates, garlic chives can become weedy. Cover all exposed soil with at least 2 inches of mulch.

9 Plant fall greens. In Bed 1, as your lettuce crop peters out, replace it with cilantro, and replace cilantro with lettuce. Lettuce or other salad greens also can be planted after onions in Bed 3. Pull bush beans in Bed 2 when the leaves begin to wither, and promptly plant spinach in their place.

FALL

10 Mulch herbs. Spread 2 inches of mulch around the base of sage to enhance its winter hardiness. Wait until spring to prune back the dead branches from sage, oregano, and mint, because the dead stems will shelter the plants' crowns through the cold winter months.

DIG THIS!
Slender, beelike insects that can hover in the air, called hoverflies, come in a range of colors and sizes, and most are mighty beneficials. Tiny hoverfly larvae consume huge numbers of smaller insects.

Harvestmen (often called daddy longlegs) eat decomposing plant material. They lack venom and cannot bite.

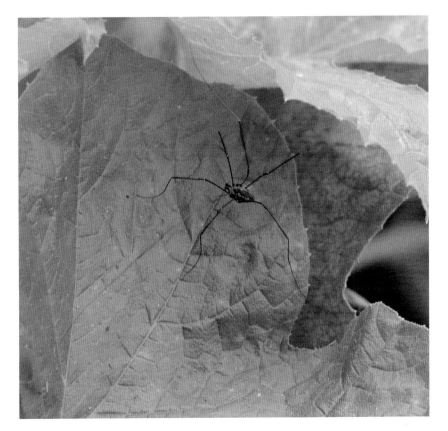

CHAPTER THIRTEEN

PREVENTING DASTARDLY DISEASES

When given half a chance at a healthy life, plants rarely get sick until after they have produced a crop. But when the right combination of rainfall and temperature comes together to give disease-causing fungi, bacteria, nematodes, or viruses the conditions they've been waiting for, bad things can happen in good gardens.

Garden diseases are caused by microscopic life-forms including fungi, bacteria, and viruses. Some can persist in soil for many years, while others can enter the garden on the wind or from the movement of insects. There is no such thing as a disease-free garden.

Healthy, well-nourished plants that enjoy plenty of light and fresh air respond to disease challenges better than stressed ones, but diseases can become an issue in even the best organic gar-dens. Learn as much as you can about vegetable diseases that are common in your area, because with plant diseases, you must think in terms of prevention rather than cure.

The big difference between insect and disease problems is that bug issues can be addressed head-on and corrected, but once a disease is afoot, the sick crop is pretty much a lost cause. You must work preventively, using two potent tools: genetically resistant varieties and protective sprays.

NIGHTMARE NEMATODES

Soils in warm, moist climates often host microscopic eel-worms, or nematodes, which form parasitic colonies inside swollen galls on the roots of host plants. These knots and galls prevent the plants from taking up nutrients and water, so infected plants grow slowly and appear thirsty almost all the time. Numerous tomato varieties are genetically resistant; simply look for a capital N after the variety's name (like 'Better Boy' VFN). Good resistance also can be had in peppers and sweet potatoes.

SUPERSTRONG VARIETIES

In the last 50 years, plant breeders have made huge steps in developing varieties that are naturally resistant to numerous common diseases. In seed catalogs, disease resistance is often abbreviated with capital letters that appear after the variety name. 'Roma' VF tomato, for example, is resistant to two soilborne diseases, verticillium (V) and fusarium (F) wilt. Similarly, PM stands for powdery mildew, which causes white patches on the leaves of many plants, including cucumber-family crops. If you live in a climate where certain diseases are widespread, use resistant varieties as your first line of defense.

In the South and Southwest, opt for maximum disease resistance in tomato and pepper plants, which are commonly affected by fusarium wilt, viruses, and rootknot nematodes. Viral resistance is also important in cucumber-family crops.

Gardeners in the North and Northwest should look for verticillium wilt resistance in tomatoes and black rot and fusarium resistance in cabbage-family crops. Virus-resistant peas are especially valuable in the Northwest, along with cucumber-family crops that resist powdery mildew.

To compare the most disease-resistant varieties of other crops, review the lists maintained by Cornell University's Department of Plant Pathology (search "disease-resistant vegetable varieties Cornell").

Choosing resistant varieties will be crucial for success with the Cajun Spice garden plan on page 176.

FIGHTING WITH FUNGI

Most diseases that infect plants' leaves are caused by fungi. By the time you can see the problem, it's too late to do much about it. Most diseases are pretty predictable, though, which gives you opportunities to try these simple preventive methods:

- **Plain milk,** when diluted in water and exposed to sunlight, briefly changes into a disinfectant compound that's murder on fungal spores yet gentle to plant leaves. Mix ½ cup milk to 2 cups water. Apply weekly to healthy plants that are at high risk for developing powdery mildew; for example, pumpkins or winter squash.

TROUBLE IN PARADISE: WHAT WENT WRONG?

Diseases often seem mysterious because we can't see them without help from a microscope. Most home gardens have only modest disease problems, but to be sure you keep the upper hand, learn to recognize symptoms of diseases that are widespread in your area.

Symptom	Likely Cause	Techniques to Try
Plant slowly wilts or rapidly collapses, or new growth stops and plant dies	Soilborne fungal diseases including fusarium, verticillium, and numerous others	Use resistant varieties; plant a different crop family on that site the following season; enrich soil with compost
New growth crinkled or distorted, with crazy flowering patterns or thickened leaves	Viruses, which are spread by small insects and interfere with DNA signaling patterns within the plants	Use resistant varieties; pull out infected plants
Leaves have white patches or numerous dark spots, or entire leaves wither and die	Airborne fungal diseases, including powdery mildew, downy mildew, early blight, and hundreds more	Use resistant varieties; treat at-risk crops with preventive milk, baking-soda, or oil sprays

Baking soda also can help prevent powdery mildew and other leaf spot diseases. Mix 1 teaspoon per quart of water, with a few drops of liquid soap added to help it stick. Baking soda is especially effective when used in rotation with very light horticultural oils.

Horticultural oils may be based on soybean, canola, or even herbal essential oils. These oils make leaf surfaces inhospitable to fungi, but they can damage leaves when applied in hot weather. Check the label of the product you buy to make sure the crop plant you want to treat is listed, and follow the label's application instructions precisely.

Pruning or pinching off expendable plant parts at the first sign of trouble is a smart intervention, too. When the lowest leaves of your tomatoes start showing dark spots from early blight (no resistance is available), clipping them off can seriously slow the spread of the disease.

DIG THIS!

Different strains of the same disease infect different types of plants. For example, the strain of the *Fusarium* fungus that causes tomatoes to turn yellow and die is different from the one that causes basil to wilt.

CAJUN SPICE
GARDEN PLAN

You don't need to limit yourself to particular varieties to grow a good garden—unless a favorite crop faces serious disease pressures beyond your control. Depending on where you live, genetic disease resistance may be required if you are to be successful growing tomatoes, peppers, or even basil. Growing resistant varieties has another advantage, too. For starter gardeners, they can help you gain the confidence you need to move ahead.

By the time the French-speaking Acadians arrived in Louisiana in the late 1700s, they were in rough shape. Those not lost at sea en route from Nova Scotia and New York established a settlement in Louisiana—a daunting climate plagued by mosquitoes and hurricanes, but the fishing was great! Against all odds, the Acadians, or Cajuns, created one of the most exciting culinary traditions in the world.

The Cajun Spice garden offers a tasty sample of big-flavor herbs and vegetables. This garden is well suited to climates with long, humid summers, which naturally face serious disease pressures. When moisture from frequent rains or heavy dews combines with warm temperatures, you had better be ready with disease-resistant varieties. In climates with shorter growing seasons, substitute ordinary potatoes for sweet potatoes as you implement this planting plan.

THE STUFF

FOR THE BEDS

- Eight 40-pound bags of compost, or about 5 wheelbarrow loads
- One 5-pound package of balanced organic vegetable garden fertilizer
- Grass clippings, shredded leaves, or other mulch material

FOR THE TOMATOES

- Three 5-foot-tall tomato cages

TOOLS

- Wheelbarrow, cart, or wagon for moving compost
- Spade or shovel
- Digging fork

THE PLANTS

BED ①
- Sweet potato, 6 slips (rooted cuttings; see page 219)
- Zucchini, 1 packet seeds (resistant to viruses and powdery mildew)

BED ②
- French or English thyme, 2 plants
- Tomato, 3 seedlings (multiple disease resistance, as in VFFNT or better)

BED ③
- Celery, celtuce, or parcel, 3 seedlings (see page 202)
- Collard, 1 packet seeds
- Greek oregano, 1 plant
- Lettuce mix, 1 packet seeds
- Marjoram, 1 plant
- Parsley, 1 packet seeds or 3 seedlings
- Sage, 1 plant
- Scallions, 20 or so seedlings or sets

BED ④
- Basil, 1 seedling or 1 packet seeds (resistant to fusarium wilt)
- Hot pepper, 2 seedlings (resistant to multiple viral diseases, especially TMV)
- Sweet pepper, 2 seedlings (resistant to multiple viral diseases, especially TMV)

NAME

Cajun Spice

FOOTPRINT

12 × 14 feet

SKILL LEVEL

Beyond beginner

WHEN TO PLANT

Midspring: thyme, parsley, celery, scallions, lettuce, Greek oregano, marjoram, and sage

Late spring: tomatoes, zucchini, basil, peppers, and sweet potatoes

Late summer or early fall: collards

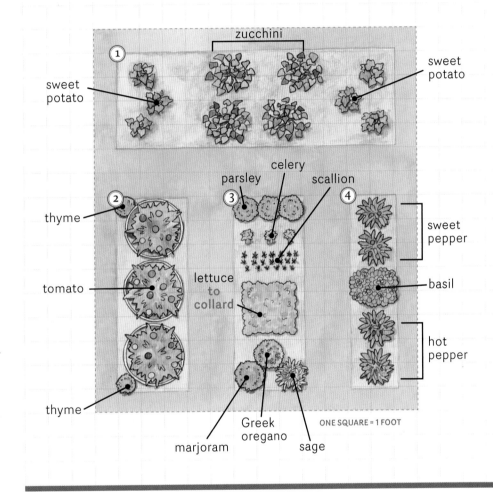

zucchini

① sweet potato

sweet potato

② thyme

tomato

thyme

celery

parsley   scallion

③

lettuce to collard

marjoram

Greek oregano

sage

④

sweet pepper

basil

hot pepper

ONE SQUARE = 1 FOOT

CAJUN SPICE
PLANTING AND CARE

MIDSPRING

❶ Prepare the beds. About four weeks before your last frost date, prepare the beds. If starting from scratch, use a spade or shovel and digging fork to remove grass and weeds from the beds. Evenly distribute the compost over the beds, and sprinkle on a heavy dusting of organic fertilizer. Check soil moisture, and whenever the soil in your garden is dry enough to crumble easily when dug, use your preferred digging tool to mix the compost and fertilizer into the top few inches of soil.

❷ Plant herbs and more. Set out thyme plants in Bed 2. Sow lettuce seeds and plant celery seedlings and scallions along with parsley, oregano, marjoram, and sage plants in Bed 3.

❸ Harvest lettuce and scallions. After the lettuce sprouts, gradually thin the seedlings to 4 inches apart, and eat the baby plants. Begin pulling scallions when they are 10 inches tall.

LATE SPRING

❹ Plant tomatoes and more. About a week after your last frost, set out tomatoes, hot peppers, sweet peppers, and basil. Direct-seed the zucchini or set out seedlings.

❺ Set out sweet potatoes. When the soil feels warm to your bare feet, set out sweet potato slips. To plant slips, open a diagonal planting hole with your hand and position the slip so that only the topmost leaves show at the surface. Bury the root and stem with loose soil and water well. Use shade covers (as described on page 114) to protect newly transplanted sweet potatoes from hot sun.

❻ Harvest spring crops. Gather lettuce, scallions, and stalks of celery as you need them in the kitchen.

EARLY SUMMER

❼ Dry herbs. Once the thyme, oregano, and parsley grow into lush mounds, gather stems for drying. When cut back by two-thirds their size, the plants will rebound quickly with a flush of new growth.

LATE SUMMER TO EARLY FALL

❽ Plant collards. Sow collards in Bed 3 in the space vacated by spring crops. See page 219 for directions for digging the sweet potatoes.

GARDEN ÉTOUFFÉE

Zucchini squash stand in for shrimp in this Cajun classic recipe, which uses many of the crops grown in the Cajun Spice garden on page 176.

¼	cup olive oil
½	cup flour
1	onion, coarsely chopped
2-4	zucchini squash, cut into 1-inch chunks
3	scallions, chopped
3	cloves garlic, chopped
1	mature sweet pepper, chopped
4-5	stems fresh thyme, chopped
3-4	stems fresh oregano or marjoram, chopped
2-3	stems fresh Italian parsley, chopped
2	tomatoes, peeled and chopped
6-8	medium okra pods, sliced (optional)
	Salt, freshly ground black pepper, and hot sauce

Make a roux by cooking the oil and flour together in a heavy pot over medium heat. Cook, stirring constantly, to a light caramel brown color. Add the onion, followed by the vegetables and herbs. Cover the pot and cook over medium-low heat for 30 minutes, stirring occasionally to limit sticking. As the vegetables release their juices, they mix with the roux to form a gravy. Season to taste with salt, black pepper, and hot sauce. Serve over hot cooked rice, quinoa, or bulgur.

CHAPTER FOURTEEN

SMART HARVESTING

Every evening when the sun goes down, the plants in your garden get busy doing what they must to recover from the stresses of the day. Solar collectors (leaves) switch to standby mode as the plants recharge themselves with moisture and nutrients. The result is that almost all vegetables are at their best in terms of both flavor and nutrition in the morning. Whenever you can harvest anything early in the day, do it!

CHILL OUT!

Most vegetables keep best when they're chilled very quickly after they are harvested—chilling maintains their flavors and nutrients at just-picked levels. When you must pick in the evening, when veggies are holding the day's heat, it's especially important to cool them down quickly unless you plan to eat them right away. Make "ice pancakes" (frozen, water-filled plastic sandwich bags), and layer them among your picked cucumbers, snap beans, or whatever. But there are several exceptions to the cooldown guideline:

- Keep harvested tomatoes and peppers at room temperature. Temperatures below 55°F (12°C) destroy important flavor compounds.

- Cure onions, garlic, and sweet potatoes in a warm, 80°F (25°C) place for up to two weeks before storing them at cool room temperatures. This drying period improves both eating quality and storage life of these vegetables.

- Regular potatoes require constant protection from light, so gather them in the evening or on a cloudy day. Garden-fresh potatoes have delicate skins, so wait until just before cooking to wash them. For storage, you can toughen skins by waiting to harvest potatoes until two weeks or so after the foliage has died back.

- Store sweet potatoes and winter squash at cool room temperatures—50 to 55°F (10 to 12°C) for squash; 60°F (16°C) for sweet potatoes. Sweet potatoes in particular would rather be warm than refrigerated.

Dry herbs in small bundles, and use them for seasoning soups, stews, and casseroles during the winter months.

PUTTING FOOD BY

The easiest crops to store—garlic, potatoes, and winter squash—will keep for months in a cool, dry place. Carrots and most other root crops can be left in the ground and dug as needed, or you can wash them and stash them in the fridge. Here is a quick guide to the most practical long-term preservation methods for several vegetables that often produce bumper crops.

Crop	Preservation Options
Cucumber, beet, turnip	Pickle, then freeze or can in a water-bath canner
Dark leafy greens (spinach, kale, collards, chard, etc.)	Blanch and freeze, or dry into flakes
Herbs	Dry or freeze
Pea (all types), snap bean	Blanch and freeze
Pepper	Blanching is optional before freezing whole or in pieces; blanched sweet pepper rings or strips dry beautifully; dry small hot peppers whole
Summer squash	Grill or blanch and freeze, or blanch and dry into chips
Tomato	Blanch or roast before freezing, dry until leathery, or can in a water-bath canner

PROVIDE DAY CARE FOR TONIGHT'S DINNER

If you don't have time to pick your leafy greens in the morning, spend 20 seconds covering the planting with a cardboard box. Or you can use a lightweight blanket held aloft with stakes. As long as the soil has adequate moisture, the shaded greens should be in reasonably good picking condition in the evening. If you forget the day-care drill, pick your salad greens as soon as you get home and chill them in ice water for 30 minutes.

PRESERVING YOUR FAVORITE HERBS

Most of the aromatic Mediterranean herbs, including oregano, sage, rosemary, and thyme, are easy to preserve by drying 8-inch-long stems in bundles of five or six. Harvest on a bright, sunny day, preferably in late morning when any overnight dew has dried. To make cleaning the stems easy, wash the plants with a fine spray of water the day before you plan to pick them. That way, the gathered stems should need only a quick swish through cool water to get them clean enough to dry.

Parsley can be dried, too, or you can freeze it in cubes of ice. The ice trick also works well with cilantro, and individual leaves of mint frozen in cubes of fruit juice are beyond cool.

The trickiest herb to preserve is basil, because it turns black when you bruise it, cut it, cook it, or freeze it. Most cooks rely on frozen partially made pesto as their primary way of preserving basil: Purée lots of leaves with olive oil, lemon juice, and salt, and freeze in cubes or other small portions. The olive oil and lemon juice help preserve a little color, so that the thawed pesto is dark green instead of black. Finish the pesto by adding garlic, toasted nuts, and grated hard cheese to the thawed cubes.

GOOD-FOR-YOU GARDEN
GARDEN PLAN

The most nutritious veggies on the planet are grown in organic gardens and picked at just the right time. Your diet automatically improves when your garden is calling to you to get out there and pick. Numerous medical conditions, from heart disorders to immune system problems, respond favorably to a diet based on exactly what gardens like to produce—dark leafy greens, sun-ripened tomatoes and peppers, and pungent onions. And, of course, getting out in the fresh air and sunshine is good for you, too.

The **Good-for-You Garden** produces a full season of dark leafy greens, including spinach in spring, chard in summer, and kale in fall and early winter. Three more nutritional superstars—broccoli, carrots, and cantaloupe—provide abundant antioxidants, vitamin C, and calcium, too. To push your garden-grown nutrition score even higher, you can grow supernutritious varieties like 'Sugarsnax' carrot, 'Health Kick' tomato, or 'NutriBud' broccoli, which are widely available from mail-order seed suppliers.

SLIPPING FROM THE VINE

Melons are famous for teasing their keepers with the "Is it ripe yet?" game. But if you stick with varieties known for their "full slip" characteristic, you will never harvest an underripe muskmelon. After the melon's rind shows good netting, start checking the stem end until you see a crack forming between the stem and the fruit. When the stem slips away with a gentle push of your thumb, the melon has reached perfection.

Unfortunately, honeydews, Asian melons, and true cantaloupes don't perform the slip trick. They must be cut from the vine when ripe. Most varieties develop yellowish rind colors, but other signs of ripeness must be learned through experience, one variety at a time.

TELL ME MORE!
FRESH OR FROZEN?

One of the reasons why garden-grown veggies are better for you is because you eat them within hours (or maybe even minutes!) after picking. Vitamin C and folate (a B vitamin) are the first nutrients to take a tumble. Even when promptly refrigerated after picking, spinach and other dark leafy greens can lose half their content of these nutrients within a few days. If you can't eat all the greens your garden produces, blanch them in a little boiling water and freeze them. When thawed and squeezed (to remove excess water), frozen chard, kale, or spinach make great additions to casseroles, quiches, soups, or even pizza.

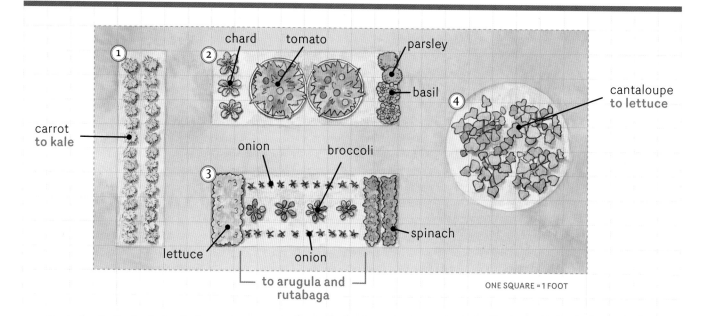

ONE SQUARE = 1 FOOT

NAME
Good-for-You Garden

FOOTPRINT
8 × 19 feet
See other uses of this bed grouping in the Easy-Care Bag Garden, page 21.

SKILL LEVEL
Beyond beginner

WHEN TO PLANT
Midspring: carrots, chard, parsley, lettuce, onions, broccoli, and spinach
Late spring: tomatoes, basil, and cantaloupe
Late summer: kale
Early fall: arugula, lettuce, and rutabaga

THE STUFF

FOR THE BEDS
- Six 40-pound bags of compost, or about 4 wheelbarrow loads
- One 5-pound package of organic vegetable garden fertilizer

FOR THE TOMATOES
- Two 5-foot-tall tomato cages

TOOLS
- Wheelbarrow, cart, or wagon for moving compost
- Hand trowel
- Spade or shovel
- Digging fork

THE PLANTS

BED ①
- Carrot (fast-maturing variety), 1 packet seeds
- Kale, 1 packet seeds

BED ②
- Basil, 1 packet seeds or 2 seedlings
- Chard, 1 packet seeds or 3 seedlings
- Parsley, 1 packet seeds or 2 seedlings
- Tomato, 2 seedlings

BED ③
- Arugula, 1 packet seeds
- Broccoli (fast-maturing hybrid), 4 seedlings
- Lettuce mix, 1 packet seeds
- Onion, about 25 seedlings or sets
- Rutabaga, 1 packet seeds
- Spinach, 1 packet seeds

BED ④
- Cantaloupe (muskmelon), 1 packet seeds
- Lettuce or other salad greens, 1 packet seeds

GOOD-FOR-YOU GARDEN
PLANTING AND CARE

EARLY SPRING

1 **Dig and enrich beds.** About six weeks before your last frost date, prepare the beds. If starting from scratch, use a spade or shovel and digging fork to remove grass and weeds from the beds. Evenly distribute the compost over the beds, and sprinkle on a light dusting of organic fertilizer. In Beds 2 and 3, mix a little more fertilizer into the spaces to be planted with broccoli, spinach, and tomatoes. Check soil moisture, and whenever the soil in your garden is dry enough to crumble easily when dug, use your preferred digging tool to mix the compost and fertilizer into the top few inches of soil.

MIDSPRING

2 **Plant cool-season seeds.** Three weeks before your last frost date, watch the forecast for a period of calm weather. Then plant the cool-season crops: parsley, lettuce, chard, carrots, spinach, broccoli, and onions. Weed early and often, and don't forget to thin direct-seeded crops.

LATE SPRING

3 **Set out tomatoes and basil.** One to two weeks after the last frost has passed, set out tomato seedlings and either sow or transplant basil in Bed 2.

4 **Plant cantaloupe.** Plant pairs of cantaloupe seeds 12 inches apart throughout Bed 4. As soon as the seedlings appear, thin until the four strongest plants remain. If you anticipate problems with cucumber beetles or other insect pests, use row covers to protect the plants (see page 40). Remove the row covers when the plants begin to bloom heavily.

SUMMER

5 **Replace carrots with kale.** As the carrots grow, maintain even soil moisture to help the roots size up quickly. Pull or dig when the soil is moist, and plant kale seeds after the carrots are harvested. Kale will usually germinate well from direct-sown seeds, or you can start seeds indoors and set them out after the carrots are harvested.

6 **Harvest broccoli and onions.** Cut broccoli heads high to encourage the development of side shoots. Pull onions after they fall over.

EARLY FALL

7 **Sow fall crops.** As nights start to cool down in August, bring Bed 3 back to life by planting arugula and rutabaga seeds.

8 **Replace melons with lettuce.** As soon as the melons are harvested, gather up the vines and compost them to short-circuit insects and diseases lurking in the debris. Direct-sow lettuce or other salad greens in Bed 4.

9 **Apply winter mulch.** To improve your garden's overall health, mulch over all vacant spaces during the winter months. Grass clippings and chopped leaves are great materials for tucking in beds for winter.

CHAPTER FIFTEEN

STRETCHING THE SEASONS

If you could change something about your climate, what would it be? Most folks want spring to come sooner, because waiting for spring is especially hard for gardeners. By using simple season-stretching hardware and techniques, you can easily add a month to the front end of your growing season.

THREE WAYS TO BRING ON SPRING

With the help of cold frames, cloches, and plastic-covered tunnels, you can start growing cool-natured crops such as arugula, kale, lettuce, and spinach before winter ends. Late in spring, you can use your frames, tunnels, or cloches to protect warm-season crops from chilly winds for a week or two after they are set out. The Six-Weeks-Sooner garden on page 188 explains the timing and method for putting these three devices to work.

You really should hold off planting tomatoes and other warm-season crops until the soil warms, because they won't grow in cold soil anyway. And stretching the growing season into fall is primarily done by planting appropriate crops from midsummer to fall, as is done in many of the planting plans in this book.

Cold Frames

Cold frames bring treacherous winter winds to a standstill, shelter plants from ice and snow, and heat up whenever the sun shines. The soil inside a frame will warm up much faster than open ground, which makes a huge difference to plants. Salad greens are surprisingly cold tolerant when grown inside frames. You can also use a cold frame to harden off seedlings grown indoors.

This simple temporary cold frame is made from a recycled window.

You can build a sturdy cold frame from 2×4s, a few box nails, and four steel corner brackets. Brackets come in different forms—some for inside the box and some for outside. The simplest (and cheapest) brackets screw into the top of a frame that's already been banged together with 3-inch box nails.

The biggest problem with any cold frame is overheating. When in doubt, it is always better to vent by securely propping open the top with sticks or bricks than to risk frying your plants. You will probably end up storing your cold frame for much of the year, when temperatures are warmer.

Cloches

Cloches are the season stretchers of choice for plants spaced more than 8 inches apart, be they spring cabbage, kale, or peppers in need of protection from drying wind. Most gardeners keep a stash of cloches made from translucent plastic milk jugs or large clear plastic bottles. Simply leaving the caps off milk carton cloches provides adequate ventilation. Plastic cloches will last for two or three years if stored out of sunlight, which causes them to become brittle.

Before cutting off the bottom of a jug, make a V-shaped slit in the top of the handle. Later, you can shove a long, slender stick through the slit and down into the soil to help hold the cloche steady in the wind.

When refashioned into cloches, milk jugs work like mini-greenhouses.

Low Tunnels

Plastic-covered tunnels are easy to set up and move, and they can cover more ground than a cold frame. Low tunnels stand steady in wind better than high ones, and tunnels that must hold up to heavy snow loads benefit from sturdy support.

Providing the framework for a low tunnel is a great use for tomato cages made of concrete-reinforcing wire, which can be opened into an arch that is placed over a bed and then covered with plastic. You can also use wire, flexible plastic pipe, or pieces of flexible sapling wood for hoops if you keep your tunnels low and tight. If you have framed raised beds, attach matching pairs of pipe brackets to the outside of the beds' sides to create sleeves for support hoops for temporary tunnels.

Overheating beneath plastic can be a problem, so the ends must be kept open on warm, sunny days. Or you can cover a tunnel with a midweight row cover, which blocks wind yet doesn't heat up nearly as much as plastic. In climates where early-spring weather quickly cycles between mild and cold, you can grow cool-natured veggies under a row cover tunnel and add a layer of plastic—or even an old blanket—when temperatures drop below about 25°F (-3°C).

Low tunnels covered with plastic or a row cover protect plants and help warm the soil.

SIX-WEEKS-SOONER GARDEN PLAN

If the scent of spring in the air makes you hungry for salad, this planting plan will start satisfying your appetite six weeks sooner than if you had sown salad greens in open ground.

In the Six-Weeks-Sooner garden, each of the three main types of season-stretching devices—cold frame, tunnel, and cloche—is used to extend the season of veggies that adapt well to chilly conditions. For example, mache and arugula started inside a frame in late winter will germinate during mild spells, and the frame's rigid top will protect the seedlings from snow.

The tunnel can be covered with a row cover, plastic, or both. The wisest strategy is to install a row cover over the entire tunnel, with all of the ends securely tucked in or weighted, and then add a layer of plastic that is left open on the ends. The plastic can be removed quickly when it is no longer needed, and you will probably need it for only a few weeks.

At the end of six weeks, just as your last frost passes, you can remove your covers to reveal a spring garden lush with greens, beets, onions, and broccoli. Along the way, you will learn which types of season-stretching devices best match your garden and the needs of your plants.

TELL ME MORE!

CAN YOU GARDEN THROUGH WINTER?

Spinach is the most cold tolerant of all vegetables. It is the easiest crop to grow through winter beneath a cold frame or tunnel as far north as Zone 4. Spinach planted in fall and grown under cover will show little actual growth in winter, because there isn't enough intense sunlight to keep the plants going. Then, when days become longer and warmer in early spring, the overwintered plants will explode with new growth.

If you live in Zone 7 or warmer, you can add arugula, cabbage, cilantro, collards, kale, and mizuna to your list of easy edibles to grow through winter. Just be ready to pop on a row cover or tunnel if winter weather turns bitterly cold.

THE STUFF

FOR THE COLD FRAME
- 1 reconditioned window frame
- 4 pieces of scrap lumber (such as 2×4s) that match the outside dimensions of the window frame
- Eight 18- or 24-inch wood stakes

FOR THE TUNNEL
- Five 5-foot-long wire, plastic, or wood hoops
- One 8 × 12-foot sheet of clear or opaque plastic

NAME
Six-Weeks-Sooner

FOOTPRINT
6.5 × 12 feet

SKILL LEVEL
Experience counts

WHEN TO PLANT
Late winter: arugula and mache

Early spring: beets, radishes, onions, and kale

Midspring: chard, broccoli, lettuce, parsley, and spinach

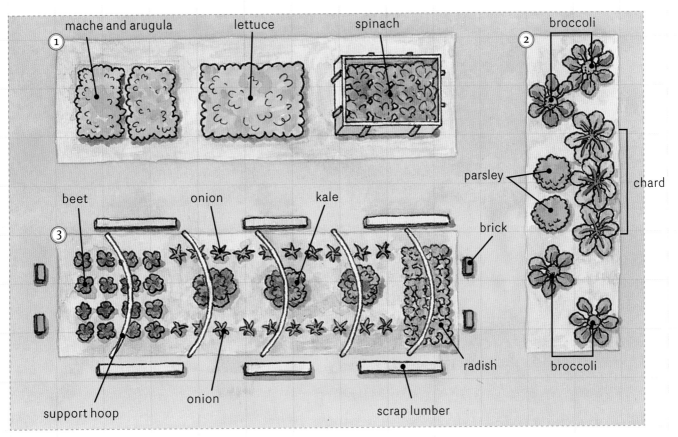

ONE SQUARE = 1 FOOT

- O One 8 × 12-foot piece of midweight row cover
- O 6 pieces of scrap lumber or firewood
- O 4 bricks or heavy stones

FOR THE CLOCHES
- O 9 cloches made from 1-gallon translucent plastic milk or juice jugs (see page 187)
- O 9 straight sticks, about 18 inches long

THE PLANTS

BED ①
- O Arugula, 1 packet seeds
- O Lettuce, 1 packet seeds
- O Mache, 1 packet seeds
- O Spinach, 1 packet seeds

BED ②
- O Beet, 1 packet seeds
- O Kale, 1 packet seeds
- O Onion, 20 sets or seedlings
- O Radish, 1 packet seeds

BED ③
- O Broccoli, 4 seedlings
- O Chard, 1 packet seeds or 3 seedlings
- O Parsley, 1 packet seeds or 2 seedlings

SIX-WEEKS-SOONER
PLANTING AND CARE

WINTER

❶ Recondition an old window. Obtain an old window frame and prepare it for garden duty. Avoid very old windows with numerous layers of paint, because lead from the paint can leach into your garden. With most windows (or shower doors), it is sufficient to scrape off loose paint and repair loose panes of glass with caulk.

LATE WINTER

❷ Set up the cold frame. About eight weeks before your last frost, or as soon as the snow melts, install the frame at one end of Bed 1. Position the four pieces of wood on the ground, and pound two stakes into the ground on the outer edge of each piece as shown at left. When you lay the window on the frame, it should slip down inside the stakes. Leave the frame in place for a week or two to warm the soil.

❸ Plant cold-hardy greens. On a mild day, lift the window frame out to plant mache and arugula. Sow seeds about 1 inch apart and barely cover them with soil. Water lightly to make sure the surface of the soil is moist, and place the window back over the bed.

EARLY SPRING

Use stakes and short pieces of lumber to make a cold frame, and top it off with a reconditioned window. When it's no longer needed on one spot, you can move the frame in minutes.

❹ Wake up the beds. About six weeks before your last frost, evenly distribute the compost over the beds, and sprinkle on a light dusting of organic fertilizer. Lightly cultivate the beds to mix in the soil amendments and fertilizer. If the soil is frozen, proceed to Step 5 without cultivating the soil.

❺ Set up the tunnel. Push five support hoops into the ground at even intervals over Bed 3. Working on a windless day, spread the row cover and then the sheet of plastic over the hoops. Secure the sides of the tunnel with pieces of scrap lumber or firewood. Secure each end of the tunnel with two bricks.

6 Plant kale, onions, and more. Wait a few days for the soil to warm. Lift one side of the tunnel and sow kale seeds down the center of the bed; plug in a row of onions along both edges of the bed. Sow a matrix of radishes ½ inch deep and 2 inches apart, and a matrix of beets 6 inches apart at the other end of the bed. Moisten the planted bed before securing the sides and ends of the tunnel.

7 Move the frame. Lift the window, scrap lumber, and stakes; install them at the middle of Bed 1 as you did in Step 2. Sow lettuce in the frame by scattering the seeds about 1 inch apart, barely covering with soil, and patting them into place with your hand. Water lightly to make sure the surface of the soil is moist, and place the window onto the support pieces.

MIDSPRING

8 Plant cloche crops. About four weeks before your last frost, set out broccoli seedlings in Bed 2 and sow or set out parsley and chard. Cover each one with milk jug cloches.

9 Move the frame again. About four weeks before your last frost, lift the window, scrap lumber, and stakes and move them to the other end of Bed 1. Install the frame as you did in Step 2. Sow spinach in the frame by planting seeds ½ inch deep and 2 inches apart. Water lightly to make sure the surface of the soil is moist, and place the window over the bed.

10 Thin and weed. Harvest tender young leaves of arugula for use in salads and cooked dishes, gradually thinning the plants to 8 inches apart. Thin beets as needed, and patrol all of your beds regularly to keep on top of weeds, which often grow beautifully beneath cold frames and cloches.

LATE SPRING

11 Take off the covers. About one week before your last frost, remove the cloches from Bed 2. Either store them or use them to provide wind protection for tomato or pepper seedlings. The tunnel can be taken down and stored, or you can move it to another bed where extra-warm conditions are needed (for example, a squash or cucumber bed). Gather up the window and its related frame and store them until next year.

PICK-OF-THE-CROP VEGGIE VARIETIES

Choosing vegetable varieties can be a lot of fun, but it comes with a risk. Seed companies make each variety sound so luscious that you wonder why their customers haven't already snapped up every last seed, but few varieties give superlative results in all climates, soils, and seasons.

MAKING GOOD CHOICES

Consider the humble snap bean. The plants may grow as long vines or knee-high bushes, and the pods may be flat or round, short or long, and green, yellow, burgundy, or striped. Inside the pods, the beans may mature to white, black, purple, or some blotchy combination. All of these "mays"—plant form, size, color, flavor, and many other characteristics—come together as a particular *variety* of snap bean. There are hundreds of snap bean varieties. There are probably a thousand varieties of tomato.

In this section, I cut to the chase on this wonderfully complicated matter of varieties. There really are superior varieties of vegetables—varieties so productive and adaptable that they are considered classics: 'Provider' bush snap bean, 'Packman' broccoli, and 'Buttercrunch' lettuce, to name a few. But sometimes you'll need to choose a variety for something other than productivity. You may need a squash that can resist a common disease like powdery mildew or a tomato that won't turn yellow and languish because of soilborne fusarium wilt. These and many other problems can be prevented by growing special disease-resistant varieties.

Many seed companies offer superlative varieties. An organically oriented seed company in your region can be your best friend as you decide what to grow in your garden. All of them publish online catalogs, and many sell seed packets in seasonal rack displays at organic food stores. To get you started, a list of excellent seed sources appears on page 226.

DIG THIS!

Heirlooms are old, open-pollinated varieties that have been around for a long time. Think of them as antique varieties.

WHAT IS A VARIETY?

For thousands of years, people have used their big brains to exploit plants as sources of food. When they discovered a great patch of something growing wild (for example, cabbage in ancient Rome), gardeners began saving and replanting seeds from the best plants. This process of *selection* eventually results in what is called a *strain*. As a strain becomes even more defined, with a cluster of stable characteristics, it can be classified as a *variety*. In this way, a vegetable's size, color, leaf form, flavor, growth rate, disease resistance, and yield potential all can be rolled into a variety name consisting of one or two distinctive words: 'Fordhook Giant' chard or 'Space' spinach, for example.

Variety names appear in single quotes throughout this book. On seed packets, variety names may appear in capital letters or in a different color ink.

Some food plants (obscure leafy greens in particular) do not have variety names; they are sold by their common and species names (botanical names, usually written in italics) only.

Open-Pollinated vs. Hybrid Varieties

Home gardeners have many occasions to choose between open-pollinated and hybrid seeds. Open-pollinated (OP) varieties are created and maintained through the selection process. Hybrids are created by crossing two specially selected parent plants. The first generation after hybrid crosses are made (called the F1 generation) often brings wonders like improved productivity and disease resistance, but subsequent generations may be just

TELL ME MORE!

OPEN-POLLINATED OR HYBRID?

When choosing between open-pollinated (OP) and hybrid (F1) varieties, consider priorities and potential problems with the crops you want to grow.

Characteristics	Open-Pollinated	Hybrid
Disease resistance	A few university-bred cucumber-family crops offer powdery mildew resistance; a handful of OP tomatoes show some disease tolerance.	Genetic resistance is the most dependable, planet-friendly way to defend high-risk crops from common diseases.
Vigor and growth rate	Generally grow slower than comparable hybrids. Some OP tomatoes and other vegetables may mature too late to be successful.	Early maturation is often crucial for warm-natured crops in cool climates and for cool-natured crops in hot climates.
Organic adaptability	Plants from organically grown or biodynamic seed, grown in biologically active soil, are likely to thrive in rich garden soil.	Often bred for high-input systems involving fertilizers, fungicides, and insecticides.
Flavor or appearance	Often more interesting and complex than hybrids and certainly more varied.	Usually bred for uniformity and shipping ability, secondarily for flavor.

plain weird as the genetic jumble settles itself into place. The opposite should happen if you become interested in saving seeds from your garden and begin collecting seeds each year from your best specimens of superior open-pollinated varieties. Over time, the strain should develop into one that is uniquely adapted to your garden.

Saving Great Seeds

The seeds inside seed packets have been professionally grown, graded, and tested for guaranteed germination. This sets a high standard for homegrown seeds, but every gardener can easily save great seeds from *something*. For top candidates, look to crops that naturally grow well in your area and are customarily harvested when they are totally ripe, or close to it. Good examples include dry beans, cantaloupe, tomatoes, watermelons, and winter squash.

Save seeds from the very best fruits borne by plants that show little, if any, signs of disease. Allow the seeds to dry at room temperature for several days, and then sort through them by hand to pick out unwanted debris. Select the largest, plumpest seeds to save and replant. If you fear there might be insects hiding away in certain seeds, store them in the freezer.

Storing Your Seeds

Except for short-lived onion, lettuce, and parsnip seeds, most seeds will last at least three years when stored in the right conditions. As you consider where to store your seed collection, ponder this equation:

$$\frac{\text{temperature (°F)}}{+ \quad \text{humidity (\%)}} < 100$$

This means that if your storage place is on the warm side (75°F/20°C), you need constant low humidity (below 25 percent) to meet good storage requirements. Better yet, keep your seeds in a cool place,

sealed inside zip-lock bags inside an airtight plastic storage box.

If you can't avoid fluctuating temperatures or humidity levels, refrigerate or freeze your seeds in airtight containers. Just be sure seeds are thoroughly dry before you freeze them; seeds that are not completely dry or have been exposed to high humidity levels can expand and burst when placed in a freezer. In humid summer weather, place seeds you plan to freeze in an airtight container with a packet of silica gel for two days before you freeze them. In winter when indoor humidity levels are usually very low, air-drying seeds for a day or two before freezing them is sufficient.

TELL ME MORE!

HOW LONG WILL THEY KEEP?

When stored in a cool, dark place with constant low humidity, vegetable seeds typically remain viable for 1 to 10 years, depending on species. Freezing can triple the storage potential of most seeds, but this list reflects average seed longevity under good but nonfrozen conditions.

1 to 2 Years	3 to 4 Years	5 Years or More
Corn	Bean	Broccoli
Lettuce	Beet	Brussels sprout
Okra	Carrot	Cantaloupe
Onion	Chard	Cauliflower
Parsley	Leek	Celery
Pepper	Pea	Chinese cabbage
	Squash	Cucumber
	Tomato	

TOP VARIETIES FOR YOUR GARDEN, CROP BY CROP

Listed by common name from A to Z, here is my guide to choosing varieties of 46 garden-worthy vegetables and 10 must-have herbs.

Arugula

Eruca vesicaria ssp. *sativa*

This rustic, full-flavored green from Europe grows to baby size in only a month, and you can have fully grown plants in less than 60 days. Arugula varieties are open-pollinated strains that vary in leaf shape, hardiness, and vigor. Try several from different seed sources to find a favorite because strains often differ, as is common in open-pollinated vegetables. Smooth-leafed varieties like **'Astro'** and **'Apollo'** often have milder flavor than **'Runway'** and other varieties with finely cut leaves.

With an insulating mulch or protective tunnel, healthy fall-grown plants will survive winter in Zone 6. Overwintered arugula will promptly develop flowers and seedpods in spring. Arugula plants that are allowed to develop mature seeds in early summer often reseed themselves for fall. Lift and move young plants that pop up in inconvenient places.

Asparagus

Asparagus officinalis

Most vegetables are annuals, but asparagus is a hardy perennial that comes back year after year, even in cold climates. The edible parts are the new buds that emerge from the ground first thing in spring. Wait until a site has benefited from several seasons of active soil-improvement techniques and is free of perennial weeds before starting an asparagus bed. Plant dormant 1- or 2-year-old roots, which are called crowns. When spread out, the crowns form a circle of outstretched roots, so only 12 plants will fill a 3 × 8-foot bed. In midsummer, the mass of ferny foliage may stand 5 feet tall. Starting the third year after planting, expect good crops of elegantly slender spears from disease-resistant 'Jersey Supreme'. Like other varieties with 'Jersey' in their names, 'Jersey Supreme' is an all-male variety that puts all of its energy into vegetative growth rather than expending it on flowers and seeds, so it

TASTY TIP In spring, only young arugula leaves have salad-worthy flavor, but arugula grown in cool fall conditions holds its eating quality much longer. In any season, use older arugula leaves in cooked dishes, because cooking makes little bug holes disappear. Or purée washed leaves with olive oil and garlic to make a wonderful pesto. Immature green seedpods add interesting flavor when chopped into salads, and you can use arugula flowers as edible garnishes.

TASTY TIP It's best to let asparagus plants gain strength for two years after planting, and then start harvesting spears in the third year. Asparagus plantings of any age benefit from being mulched with compost or manure covered with a layer of straw or hay each winter—an easy way to maintain high soil fertility while keeping out weeds.

tends to be very productive. Ontario-bred 'Guelph Millenium' tolerates extreme cold. For awesome springtime special effects, sow johnny jump ups (*Viola tricolor*) once and then let them naturalize among clumps of 'Purple Passion' asparagus. The charming edible blossoms of these wild pansies will appear in abundance just as the violet-blushed asparagus spears push up in spring.

Basil
Ocimum basilicum

A fast-growing annual herb with an uncompromising need for warm weather, basil comes in an array of types. Why not grow two or three different kinds every year? You can set out some plants as seedlings in spring and then sow more seeds right in the garden in early summer, after the soil has warmed. Basil rushes to flower, but clipping off the bloom spikes regularly can keep plants productive for many weeks. On the other hand, allowing selected plants to shed mature seeds may lead to welcome squads of volunteer seedlings that show up like clockwork after the first warm rains of summer. Basil reseeds more successfully in warmer climates than in cooler ones. To get to know this incomparable garden herb, try mixing and matching among four different types, starting with the smallest:

Dwarf. Dwarf or "globe" basils such as 'Spicy Bush' and 'Aristotle' fit into tight spaces, have a naturally neat growth habit, and are very slow to flower. They are great for edgings and containers. These are the best basils to try as potted plants kept indoors through winter.

Genovese. Flavorwise, it's hard to go wrong with any variety described as a Genovese type, most of which have large, slightly puckered leaves. Downy

mildew of basil has become a growing threat in recent years, but genetic resistance is available in 'Prospera', 'Rutgers Passion', and 'Amazel'.

Purple or red. Add color to the garden with dark-leafed varieties such as 'Red Rubin', which looks stunning when grown near sage or other plants with light-colored foliage. Whether they are called red or purple, these varieties have dark leaves that may be flat, ruffled, or streaked with green. For a fun backyard breeding project, grow purple and green basils side by side, let them make seeds, and save and replant them. Expect some really splashy basils!

Scented. Just for fun, try subspecies of basil that carry scents of cinnamon, lemon, and even anise or camphor; of these, lemon basil is the most recipe friendly.

Beans
Phaseolus vulgaris and other species

Most of the beans we grow and eat are descendants of plants that were domesticated in the Americas. Further refinements in breeding have led to a huge variation in the basic bean, almost all of which are easy to grow. Snap or green beans, which are harvested young and tender, top the charts in terms of ease of culture. Except for fava beans (see Not Your Average Beans on page 199), all beans are warm-season crops that are planted in late spring, after the soil has warmed. Beans can be started indoors and transplanted, but it is much easier to simply sow the seeds where the beans are to grow.

Sorting through snap beans will require you to choose among three major characteristics that are under strict genetic control: plant growth habit (bush or pole), pod type (flat, round, or superslender

BUSH OR POLE?

Look for a good overall fit when deciding whether to grow bush beans, pole beans, or some of each type. For planning purposes, regard varieties described as "half-runners" as pole beans. When given vertical support, half-runner beans typically climb 5 to 6 feet—about half the vine length of most pole beans grown in gardens 100 years ago. Here are the general differences to consider:

Characteristic	Bush	Pole
Growth rate	Rapid (50+ days)	Moderate (60+ days)
Bearing habit	Concentrated pod set, ideal for canning/freezing or planting before or after other vegetables	Extended harvest over several weeks, ideal for fresh eating
Space requirements	Good productivity when grown in double or triple rows	Excellent productivity due to use of vertical space
Ease of culture	Among the easiest vegetables to grow	Easy, but requires trellising and monitoring for insect problems

French filets), and pod color (green, yellow, or purple). The growth habit question is addressed in the Bush or Pole? comparison chart above. Once you have chosen a growth habit, fill out your planting list with easy-to-grow varieties such as these:

Flat pole: green 'Northeaster' (55 days), 'Hilda' (60 days)

Round pole: green 'Kentucky Wonder' (67 days), purple 'Purple Pole' (67 days)

Filet pole: green 'Fortex' or 'Emerite', yellow 'Monte Gusto' (all about 60 days)

Flat bush: green 'Roma II' (53 days), yellow 'Capitano' (54 days), purple 'Sequoia' (55 days), variegated 'Dragon Tongue' (60 days)

Round bush: green 'Provider' (50 days), purple 'Royal Burgundy' (55 days), yellow 'Rocdor' (52 days)

Filet bush: green 'Maxibel' (50 days), yellow 'Soleil' (57 days)

Double-Duty Soup Beans

These days, most people define garden beans as snap or green beans, which of course have edible pods. But it was not so long ago that gardeners routinely harvested green beans and dry beans from the same plants, and you can still do so today. Many beans traditionally grown for harvesting their beans only, for example, 'Taylor's Horticultural' or French flageolets, make great snap beans when harvested very young. And thinning the pods a bit for fresh eating may be good for those left behind, resulting in bigger dry beans for the winter kitchen. Other varieties to use as double-duty beans include 'White Half Runner', 'Cherokee Wax', and 'Tiger's Eye' (all about 55 days to green beans, or 85 days to mature dry ones). The big, meaty pods of scarlet runner beans make great eating when they are young and tender, too.

NOT YOUR AVERAGE BEANS

Every climate has some quirky or extreme mini-season. Often this can be filled with the right specialty bean.

Fava beans, *Vicia faba* (75+ days to maturity), can be a triumph in cold, clammy weather, and they benefit the soil by keeping nitrogen-fixing bacteria busy. On the downside, favas planted in early spring occupy space well into early summer, and productivity is modest at best. Grow a small experimental plot of these upright, nonvining plants before committing a lot of space to favas, or use them as a cover crop.

Runner beans, *Phaseolus coccineus* (60 days to maturity), are often grown for the beauty of their flowers alone, but both the immature pods and mature beans are delicious. This is a true multipurpose plant to find a place for at least every few years. Most varieties develop long vines that require a trellis. Seeds are most often sold simply as scarlet runners, but named varieties include red 'Scarlet Emperor' and 'Magic Beanstalk', red-and-white 'Painted Lady', and salmon pink 'Sunset'.

Southern peas, *Vigna unguiculata* (70–80 days to maturity), include familiar black-eyed peas as well as many southern summer standbys like 'Pinkeye Purple Hull' and 'Mississippi Silver'. Best in warm, humid climates, most southern peas are bush varieties, but 'Red Ripper' and a few other heirloom varieties develop long, twining vines.

Yard-long beans, *Vigna unguiculata* ssp. *sesquipedalis* (80 days to maturity), come from tropical Asia. They are more closely related to purple hull peas and other southern peas than to garden beans. Increasingly popular in warm climates as a pest-resistant, hot-weather alternative to snap beans, yard-longs love warmth. 'Red Noodle', 'Mosaic', and other varieties with purplish red pods make great edible ornamentals. All varieties develop very long vines that require a sturdy trellis.

Lima beans, *Phaseolus lunatus* (85 days to maturity), are outstanding in warm climates where hot, muggy nights cause other beans to take a summer siesta. Limas are slow growing and rarely produce heavy crops, plus it's time consuming to shell them. Mature limas that are gathered when the pods dry to tan are easier to shell than small, green lima beans. In addition to tolerating humid heat, bush varieties like 'Fordhook 242' and pole varieties including 'Christmas' are rarely bothered by insects.

Tepary beans, *Phaseolus acutifolius* (75–85 days to maturity), include many drought-tolerant strains developed by Indigenous people of the Southwest. These are the best beans to grow in summer in hot, dry climates. Tepary beans are primarily used as dry beans, but the young, green pods of some varieties also can be eaten like snap beans. Growth habit varies with variety; most are lanky bushes that develop short twining stems.

Beets

Beta vulgaris

Beets are closely related to chard, and you can use beautiful young beet greens to bring color and crunch to salads and sandwiches. Yet beets are grown primarily for their juicy roots, which are usually deep red but also may be golden yellow or red marked with white. Beets are usually planted in spring, starting about two weeks before the last frost. In many climates, a second crop can be grown from late summer to fall.

Fast-growing hybrids are often rated at 55 days to maturity, but very few beets will be ready to pull in such a short period of time. Be prepared to wait longer for your crop to grow as big and beautiful as it can be, which will probably take about 70 days. You don't have to wonder when your beets are ready, because the roots pop up out of the ground as they swell. Hybrid varieties deliver fast, uniform growth, so you might start with supersweet 'Boro' or 'Red Ace' before trying more interesting open-pollinated varieties like 'Golden', elongated 'Forono', or red-and-white-ringed 'Chioggia'.

Bok Choy

Brassica rapa Chinensis group

This sturdy little vegetable deserves a place in more gardens because it's fast and easy to grow and succulently delicious to eat. Tremendously popular in southern China and Japan, bok choy is also written as pac choi and pak choy; the English pronunciation of all three is similar. A cool-season variation on good old mustard cabbage, bok choy is a top crop to grow in spring and fall. In either season, you can sow the seeds directly in the garden, or start them indoors and set them out as seedlings.

Varieties vary in size (5 to 15 inches tall at maturity) and stem color (white, green, or tinged with purple). Small and tender single-serving-size plants with thick white stalks like 'Mei Qing' (45 days) are an ideal fit in any garden; very small varieties like 5-inch-tall 'Toy Choy' (35 days) are great for containers. The leaves of 'Red Choy' turn red as the plants mature. In addition to these and other bok choys valued for their leaves, a few varieties have been selected for their tender sprouting stems, which are gathered just as the first flowers open. Often called choy sum or Chinese flowering cabbage (*B. parachinensis*, sometimes listed as *B. rapa*), these are fine plants to grow in cool fall weather. Most are green, but a few varieties, including 'Kosaitai' (50 days), bear beautiful purple stems.

Broccoli

Brassica oleracea Italica group

Broccoli can be tricky to grow because it can react badly to periods of very hot or very cold weather—sometimes by refusing to form a head at all. Then again, the weather can go in your favor, so you may enjoy great success on your first try.

The biggest challenge with this crop is finding the best planting dates, which may be in spring, early summer, or late summer, depending on your climate. Do your learning with tried-and-true, fast-maturing hybrids like 'Packman', 'Gypsy', or 'Corvina', all of which produce heads about 60 days after transplanting. When you gain confidence with broccoli, experiment with other vigorous varieties like 'Belstar' (66 days), 'Fiesta' (65 days), or 'Batavia' (55 days) hybrids; all of these varieties produce plentiful crops of smaller side shoots after the large central head is harvested, which is a big plus in the home garden.

The same tender vegetable sold as Brocollini in markets is easy to grow using special varieties like 'Apollo', 'Artwork', or 'Aspabroc'. Promptly harvest the first little heads as soon as they appear to stimulate the production of dozens of long-stemmed side shoots. These tender-stem broccolis grow well in both spring and fall, and they are the best type of broccoli to grow in containers.

Growing more than one type of broccoli provides a little protection from crop failure, because some varieties are more sensitive to weather stresses than others. You also can prevent problems by using cloches when you set out seedlings in spring (see page 187), and by keeping the plants' roots cool and moist by applying mulch after the weather turns warm in summer.

For warm climates, where winter temperatures seldom fall below 20°F (-7°C), you can grow overwintering varieties such as 'Purple Sprouting' and 'Bonarda', which stand as small plants through winter and explode with growth in spring. These varieties must be exposed to significant cold to trigger sprout production, but the 'Santee' and Brazilian-bred 'Pircicaba' varieties are less choosy and will produce excellent fall crops from seeds started in early summer.

Cabbage

Brassica oleracea Capitata group

Cabbage is easier to grow than broccoli or cauliflower, because it's much less picky about planting dates. Still, try to get seedlings in the ground three to four weeks before your last spring frost date, and use milk jug cloches to protect them from cold winds. In many areas, a second crop can be started indoors in midsummer and set out in August for harvest in late fall.

First-timers with small beds will love the firm, softball-size heads of green 'Tiara' (63 days) or 'Katarina' (65 days), which perform well when planted at close, 16-inch spacing. Small, crinkled savoys like 'Alcosa' (72 days) and pointed 'Caraflex' (68 days) also are good choices.

Days-to-maturity ratings for cabbage vary from 55 to over 120 days, but they are rough estimates at best. Cabbage will grow steadily in perfect weather, but it's also inclined to hunker down and wait out spells that are too cold or too hot, and that delays maturity. Grow fast-maturing varieties in spring and again in fall if you live where summers are hot, keeping in mind that cabbage that matures in mild or cool weather tastes much better than cabbage that heads up when temperatures are above 80°F (20°C). In moderate or cool-summer climates, slower-growing varieties will produce prize-winning heads when they size up in the fall. Many of the best "hard-headed" varieties for winter storage, for example, red 'Ruby Perfection' or green 'Late Flat Dutch', mature about 90 days after planting.

Carrot

Daucus carota

You may get lucky, but be forewarned that growing a good crop of carrots requires attention to detail. The first challenge is getting the seeds to sprout, which takes 10 days or more. Keep the seeded bed moist and be patient. When planting carrots in summer, you will need to shade the seeded bed and water it daily to get the seeds to sprout. And although carrots are considered untransplantable, I get a 70 percent survival rate when transplanting three-week-old seedlings started indoors. In hot summer weather, this often gives me a better stand than I can get with direct-sown seeds.

Among carrot varieties, there are four major types, all with distinctive differences in their root shapes and textures. Getting familiar with their characteristics will improve your crop as you find the best matches for your site and soil.

Nantes types are fast and easy to grow, and adapt to a range of climates and soils. These little beauties make up for their modest 5- to 7-inch length by developing remarkably sweet, crisp roots. When sown in spring, early hybrids like 'Yaya' and 'Mokum' mature in less than 60 days, with open-pollinated 'Early Nantes' needing two weeks longer. If your soil stays cool into early summer, try 'Bolero', the main season (75-day) variety used as a comparison in taste tests. For a change of color, it's hard to beat 'Gold Nugget' (68 days) or gorgeously bicolored 'Cosmic Purple', perhaps the most salad-worthy of all carrot varieties. There is even a miniature Nantes for containers called 'Little Finger' that produces 4-inch carrots in about 60 days.

Nantes carrots also can be sown in summer for harvest in fall, but because they are not the best storage carrots, most gardeners choose a heftier type for the summer-to-fall slot.

Chantenay carrots develop stocky, conical roots, broad at the shoulder tapering to a pointed tip. These become sweeter as the soil cools in fall. The thick roots adapt well to clay soil as long as it has been improved with plenty of organic matter (but no manure, which can cause formation of forked or hairy roots). Chantenays are among the finest-tasting carrots when allowed to mature in cool fall soil. 'Red Core Chantenay' and 'Royal Chantenay' (both about 72 days) have legions of devoted fans.

Imperator carrots are so long that they need deep, well-worked soil to thrive. The long, tapered roots break easily, so they must be harvested carefully, too. Among orange Imperators, 12-inch-long 'Sugarsnax' (68 days) and 'Tendersweet' (75 days) combine high nutrition with great flavor, texture, and disease resistance. Lemon-hued 'Yellowstone' (72 days) makes a beautiful companion variety for fresh eating. Very dark-fleshed varieties like 'Purple Haze' (70 days) or 'Atomic Red' (74 days) are at their best when cooked and make a great vegetable for grilling.

Danvers carrots make fabulous juice, and the sturdy roots store well, too. These heavy, thick-rooted carrots need deep sandy loam or fertile raised beds to perform well. They tend to grow best in climates where nights stay cool throughout their growing season. Varieties with Danvers in their names typically mature in about 80 days, but the beautiful, bicolored 'Dragon' variety (90 days) is well worth the wait. Its big purple roots with orange cores become extra sweet when they mature in cool fall soil.

Cauliflower
Brassica oleracea Botrytis group

Another variation on cabbage, cauliflower is a crop that I left out of the planting plans in this book, for several reasons. Unlike its close cousins (broccoli, cabbage, and kohlrabi), cauliflower are large-framed plants that cannot be grown at close spacing. In addition to needing rich, fertile soil and spacing of at least 28 to 30 inches between plants, cauliflower must be planted at exactly the right time for your climate. Spring crops sometimes do well, but cauliflower that forms heads in early to midfall, at about the time of your first frost, tends to have the best flavor and texture.

If you decide to take on the challenge of cultivating cauliflower, keep in mind that varieties rated at more than 79 days to maturity—for example, white 'Symphony' (95 days) and purple 'Graffiti' (80 days)—form big, heavy heads and grow best in fall, or where summers are mild.

In most areas, fast-maturing hybrids like 'Snow Crown' (50 days) are better choices. Orange 'Flame Star' (62 days) is also easy to grow, or you can try purple 'Violet Queen' (54 days) or lime green 'Verdi' (60 days). Little can go wrong with 'Fioretto' (70 days), which bears loose clusters of little heads on long, tender stems.

Recent crosses between broccoli and cauliflower have produced cauliflowers with heads composed of intricately spiraled domes. Challenging yet fun to try, lime green 'Veronica' Romanesco cauliflower (80 days) takes forever to head up, but you may decide the reward is worth the wait.

Celery
Apium graveolens

Most of us regularly buy celery at the store, but few of us grow it in our gardens. This is based on a fundamental misconception about what this plant really is. The long, tall supermarket version of celery is a carefully engineered creation, grown on special rich soils using tricky techniques. The garden version is looser, leafier, and darker green, but it's also more flavorful. Every gardener should try growing some type of celery; all are easy to start indoors and transplant in spring, while the soil is still cool. Be ready to provide water, because the one thing celery requires is plenty of moisture to satisfy its thirsty fibrous roots. On the plus side, celery and its close relatives can tolerate a few hours a day of shade.

Traditional celery varieties include 'Utah 52-70 improved' (110 to 120 days), but you can get small hearts from 'Tango' after about 84 days. Several heirloom celery varieties blush red where they are touched by the sun, including beautiful 'Redventure' (85 to 95 days).

Cutting celery (80 days) has narrower stems and a bushier growth habit than regular celery, but it's also incredibly easy to grow. When you need celery flavor in cooking, simply pull off a few stems and start chopping, leaves and all.

Parcel (think of it as a cross between celery and Italian parsley) is similar to cutting celery but with a more parsleylike leaf shape. Young and healthy plants are surprisingly cold hardy, often surviving winter in Zone 6.

Celeriac (*A. graveolens* var. *rapaceum*), or root celery, takes all season to grow to harvestable size, but the trouble-free plants need little attention beyond regular watering. Instead of stout stalks, this celery sister develops a dense, nutty-sweet root in fall. Celeriac cubes sautéed in butter are a unique culinary treat. Dependable varieties include 'Diamant' and 'Brilliant', both rated at 110 days to maturity.

Chard
Beta vulgaris Cicla group

Also called Swiss chard, this crop holds superstar status among edible ornamentals. It's easy to grow from seed and comes in a rainbow of colors. Cooked chard can stand in for spinach anytime (they are closely related plants). All varieties attain picking size in about 55 days, and they remain productive for months if kept watered. You might start with a packet of 'Bright Lights' or another variety that's really a mix of colors, or go bold from the start with a red-, pink-, or yellow-stemmed variety. Red-stemmed, red-veined varieties like 'Ruby Red' and 'Rhubarb' are easy to grow, and 'Peppermint' has a similar stained-glass beauty. If your main goal is high productivity, choose white-stemmed 'Fordhook Giant'—in university-sponsored field trials, no other variety could compare yield-wise. Look for miniature varieties like 'Pot of Gold' for growing in containers. See page 128 for tips on working with chard seeds, which often contain multiple capsules within each wrinkled "seed."

Chinese Cabbage
Brassica rapa Pekinensis group

Gardeners who think they can't grow crisp heads of anything will be pleasantly surprised by Chinese cabbage, which stands as a rosette of green leaves for only a few weeks before developing dense heads composed of celery-crisp leaf stalks and lightly crinkled leaves. Chinese cabbage matures much faster than regular cabbage and does not require especially rich soil. If you can grow lettuce, you can grow Chinese cabbage. In most climates you can grow two crops—one in spring and one in fall. You can direct-sow the seeds, or start them indoors and set out the seedlings when they are three weeks old.

Chinese cabbage varieties vary in shape and size; whatever the shape, small varieties mature two to three weeks faster than the big boys.

Michihili types grow into upright cylinders 12 to 20 inches tall. Full-size varieties including 'Monument' and 'Michihili' need 80 days to mature and are best grown in fall.

Napa types form short, barrel-shaped heads. Scaled-down 'Minuet' sizes up fast, in just under 50 days, as do other minis like 'Little Jade' and 'Wa Wa Tsai'. Red-blushed Chinese cabbage are rarely seen in markets, but arresting 'Red Dragon' (65 days) is definitely worth adding to the fall garden.

Chives
Allium schoenoprasum

The most delicately flavored member of the onion family, chives grow as hardy perennials. You can harvest (and dry) the hollow leaves as soon as they appear in spring and intermittently all summer. The pink or lilac spring flowers are edible, too, or you can use them as cut flowers. Chives propagate themselves by dividing themselves into clumps and by shedding seeds. They are well behaved in most climates, but they can shed so many seeds that they become weedy in cold climates. Prevent this problem by harvesting the blossoms as cut flowers or trimming off the flowers as they fade to brown. Garden cooks will want to keep two clumps going— one of a very narrow-leafed variety like 'Fine Leaf' for eating fresh, and a larger-leafed variety such as 'Staro' for drying. It's also fine to start with a nameless clump given to you by a local gardener. The fact that pass-along chives have proven themselves in your climate is worth more than a fancy variety name. (See also Garlic Chives, page 207.)

Cilantro
Coriandrum sativum

Sometimes called Chinese or Mexican parsley, cilantro is a big-flavored herb used generously in Mexican, Szechuan, or Thai dishes, or you can mix the leaves with lettuce and other greens in salads. Seedlings are usually sown where they are to grow and then thinned to 8 inches apart, but very young purchased or indoor-grown seedlings can be transplanted if you keep them moist and handle them gently. Some varieties like 'Calypso' and 'Santo' are slow to bolt, especially in late summer and fall, but any cilantro will bolt quickly when days are lengthening in spring and early summer. Plant 10 or so seeds every three weeks from spring to late summer to have an intermittent, if not continuous, supply. Cilantro will overwinter with a protective mulch, cloche, or tunnel in Zone 6. When overwintered or spring-sown plants are allowed to bloom and produce mature seeds in summer, almost every last one will germinate when replanted in early fall.

Collards
Brassica oleracea Acephala group

Closely related to better-known kale, collards are an anchor crop for the fall garden. Easily grown from seeds sown directly in the garden in late summer, collards become sweeter as fall weather cools down. In much of the South, gardeners gather collard leaves all winter, but some folks don't know that the green, unopened flower buds that appear in spring are edible, too, as are the immature green seedpods. And even though hardly anyone does it,

more gardeners should try growing a quick spring crop of collards to eat as hand-size baby greens. In Europe, collards grown this way are called "spring leaf cabbage."

If collards usually survive winter in your area, consider growing open-pollinated varieties like 'Champion' (60 days) or 'Green Glaze' (79 days), which has a leaf surface that makes it unappealing to leaf-eating caterpillars. If you allow your best plant to develop ripe seeds each summer, and gather them for replanting in fall, you will never need to buy collard seeds again. Where time is short, hybrids like 'Top Bunch' (50 days) and 'Flash' (55 days) make a quick crop of tender, cabbagelike greens.

Corn, Sweet
Zea mays

Sweet corn requires warm conditions, very fertile soil, and lots of space, but sun-ripened ears are so delicious that many gardeners put sweet corn on their planting list. Never try to push the spring season by planting sweet corn too early, because the seeds will rot when planted in cold, wet soil. You can start sweet corn indoors, but it will quickly outgrow its containers, so be prepared to set out the seedlings soon after they sprout. Early varieties can be grown at close, 10-inch spacing, but allow at least 12 to 14 inches between plants when growing taller varieties that mature later in summer. If you love sweet corn, consider planting varieties that mature at different times, as is done in the Sweet Corn & Company garden plan on page 158.

Before you ponder which varieties of sweet corn to grow, it helps to understand that there are several genetic types of sweet corn. The sweetest type is **supersweet** (often abbreviated as *sh* or *sh2*), and supersweet varieties must not be grown near the other types of corn. If the pollen of another type pollinates a supersweet, the resulting ears will be disappointingly tough and starchy. Instead, I suggest avoiding supersweet types and working with *su* (**normal sugary**) or *se* (**sugar extender**) varieties, because they're easy to grow, they don't require isolation from other types, and their flavor is sweet but doesn't cross the line into sticky-candy sweetness. All of the varieties below are *su* or *se* varieties.

Early varieties mature in less than 75 days from planting, and some tolerate cold soils. The plants grow only about 5 feet tall, and each will produce at least one smallish ear. Some will bear two. Yellow '**Sugar Buns**' or '**Early Sunglow**' make great season openers, or you can try an early bicolor like '**Sweetness**'.

Midseason varieties are ready to pick 80 to 90 days after planting, and they usually produce big, well-filled ears with plenty of flavor. Expect 6-foot plants to bear two ears per plant. Yellow '**Bodacious**' and bicolors '**Delectable**' and '**American Dream**' are famous for producing sweet, melt-in-your-mouth ears.

Late varieties need more than 90 days to reach maturity, but they're worth it if you can't get enough sweet corn. Give high priority to varieties that develop tight husks. These limit feeding by corn earworms, which are often found in the tips of sweet corn in late summer. White '**Argent**' and '**Silver Queen**' are excellent choices, or you can opt for yellow in '**Miracle**'.

Cucumber
Cucumis sativus

Cucumbers are easily grown from seeds sown in late spring, or you can set out purchased seedlings. You can allow the vining plants to ramble over mulched ground, or save space by training them to cling to a trellis. Cucumbers don't climb well on their own, but if you push the vine tips through the openings in a trellis, the plants will usually hang on nicely with help from their curling tendrils. Here are the five major types you might grow in your garden.

American salad cucumbers have a uniform oblong shape with dark green skins, just like the cukes at the store. Peeling makes older varieties like '**Marketmore 76**' (66 days) and '**Straight Eight**' (63 days)

easier to digest; many modern hybrids, including '**Sweet Success**' (58 days) and '**Sweet Slice**' (62 days), don't produce the chemical compounds that cause people to burp.

Pickling cucumbers bear small oblong fruits with thin, often bumpy skins. The fruits must be picked daily when the crop comes in, because a perfect 4-inch cucumber will become oversize and overripe in only two days. Prompt picking also encourages the plants to produce for a longer time. '**County Fair**' (48 days) and '**Little Leaf**' (55 days) are especially valuable for their resistance to bacterial wilt, the most common cause of cucumber crop failure.

Middle Eastern varieties, also called Beit Alpha cucumbers, have such thin skins that they need no peeling. Varieties like '**Diva**' (58 days) and '**Picolino**' (60 days) are best grown on trellises or in a greenhouse. They are best eaten fresh.

Oriental and Armenian cucumbers bear long, curved fruits on rambling vines that must be trellised to prevent excessive kinking and curling of the fruits. The 12-inch-long fruits of hybrid '**Tasty Jade**' (54 days) are quite uniform, but expect some variation in fruit size and shape with open-pollinated favorites like '**Suyo Long**' (65 days) and '**Yard-Long Armenian**' (60 days). All are considered burpless.

Heirloom varieties come in an array of shapes and colors, often with subtle flavor notes. Round '**Lemon**' cucumbers (65 days) have a fruity undertone. Varieties with white or pale yellow skin like '**Boothby's Blonde**' (65 days) are known for their crisp, juicy texture.

Dill
Anethum graveolens

A fast-growing annual, dill is easy to grow from seeds sown in spring. Go ahead and try direct-seeding this one, because it's easy to recognize the ferny first true leaf when it appears. Keep the babies well weeded, thin them to at least 12 inches apart, and you will be rewarded by stately plants topped with yellow flowers within about 65 days. Tie the burgeoning stems of tall varieties like 'Bouquet' to stakes. Packets of seeds simply labeled "dill" (or a few dill seeds pilfered from your spice cabinet) will grow into plants 4 to 5 feet tall, but 'Fernleaf' is more compact at about 30 inches. Dill foliage, flowers, and seeds are packed with flavor and useful in flower arrangements, too.

Edamame
Glycine max

Whether you call them green soybeans or stick with their Japanese name of edamame, these stylish legumes are so easy to grow that they should be in every summer garden.

High in protein, with the nutty succulence of sweet corn, edible green soybeans thrive in humid heat. Wait until after the soil has warmed to plant the seeds, which are always direct-sown. In warm climates with warm summers, there is usually time to grow edamame in space vacated by spring salad crops.

A few fast-maturing varieties like 'Envy' (75 days) can be grown in short-summer areas; where summers are long and warm, try different varieties until you find the perfect one for you. You might start with 'Sayamusume' (75 to 85 days), which produces well and has won taste tests in a range of climates. Compact 'Chiba' (83 days) is a good choice, too, or you can try the 'Be Sweet' variety developed for extrasweet flavor.

Eggplant
Solanum melongena

Eggplant grows slowly from seeds, and the babies need a lot of light, so for most folks, it's advisable to buy eggplant seedlings. Wait for warmth before planting the seedlings in the garden, or grow the plants in black plastic containers, which warm up quickly on hot days. Long, slender Asian varieties like 'Orient Express' (65 days) or 'Ping Tung Long' (70 days from transplanting) give impressive yields, or you can try small-fruited varieties like compact

'Patio Baby' (60 days) for small beds or containers. Where summers are long and warm, look for disease-resistant varieties of traditional eggplant such as 'Black Beauty' (70 days), or try light-skinned varieties like white 'Casper' (70 days) or lime green 'Thai Long Green' (80 days), which require no peeling when picked young. White-skinned varieties are sometimes bitter tasting; eggplants with dark purple skins tend to have the best flavor.

Garlic
Allium sativum

Packed with flavor and beneficial nutrients, garlic has the distinction of being the lead vegetable to grow from fall to spring. As long as you choose a type that fits your climate and get the cloves into the ground in midfall, you can expect great success with this trouble-free crop. See page 41 for tips on growing garlic and harvesting the scapes (curled, edible flower stalks) and bulbs. Garlic includes two subspecies, often referred to as softneck and hardneck types, plus there are many subdivisions and crossovers between these two groups.

Softneck types (*Allium sativum*). Often called artichoke types, softneck varieties grow best in mild winter areas. These varieties resemble familiar grocery store garlic. Large bulbs are composed of 12 to 20 cloves, with the largest cloves on the outside of the bulbs. Most softneck garlics don't send up scapes, though a few sometimes do. Cured bulbs store up to a year and are great for braiding.

Excellent softnecks include 'Red Toch', 'Inchelium Red', and 'Nootka Rose'. 'Burgundy' and other Creole varieties have fewer, larger cloves compared to other softnecks, with deep burgundy or silver skins. Flavor is full and moderately spicy. The plants often produce weak scapes, and the bulbs store well. Creoles grow best where winters are mild and summers are hot.

Hardneck types (*Allium sativum* var. *ophioscorodon*). The stiff base of the flower scape produced by these cold-hardy varieties makes them impossible to braid, but on the plus side you get to harvest tender scapes (see page 41). These varieties grow best in cold-winter climates. Porcelain varieties like 'Music' have thick, parchmentlike wrappers covering six or more large cloves with rich, complex flavor that holds up well when cooked. The bulbs store well, too. Purple-striped varieties like 'Chesnok Red' develop 8 to 12 medium-size cloves, with purple stripes and blotches on cloves and bulb wrappers. Easy to peel and great for baking, purple-striped types store for six months or more.

The hardiest garlics of all are the hardnecks known as rocambole types. These come in a variety of colors, and all send up double-looped seed scapes. Famed for their strong, rich flavor, rocamboles like 'Spanish Roja' and 'Killarney Red' produce 6 to 11 cloves that are easy to peel. Cured bulbs store for three to five months.

Garlic Chives
Allium tuberosum

Commonly sold by species rather than variety, garlic chives produce plenty of tender flat leaves for snipping into soups or salads in spring. Then late summer brings a beautiful show of fragrant white flowers. Many gardeners grow garlic chives for their blooms alone. This stalwart perennial is hardy in Zone 3; it can be started from seed or by planting divisions taken from established clumps. Garlic chive seedlings can invade neighboring beds and gardens because it's an abundant seed producer; this tendency is strongest in cold climates. Gathering the vase-worthy white blossom clusters in late summer literally nips this potential problem in the bud. (See also Chives on page 203.)

Kale
Brassica oleracea, B. napus

The easiest of the cabbage cousins to grow, kale is also amazingly tolerant of cold weather. Seedlings started indoors can be set out under cloches more than a month before the last frost in spring. The spring crop will produce beautiful cooking greens in early summer. If you gather the older leaves at least once a week, new ones will constantly emerge from the plants' centers. Most gardeners pull up their spring crop when the weather turns hot, but spring-sown plants will bear all summer where nights remain cool. Start a second round of seeds indoors in summer, because kale is a star player in the fall garden. Plants that are well rooted when cold weather comes will stand well into winter and will live to see spring in mild-winter climates. To keep the leaves in top condition in cold weather, cover the plants with a row cover tunnel (see page 187) when temperatures are expected to drop below 25°F (-4°C).

Experiment in spring and fall with excellent eating varieties like frilly 'Siberian', vigorous 'Red Russian', or dark green 'Lacinato' or dinosaur kale (60 days), which passes easily for spinach when cooked. Very frilly varieties like 'Redbor' (50 days) perform best when grown in fall. Try several varieties to get to know their talents and quirks. Varieties listed as ornamental because of vivid leaf variegation or dazzling texture are edible and look great on the plate, but don't try to build a meal around them. They often lack the flavor and nutrition of culinary kales.

Kohlrabi
Brassica oleracea Gongylodes group

Easier to grow and more forgiving of bad weather than closely related broccoli or cabbage, kohlrabi forms a crisp bulb *above* the ground, and the plants have a neat, upright growth habit. Wash, peel, and then grate raw kohlrabi into salads or slaw, or cook bite-size pieces to serve as a vegetable. In terms of taste and texture, kohlrabi resembles the crisp inner stems of broccoli. Young kohlrabi greens are edible, too; purple-leafed varieties in particular are sometimes used in salad mixes.

Kohlrabi matures so fast that most gardeners can grow it in spring and again in fall. Very fast-maturing varieties like purple 'Kolibri' or pale green 'White Vienna' (both 45 days) are great as long as growing conditions are perfect, but spurts of heat, cold, or wet or dry weather can cause them to crack. Cracking is less of a problem with slower-growing varieties like 'Early Purple Vienna' or

'Konan' (both 55 days). For your fall crop, consider growing a big storage variety like 'Superschmelz' (60 days) or 'Kossak Giant' (70 days). As long as they size up in cool weather, the 8- to 10-inch bulbs of these varieties will keep for weeks in a refrigerator or other cool place.

Leek
Allium porrum

In addition to being a delight in the kitchen, leeks are among the most architectural of vegetables. Their neat upright form and strappy texture bring a handsome touch to any bed, so consider interplanting leeks with other cool-season vegetables like potatoes, carrots, or beets. Start with fresh seeds each year, and start them indoors beginning in late winter. Be advised that purchased seedlings can be hard to find!

Leeks grown in gardens tend to be tall and slender. You can increase the length of the white shaft by deeply mulching the plants as they approach maturity. Until then, a 2-inch mulch of clean hay or straw will limit how much mud gets splashed onto the plants, so you will find less grit in your leeks as you trim and wash them before cooking.

Like other onions, some varieties may adapt to life in your garden better than others, so try several before settling on a favorite. Fast-growing 'Lincoln' or 'King Richard' (60 days for babies, 80 for full-size plants) can be sown thickly, and you can eat the thinnings like scallions; then give the thinned plants more time and room to develop into full-size leeks. The soldierlike stature and blue-green tint of slower-growing fall leeks such as 'Tadorna' (100 days) and 'Blue Solaise' (100 to 120 days) make them hardworking texture plants in any garden. These are the big leeks often seen in stores.

Lettuce
Lactuca sativa

The types of lettuce you see in supermarkets are but a small sample of the varied lettuces available to gardeners. It will take a lifetime of gardening to try them all, which sounds like a life well spent to me. Lettuce is easy to grow in spring and fall. Start from seeds sown in the garden, or you can start some seedlings indoors or in a cold frame (as on page 186) to get a head start on salad season. Once you learn how simple lettuce is to grow from seed, you will have trouble justifying the cost of purchased seedlings.

Supereasy varieties include 'Black Seeded Simpson' green leaf lettuce (45 days), 'Red Sails' red leaf lettuce (45 days), and 'Buttercrunch' Bibb lettuce (55 days). You can sample an array of colors, textures, and forms by planting a blend of varieties. Most mail-order seed companies offer several lettuce blends from which to choose, and you will also find them in retail racks. Salad green mixtures sold as mesclun (see facing page) often contain lettuce along with more pungent greens. Whether in mixtures or individual packets, buy fresh seeds each spring, because tiny lettuce seeds have a short shelf life. Plant seeds left over from spring in fall.

Lettuce is generally easy to grow, but until you get to know this crop, stay away from the very frilly Lollos, which are often the first ones to turn bitter and bolt. Also avoid hard-headed iceberg varieties unless you live in a cool climate. So-called French crisp or Batavian varieties like green 'Nevada' (55 days) and red-blushed 'Magenta' (50 days) form elongated crisp heads, and they're easier to grow (and more nutritious) than icebergs.

Marjoram
Origanum majorana

A marginally cold-hardy perennial herb usually grown as an annual, marjoram has a low, mounding habit. Sometimes called sweet marjoram, this oregano cousin carries mild oregano flavor with sweet undertones; it is an excellent kitchen herb to dry. Usually sold simply as marjoram, you can start with either seeds or plants each spring, or you can try overwintering plants indoors (they will die if they freeze). Regular marjoram is easy to grow from seed or cuttings. 'Variegata' is less vigorous, and features green leaves splashed with cream.

Melon

Cucumis melo

The most challenging of the cucumber family to grow, melons require warmth, space, and protection from predators. They are prey to several insects and diseases, so most organic gardeners keep them under row covers until the plants start to bloom and set fruit. Insect pollinators are needed for pollination, and cucurbit pollinators are most abundant from midsummer on, so never rush to plant melons too early. Where needed, the row covers can go back on while the crop ripens to provide protection from birds and groundhogs.

Muskmelons (commonly called cantaloupes) are the easiest melons to grow because they mature quickly. Perhaps the best starter variety is 'Minnesota Midget' (70 days), a vigorous little variety suitable for small beds or roomy containers that also can be trained to a trellis. You can save the seeds of this fine old open-pollinated variety, adding to its garden value.

For fantastic flavor in a small package, try hybrid 'Sugar Cube' (80 days), a terrific trellis vine that produces a heavy crop of personal-size cantaloupes. The vines are highly resistant to powdery mildew, so they prosper even in bad mildew years. The same is true of full-size 'Hannah's Choice' and 'Sarah's Choice' (both about 76 days), which are frequent taste-test winners. Like other large muskmelons, they are best grown in widely spaced raised hills. As they run over mulched ground, the vines become a knee-high sea of green.

Mesclun

Mixed species

Mesclun is not a plant but rather a mixture of salad greens that are cut when young. In the language of gardening, the "spring greens" and "baby lettuce blends" you buy at the supermarket translate into mesclun. It comes in endless variations. Spicy mixtures include mustards, arugula, and other big-flavored greens, whereas all-lettuce blends are dependably mild.

In addition to cutting handfuls with a sharp knife, you can pinch off individual leaves and/or harvest your mesclun by thinning the plants. Mesclun offers an easy way to get to know several salad-worthy species in one packet, so it's a great choice for new gardeners who want to experiment with offbeat greens. All mesclun mixtures grow best in cool weather and benefit from regular water. They are ready to start cutting in about 35 days from planting. If you leave their roots and crowns intact when harvesting, most plants in mesclun mixtures will grow back after the first, second, and (sometimes) third cuttings.

Mint

Mentha species and hybrids

Mints are vigorous plants that spread by sending out wandering roots an inch or two below the soil's surface. For this reason, many gardeners wisely grow mints in containers, or in dedicated beds where their spread can be easily kept in check.

Peppermint (*Mentha* × *piperata*) is the most often-used culinary mint, and it is easier to keep under control than spearmint. Interesting peppermint variations include chocolate mint, which often shows pronounced red coloration. Lime-scented Cuban mint, often called mojito mint (*Mentha* × *villosa*), is a restrained grower with fresh, clean flavor for drinks. You can begin with nursery-grown plants or root stem cuttings shared by a friend or from a purchased package. Three- to 4-inch-long stem tips develop roots quickly when set to root in moist potting soil or plain water.

Mizuna

Brassica rapa var. *japonica*

This variation on mustard, selected in Japan for cold hardiness and ease of culture, is often a runaway hit in gardens. You will see it in spicier mesclun mixtures, but mizuna is so vigorous and pretty that it is often grown on its own. Most at home in the fall garden, mizuna's flavor is improved by light frosts, and cooking further tames its taste. Moderate overnight freezes won't damage the plants, but single-digit freezes that persist for several days often kill them. Plants that survive winter bloom first thing in spring. If allowed to ripen and shed its seed crop, mizuna will self-sow for fall.

Seeds sold as mizuna often produce green fringed leaves with white petioles (basal leaf veins). 'Ruby Streaks' is a more colorful red-tinted version. Mild and buttery 'Komatsuna' comes in green and red forms and has more rounded leaves. Smooth-leafed 'Vitamin Green' offers another variation, with large leaves produced over a very long season. All mizunas are ready to start cutting about 40 days after planting.

Mustard

Brassica juncea, B. rapa

Of all the leafy greens you can grow in fall, mustard is the easiest and the most varied. Technically, mizunas (page 209) are mustards, as are bok choys (page 200) and Chinese cabbage (page 203). Yet plain old mustards are anything but plain, and they're useful as cooking greens, edible ornamentals, or even cover crops. (Try sowing mustard into sweet corn stubble in fall; the roots will take up nitrogen the corn left behind, and the broad leaves will shade out weeds.) Overwintered and spring-sown mustard promptly blooms and sets seed. Allow a few seed-bearing branches to mature until the seed pods fade to tan, and gather the best ones for cooking and replanting.

Frilly green-leafed varieties like 'Green Wave' (50 days) cook into savory greens, and the raw leaves make fine garnishes. Keep a packet of a red-leafed variety like 'Osaka Purple', 'Garnet Giant', or 'Red Giant' (all 45 days) in your seed box at all times. In any season except midsummer, you can fill gaps in beds with these colorful mustards.

Okra

Abelmoschus esculentus

Best adapted where summers are long and hot, okra is a great crop to plant just as spring turns to summer. Soaking the hard seeds overnight before planting speeds germination. If your climate is marginal for okra (many are!), stick with either compact 'Jambalaya' (50 days) or red-blushed 'Candle Fire' (60 days). In warmer areas, try a season or two of 'Clemson Spineless' (56 to 70 days) before moving on to the numerous nifty heirlooms valued by seed-saving okra lovers. Days to maturity vary with growing conditions, because okra's growth rate slows down when it's cool and speeds up when it's hot. Warm temperatures also make okra pods grow faster, so those that are produced in the heat of late summer are especially tender. Use pruning shears to clip pods every three days, because pods quickly become overripe. Pods more than 6 inches long are usually quite tough, so harvest often to get them young.

Onions

Allium cepa

Familiar bulb onions are easy to grow, but it's important to match varieties to your climate. Onions form bulbs in response to changes in day length, but different varieties have different "trigger points" that stimulate bulb formation. Short-day varieties start to form bulbs as soon as day length exceeds 10 to 12 hours, but long-day onions won't start to bulb until days are 14 to 16 hours long. Ideally, you want the onions to keep growing as long as possible before lengthening days trigger them to bulb, so different varieties work in the southern, central, and northern regions.

Short-day onions. The sweetest onions are short-day varieties that grow best in mild-winter climates, where they can be planted in October and harvested in April and May. The old 'White Bermuda'

TASTY TIP In addition to traditional bulb onions, try growing other alliums, including leeks (page 208), scallions (page 216), and shallots (page 217). A garden cook can never have enough fresh onions.

variety is the grandpappy of many modern short-day varieties, including 'Pumba' and other **Granex** hybrids (the ones grown as **Vidalias** in Georgia) and 'Texas 1015' (the famous Texas supersweets). These and other short-day onions mature in about 150 days when planted in fall, or 80 days from early-spring planting. Although sweet, most short-day onions do not store well because they contain so much water. After harvesting, keep them in the fridge.

Intermediate-day onions. In the upper South and mid-Atlantic regions, intermediate varieties like 'Super Star', 'Candy', and 'Red Candy Apple' (all about 100 days) produce beautiful onions with a balanced, spicy-sweet flavor. When properly cured they will store for several months. These are sometimes called day-neutral varieties because they can be grown in a wide range of climates, including short-, intermediate-, and long-day areas.

Long-day onions. Most of the long-day varieties that grow best in the North form hard, pungent onions that store for a long time. Good varieties include 'Patterson', 'Red Bull', and 'New York Early', all about 110 days. Many small specialty onions grow best in northern climates, too.

Oregano
Origanum vulgare, O. onites

Oreganos are quite variable in size, flavor, and growth habit. Some strains can be grown from seed, while others are better purchased as plants that have been grown from root cuttings. **Greek oregano** (*O. vulgare* ssp. *hirtum*) has the best flavor for cooking of all oreganos that can be grown from seed. The best-flavored strains of **Italian oregano** (*O. onites*) are propagated from rooted stem cuttings; you can also grow them from plants. Italian oregano is hardy only in Zone 8 and warmer.

Hardy in Zone 5, dormant Greek oregano can be potted up and overwintered in an unheated garage in cold climates. When the plants bloom in summer, they are often abuzz with tiny insects, many of whom play beneficial roles in the garden.

TASTY TIPS Oregano stems of any species are easy to root in water or moist potting soil. If you buy some fresh oregano that you particularly like, try rooting a few stems to grow in your garden.

Oregano holds its flavor well when dried and stored in a cool, dry place. Try making your own herbal blends by mixing dried oregano with thyme or marjoram.

Parsley
Petroselinum crispum

A biennial herb hardy in Zone 5 or 6, parsley is most often grown as an annual. Seeds are slow sprouters, so sow generously, especially when direct-seeding outdoors. Buy fresh seed every other year, because parsley seeds lose viability faster than many other types of seeds. Seedlings started indoors can be transplanted if the roots are handled very gently. All parsley tastes best fresh, but dried parsley is better than no parsley at all in the middle of winter.

There are two major types: Italian (flat-leafed) and curly. Both reach full size about 75 days after planting, but you can start picking after about 60 days. Italian varieties like 'Dark Green Italian' or 'Giant of Italy' grow 18 inches tall, and they are preferred for cooking because of their distinctive parsley flavor. Curly varieties such as 'Forest Green' or 'Krausa' stay more compact and form lush mounds of pickable parsley. They make great edging plants in the garden, and they combine easily with flowers or other herbs.

Parsnip
Pastinaca sativa

Parsnips are woefully underrated in the garden and in the kitchen. When planted from spring to early summer, the big, robust plants produce white, carrot-shaped roots by fall. You can dig them then or wait and gather them in winter. A wonderful root vegetable for the roasting pan or grill, parsnips also can be mashed with potatoes or sautéed in butter and enjoyed by themselves.

In the garden, parsnips are a slow yet carefree garden crop. Simply sow the seeds in spring and be patient while they germinate. After you thin the seedlings to 10 inches apart, your parsnips should need little care beyond occasional watering during dry spells. Cool soil temperatures improve the quality of parsnip roots, so delay digging until nights cool down in fall. Open-pollinated varieties like 'Hollow Crown' and 'All American' mature in 100 days or so—about the same time needed to grow hybrids like 'Javelin' or 'Gladiator'. Uniformity is the big benefit of going hybrid with parsnips. But whatever variety you decide to grow, don't discard parsnip roots that are kinked or forked. Once they are peeled and pared, they will look and taste as good as the perfect ones.

Pea

Pisum sativum

A delightful crop to grow in spring, garden peas come in three forms—snap peas, snow peas, and shelling peas. The first two are the most productive types because you eat both the pods and the peas inside. Long-vined varieties that need a trellis include 'Sugar Snap' snap peas (62 days) and 'Oregon Giant' snow peas (70 days). Compact varieties like 'Sugar Ann' snap pea (52 days) and 'Oregon Sugar Pod II' snow pea (70 days) need very little support because they grow less than 3 feet tall.

These varieties grow into pretty plants, but you can maximize your peas' value as edible ornamentals by using varieties that produce colorful blooms and pods. For example, 'Golden Sweet' snow pea (61 days) features purple blossoms and lemon yellow pods, while 'Sugar Magnolia' snap pea (70 days) has plump purple pods.

Shelling peas give a more modest return per square foot, but if you love peas you will want to grow them. Improved varieties like early 'Premium' (51 days) and disease-resistant 'Maestro' (60 days) or 'Green Arrow' (65 days) pack their pods with sweet green pearls. They are so tasty eaten straight off the vine that many will not make it into the kitchen, much less the freezer, so grow a lot.

Regardless of which types you grow, get your peas in the ground early because they need to produce their crop before days warm beyond about 85°F (30°C). Hot weather causes mature plants to shed their blossoms rather than setting more pods. Peas are easy to trellis because the curling tendrils latch onto whatever they can find—string, netting, garden fencing, or nearby plants. Pick peas daily when they ripen, preferably in the morning or evening when the pods are cool. When peas become overripe, their sugars quickly change to starches, and then they're not as sweet.

Pepper

Capsicum annuum

A warm-season crop native to the American tropics, peppers bring spice and color to the summer garden. Like tomatoes, peppers require warm soil and abundant sun, and they stay in the garden all summer long. Mulch your peppers to help keep the soil moist, and don't judge your crop by the fruits you harvest in midsummer. Peppers are famous for producing modestly during summer, followed by a heavy harvest in early fall. Plants often need to be tied to a stake to keep them from falling over when they are holding numerous fruits.

Peppers come in sweet and hot versions, as well as every imaginable spiciness level in between. When deciding which types to grow, you can't miss by sticking with the same types you buy at the store, only with a more garden-friendly twist toward smaller fruit size.

Take sweet peppers, for example. The big red, yellow, and orange bells that are costly to buy also can be difficult to grow. (Most of the colorful sweet peppers sold in grocery stores are grown in large-scale greenhouses.) Yet you can easily grow sugary-sweet, fully ripe peppers in your garden if you grow smaller-fruited varieties *and* give the crop enough time to ripen all the way. Both flavor and nutritional value improve dramatically as peppers change to their mature colors. Depending on variety, peppers may mature to red, orange, or yellow.

TASTY TIP If your pepper plants start to tilt late in the season as they load up with fruit, you can tie them to stakes with strips of soft cloth. Or simply cushion their fall with a mat of dry hay or other clean mulch.

But back to size. Opting for smaller peppers means more peppers sooner, and for a longer time, with way fewer puckered or blemished fruits compared to big, blocky bells. In fact, once you've grown the incomparable varieties described below, you will probably lose interest in gigantic bells. These pint-size sweet peppers are really that good.

'Lipstick' (73 days to red ripe) bears 4-inch-long, conical fruits with glossy skins and fruity-sweet flesh with smoky flavor undertones—exactly what you would expect of a well-mannered cross between a soft-fleshed pimento and a crisp bell. In addition to excellent fruit quality, the abundant blossoms successfully set fruit under adverse conditions, so you'll get a steady supply for the kitchen. Use 'Lipstick' raw or cooked; it's great for adding color to homemade pickles.

'Carmen' (80 days to red ripe) bears 6-inch-long, smooth, conical fruits with the same great cooking qualities as old-fashioned bull's horn types, which were selected in Italy for complex sweet flavor that expands even more when roasted. With fruits only half the size of her forebears, 'Carmen' produces many more to savor and over a much longer

WARMING UP TO HOT PEPPERS

Some folks are crazy for hot peppers, but for most of us, two plants will produce all the fresh, dried, or frozen hot peppers we really need. If you get good pepper weather, one plant each of dependably hot 'Hungarian Hot Wax' (83 days to red ripe) and 'Cayenne' (78 days to red ripe) will likely give you a year's supply. 'Cayenne' peppers have thin walls, so they are especially easy to dry whole, even if you live in a humid climate. All small-fruited hot peppers—including edible ornamental varieties with showy fruits or foliage—are very easy to grow, though it's important to wait until the fruits are mature to rate their heat. Hot weather turns up the heat in hot peppers.

season. These peppers will carry a pizza with style, they go great on kebabs, and eating them stuffed and grilled will send you to pepper heaven.

'Jimmy Nardello' bears long, skinny fruits (80 days to red ripe) that won't win any beauty contests, and if you sample them raw you may wonder what all the fuss is about. Fine. Now cut a few bright red fruits into bite-size pieces and braise them in a little oil or butter until they just begin to soften. Taste. That singular fruity sweetness is what gives

SWEET *AND* HOT?

You will rarely find them in stores, but as a gardener you have the chance to grow peppers that are mildly spicy with strong sweet notes to back up the fire—what pepper aficionados call sweet-hot varieties. Like other sweet-hots, 'Mariachi' (80 days to red ripe) earns only one star for spiciness, and some fruits may seem to have no fire at all. This is a great pepper if you like just a little kick, and its 4-inch size makes it great for stuffing and grilling. 'Mariachi' can bear a bit late if the weather is too hot or too cool, but you won't have that problem with 'Garden Salsa' (75 days), a cooled-down cayenne, or any of several low-burn jalapeños, including orange 'NuMex Pumpkin Spice' (80 days to orange ripe) and 'TAM Jalapeno' (75 days to mature green).

'Jimmy Nardello' the ability to bring extraordinary succulence to summer sandwiches or pasta dishes. Plus, Jimmy is very easy to grow.

All of the above peppers ripen to red, but if you want peppers that ripen to other colors, there are several worthwhile candidates. Again, choosing small-fruited varieties over big bells will give you a heavy crop that starts early and stays late. 'Sweet Banana' (75 days) often holds ivory, orange, and red fruits at the same time, and 'Cornito Giallo' (75 days) is like a half-size Italian roasting pepper that ripens to orange. You can tell by the way 'Tangerine Dream' (75 days to orange) holds its crisp fruits high, where you can't miss them, that it was bred to be an edible ornamental. In a small garden where looks count, all small-fruited peppers—sweet and hot—can be as beautiful as they are productive.

Potato

Solanum tuberosum

The common potato can become a gardening passion once you discover the many colors and flavors available in distinctive varieties. One good way to get to know this versatile veggie is to plant a small bag of store-bought mixed gourmet potatoes. As long as they are not big baking potatoes, which need a long, cool growing season, they should multiply themselves 10 times over in three to four months. Or start with named varieties sold as "seed potatoes." These are not really seeds but mature potatoes especially grown and selected for replanting. Organically grown potatoes purchased at the store can be used as seed potatoes.

Early varieties are the mainstay of home gardeners because they can be planted early, two to three weeks before the last spring frost, and make a crop in less than 90 days. In most climates, there is enough time to grow a second vegetable after early potatoes are harvested or maybe even a third in warm climates. The parade of stellar early varieties is led by 'Red Norland', a top-producing variety that will load you up with gourmet quality red-skinned new potatoes. Garden standouts that are expensive or impossible to buy in stores include 'Red Gold' (red skin, waxy yellow flesh) and 'Caribe' (purple skin, flaky snow white flesh).

Midseason varieties often are worth waiting an extra month for, especially spotted, yellow-fleshed 'Pinto Gold' or flaky 'Adirondack Blue'. 'Red LaSoda' can be gathered young, as new potatoes, or you can let them mature into red-skinned potatoes for storage.

I put elongated fingerlings in the midseason category, too, though most catalogs list pink-flecked 'French Fingerling' as midseason and tan-skinned 'Russian Banana' as late. These and other fingerlings may stick to a slow schedule their first year, but after that they will get earlier, either by presprouting themselves indoors or by growing from little tubers hiding in the soil (they're easy to dig and move). Try them. You'll like them.

Late varieties need 110 days or more of growing time, with cool soil temperatures as they size up. These cool-climate specials often produce very large potatoes that keep for a long time in cool storage. 'Butte' is a fine-tasting all-purpose brown-skinned potato that performs well when grown organically in the Midwest; 'Katahdin' and 'Kennebec' rule in the Northeast.

TASTY TIP To grow potatoes in warm climates with short springs, try interplanting them with sweet corn, sunflowers, or tall trellised tomatoes. As summer heats up, the tall crops will provide cooling shade for the potatoes—a planting practice followed in the Andes in South America for thousands of years.

Pumpkin
Cucurbita species

Big Halloween pumpkins need a lot of space to run, but pumpkins that produce small fruits often have shorter vines, making them an easier fit in home gardens. Very tiny pumpkins that fit in the palm of your hand can be trained to run up a trellis, and many people allow the vines of small and midsize varieties to mingle with sweet corn plants, as is done with butternut squash in Sweet Corn & Company on page 158.

Pumpkins can be planted in late spring, which is the best planting time in cool climates. But in areas where fall lasts well into October, small-fruited pumpkins planted in July will make a good crop. You can sow pumpkins from seed, or start the seeds indoors and set out seedlings when they are three weeks old.

If your main motive in growing pumpkins is to make fabulous pies, you may be better off growing butternut or buttercup squash. Compared to these dense-fleshed winter squash, good old pumpkins taste weak and stringy—with a few notable exceptions. Time-tested open-pollinated varieties like 'Winter Luxury' and 'Baby Pam' (both 105 days) produce small, pie-worthy pumpkins. Better yet, opt for one of the pumpkin-shaped winter squash classified as *Cucurbita moschata*, because this species has a much higher level of natural pest resistance compared to regular pumpkins. Varieties of this species taste great and will last in storage for many months. Excellent choices include dramatically lobed 'Fairytale' (110 days) and 'Long Island Cheese' (108 days), which is shaped like a wheel of cheese.

Radish
Raphanus species

Most gardeners are familiar with round salad radishes, not all of which are red! Gardeners can dote on purple 'Purple Plum' (30 days) or blushing 'Pink Beauty' (26 days) for salads and slaws or grow a multicolored mixture such as 'Easter Egg' (30 days).

In any color, small round radishes like these are easy to grow as long as the soil is kept constantly moist. Uneven soil moisture leads to cracking.

Beautiful elongated radishes like 'French Breakfast' (21 days) and 'White Icicle' (30 days) often have a spicy bite, which calls for a special food approach. In France, good bread and butter served with these easy-to-grow beauties is breakfast fare that will wake up your palate in a hurry. Germans use these flavorful radishes to add crunch to pretzels with mustard.

Daikon radishes grow really, really well in fall. They pop up out of the ground as they size up, and some can be huge. Shape and color vary. Japanese 'Minowase' (50 days) develops long, white roots, while 'Watermelon' (60 days) produces round red roots the size of baseballs. Browse through some books on Asian cooking to find tempting ideas for using these incredibly productive radishes. They can be foundation vegetables in spicy fermented relishes such as kimchi.

Storage radishes like 'Black Spanish' (55 days) are a great choice if you want to grow more of your own fresh food to eat throughout the winter. These dense-fleshed radishes will keep for months in a refrigerator or cold cellar.

In addition to eating radish roots, the tender young seedpods provide toothsome bites, too. A few varieties including 'Rat Tail' (50 days) have been selected for large seedpod size. Popular in South Asia, rat tail radishes bear 6- to 8-inch green pods on big plants that may need staking. Harvest radish pods when they are still crisp and tender, and use them like snow peas in soups and stir-fries.

Rhubarb
Rheum rhababarum

Like asparagus, rhubarb is a long-lived perennial that requires very fertile, well-drained soil. The edible parts are the thick, juicy stems. Cut off and compost rhubarb leaves, which contain dangerously high levels of oxalic acid. Hardy in Zone 4, very large varieties like red-stemmed 'Victoria' can grow 4 feet wide and tall, so be sure to give the plants plenty of space. Red-stemmed rhubarb is the most popular type, but primarily green-stemmed varieties like 'Macdonald' and 'Glaskins Perpetual' produce up to twice as many sound stems. Cut all you like until early July. After that, let the plants grow freely for the rest of the season. For best performance, plants should be dug, divided, and replanted in a fresh spot every six to eight years.

Rosemary
Rosmarinus officinalis

A woody perennial herb hardy often in Zone 6, rosemary leaves are a favorite choice for flavoring meats, casseroles, soups, and even breads. Varieties differ in size and flavor; trailing varieties tend to have strong pine flavor, while more upright strains boast a fuller rosemary bouquet. 'Arp' and 'Hill Hardy' tolerate more cold than other varieties. Named rosemary varieties are propagated vegetatively, by rooting stem cuttings, so you will need to buy them as plants rather than starting from seeds. In cold climates, pot up your rosemary in fall, but leave it outdoors until the first hard freezes come. Keep the dormant plant in a cool garage until spring, and then replant it in your garden. A single plant is sufficient for the needs of most garden cooks.

Rutabaga
Brassica napus Napobrassica group

This star crop of the fall garden deserves wider use in gardens and at the table. I suggest changing the name to "butter root," which is what rutabagas taste like when cut into cubes and roasted. Rutabagas are as easy to grow as turnips, but they need a little more time in the ground. Plant them after fast-maturing spring crops, or just as summer heat breaks in climates with long, lingering falls. Most people direct-seed rutabagas, but if planting conditions are horribly hot, you can sprout the seeds indoors and set them out as soon as they produce their first true leaf. Keep the babies moist and shaded for a few days after transplanting them. Mature rutabagas can be left in the garden until the first hard freeze, when overnight temps fall below 25°F (-4°C). Hybrids like 'Helenor' (90 days) excel in uniformity, but fans of garden food dream of the dense yellow flesh of 'Laurentian' (95 days). 'Nadmorska' (90 days) can bring diversity to the rutabaga patch with its elongated, green-shouldered roots.

TASTY TIP
Pests in general ignore rutabaga, which is crucial for a crop grown during the height of bug season.

Sage
Salvia officinalis

This 20-inch-tall woody perennial is hardy in Zone 5 and warmer, but you are wise to start new plants from rooted cuttings every other spring to make sure you always have young, vigorous plants. Culinary sage features luminous gray-green leaves that make it a wonderful neutral in any garden. In mid- to late summer, the plants produce beautiful blue flower spikes, which are popular for frying into fritters or sprinkling on salads. Sage leaves are very easy to dry.

Garden-variety sage is fine for most gardeners, and it's easy to start from seeds. Or you can look for special vegetatively propagated varieties to meet your unique needs. Compact 'Berggarten' is great for tight spaces, while the foliage of 'Tricolor' features pink and white stripes. Variegated sages make great edible accent plants, but they are not as tall, hardy, or willing to bloom as green-leafed plants.

Scallions
Allium cepa, A. fistulosum

Whether you call them green onions or scallions, these are the only types of onions that many people will eat raw. Scallions are easy to grow, too, and by

TASTY TIP To avoid attracting the attention of onion root maggots, it's a good idea to move multipliers and other perennial onions to a new location every fall.

growing your own you can explore the types that make up this varied group.

True green onions are simply bulb onions that are pulled young, before they even think about forming a bulb. The surest way to grow this type of scallion is to plant inexpensive onion sets—small, dormant bulbs, sold by the pound at garden centers in spring. Sets are an iffy way to grow bulb onions because they are very prone to bolting, but they're the no-brainer way to grow green onions.

Scallions also are fast to grow from seed, and the seedlings are easier to keep weeded compared to other onions because they can be grown at tight, 1-inch spacing. Direct-sow in midspring, after the soil has begun to warm, to get best germination. Early and pencil-straight, 'Guardsman' (55 days) makes a great season opener, and vigorous 'Parade' (65 days) can be sown every three weeks from spring to late sumer. 'Apache' (65 days) has pretty purple shanks that set it apart from other scallions.

These varieties are interspecies hybrids, but 'Evergreen Bunching', 'Summer Island', and other varieties classified as *A. fistulosum* can behave as perennials in hospitable climates. For best performance, dig, divide, and replant selected mother clumps in both spring and fall.

Finally, many gardeners opt for multiplying onions, which go under various names, depending on whom you ask. Most often shared among gardeners as pass-along plants, multipliers can be harvested as scallions from spring to early summer. Then let the plants bloom and set bulblets—fleshy corms that multipliers produce instead of seeds. Collect the bulblets and replant them in fall.

Shallot
Allium cepa

Closely related to bulb onions but much more cold-hardy, shallots are customarily planted in fall, just like garlic. They do, however, require a bit more babying. Plant the mother bulbs in a very well-drained, fertile bed, and top off the planting with a thick winter mulch. You can plant shallots purchased at the supermarket or mail-order named varieties. So-called gray shallots are especially valuable in cold climates. In areas above the 35th parallel (Zone 6 and colder), varieties like 'French Red' and 'Dutch Yellow' deserve a trial.

You can save money and avoid shipping restrictions by starting seed-sown varieties indoors in late winter, and setting out the seedlings in midspring. Varieties like 'Ambition' (120 days) and 'Conservor' (110 days) will form a mix of single bulbs and small clusters that will store for a year. 'Davidor' (95 days) does not store as long, but it is the best-adapted variety for southern latitudes.

Spinach
Spinacia oleracea

Valued for salads and cooking, spinach is on every gardener's planting list. Lengthening spring days trigger spinach to bolt (produce flowers and seed), after which the leaves' flavor and texture go downhill. Try upright 'Seaside' (40 days), smooth-leafed 'Space' (39 days), or another bolt-resistant hybrid in spring. Fall is a better time to experiment with unusual large-leafed varieties like 'Giant Winter' and 'Viroflay' (both 50 days), or beautiful red-stemmed 'Beaujolais' (32 days). Spinach seeded in fall will survive winter in all but the coldest climates with protection from a cold frame or plastic tunnel. 'Giant Winter' and 'Winter Bloomsdale' (45 days) work especially well when grown from fall to spring. Spinach is a nitrogen-hungry crop, and overwintered plants in particular benefit from booster feedings with a water-soluble fertilizer.

Squash
Cucurbita species

Wonderfully productive and easy to grow, squash come in dozens of shapes and sizes. Those that are customarily eaten young are called summer squash, while those that ripen fully in the garden are winter squash. The hard rinds of winter squash make them easy to store at room temperature for many months, which is one of the easiest ways to extend your garden's productive season. Botanically speaking, there is quite a bit of crossover between summer and winter squash.

Cucurbita pepo is the most common species grown in gardens. *C. pepo* includes all summer squash (yellow squash, zucchinis, and pattypans) and three types of winter squash: acorn, delicata (sweet potato squash), and spaghetti squash. Many pumpkins also belong to this species. Representatives of this species are vigorous, grow fast in warm weather, and are often phenomenally productive. Young acorn squash can be eaten like summer squash.

One drawback of *C. pepo* squashes is that squash vine borers and squash bugs just love them to death. To prevent damage, use row covers as described on page 40. Sadly, flavor in acorns is often weak compared to other winter squash, but delicatas excel as single-serving-size stuffing squash.

Among summer squash, yellow zucchinis like 'Golden Glory' (50 days) contrast beautifully with dark green varieties like 'Raven' (48 days). Tricolored 'Sunburst' pattypan (55 days) offers a versatile twist in color, taste, and texture. In yellow squash, old timey 'Yellow Crookneck' (58 days) is hard to beat for overall flavor. Some of the better storage squash within this species include mildew-resistant 'Sweet REBA' acorn (85 days), compact 'Bush Delicata' (100 days), and yellow-orange 'Small Wonder' spaghetti squash (80 days).

Cucurbita moschata is the top squash species for pest resistance. This species is represented by several types of winter squash: butternut squash, "cheese" pumpkins, Tahitian squash, and a few Japanese heirlooms. You'll appreciate the excellent vine borer resistance that *C. moschata* squash offer, and the flavor and quality of mature fruits are excellent. As an added bonus, the immature fruits of this species taste great when handled like summer squash. Fruit shape, rind color, and flavor vary tremendously with variety.

The biggest challenge in growing *C. moschata* squash is allowing enough room for the vigorous vines to run, though they don't need as much space as species with larger leaves. Also, older varieties are susceptible to powdery mildew, which weakens the vines and compromises flavor.

Open-pollinated 'Waltham' butternut (100 days) will become a permanent garden resident if you save and replant the seeds. The flesh of stuffable 'Futsu Black' (100 days) is spiced with hazelnut undertones, and the fruits ripen reasonably fast. Also try heirloom pumpkins that fall within this species, including squat, round 'Long Island Cheese' (108 days) and 'Musque de Provence' (125 days), which looks like Cinderella's carriage. If you live where summers are long and hot, by all means try gigantic 'Tahitian' (110 days). As the fruity flesh of this heirloom variety roasts, abundant natural sugars caramelize the pieces.

Cucurbita maxima includes the big 'Blue Hubbard' squash as well as smaller varieties in several colors. For overall flavor and keeping quality, buttercups and other select variations are always worthwhile. The large-leafed, vigorous vines develop supplemental roots where the stems touch the ground, which gives them an edge against pests. Several heirloom varieties are highly rated for flavor, and well-grown fruits of this species are highly prized for pies. Be aware that some varieties taste much better than others.

C. maxima squash have their weaknesses, too. Big Hubbards are tremendously attractive to squash vine borers, and plants of this species need plenty of room to run. 'BonBon' buttercup (95 days) is famous for its use in delicious pies, while 'Sweet Meat' has a distinctive gray rind. Many gardeners love the elongated fruits of 'Georgia Candy Roaster' (100 days), which holds up well to humid heat.

WARM-CLIMATE WINTER SQUASH

Hot, humid summers can be tough on many types of winter squash, but heat-loving cushaw squash (*Cucurbita argyrosperma*) run on hot sun, tolerate moderate drought, and produce huge fruits that often weigh 10 to 20 pounds. The smooth, creamy flesh actually becomes sweeter in storage, and you can roast the seeds. Some pumpkins fall into this species, and canned pumpkin is often really cushaw squash. Varieties like **'Orange Cushaw'** and **'Tequila Black'** mature in about 120 days.

Sweet Potato
Ipomoea batatas

In areas with hot, humid summers, it's hard to beat sweet potatoes as a tasty, nutritious, and very low-maintenance summer crop. Grown from "slips"—the stems that sprout from the end of a sweet potato when it emerges from dormancy—sweet potatoes cannot be planted until the soil is downright warm to the touch—May or June, even in the South. Once established, the vines run like mad, forming a lush ground cover that shades the soil and suppresses weeds. Dig the tubers in early fall, before the soil gets cold, and cure them in a warm place for a week or two before storing them where temperatures stay above 55°F (12°C).

Most gardeners like fast-maturing varieties such as **'Covington'** (90 days), a dependable producer of high-quality tubers. **'Georgia Jet'** is a little faster at 80 days, but in some gardens it tends to "lunker"— produce one or two huge tubers instead of a pretty cluster of five or six. (Lunkers are perfectly edible.) If you live in prime sweet potato country (Zones 7 and 8), experiment with delicious **'Murasaki'** (100 days), with purple skin over white to pale yellow flesh. **'Vardaman'** (100 days) produces beautiful bronze-blushed foliage and long, slender tubers. White-fleshed sweet potatoes are rare in gardens, but their creamy consistency makes them ideal for mashing.

TASTY TIP If you want to try a sweet potato variety that a friend or neighbor just planted, simply take 4-inch-long stem tip cuttings and root them in moist potting soil or water. They will be nicely rooted and ready to set out in about two weeks.

Thyme
Thymus species and hybrids

Actually a group of related herbs, thymes look good, taste great, and attract scores of buzzing insects when they bloom in summer. Be careful when choosing plants, because the heavy-blooming ornamental thymes used as ground covers leave much to be desired in the kitchen. Instead, try strains of less showy culinary thymes in your food garden.

Often called **English** or **French thyme**, the best species for cooking and drying, *Thymus vulgaris*, is a hardy perennial that can survive winter in Zone 4. It is also easy to grow from seed, which may be sold as *T. vulgaris* or as a strain. **'German Winter'** generally has dark green leaves and a compact growth habit, while faster-growing French or "summer" thymes have softer stems that quickly regrow after they are cut back. **Lemon thymes** (*T. citriodorus*) are a bit less flavorful than their upright cousins, but their spreading growth habit makes them indispensable for containers or for billowing over the edges of beds.

Tomatoes

Lycopersicum esculentum, also known as
Solanum lycopersicum

Variety determines whether a tomato is big and tangy or small and sweet and whether it ripens to yellow, orange, red, or even green. Growth rate, disease resistance, and growth habit are under genetic control, too, so choosing garden-fit varieties is fundamental to success.

Sorting through hundreds of tomato varieties gets complicated fast, but you can avoid confusion by starting your tomato-growing career with widely adapted, tried-and-true selections. Here's my rundown of a dozen remarkable varieties every gardener should try at least once:

'Sungold' cherry (58 days) wins taste tests with its sweet, fruity flavor, and it contrasts beautifully with red cherry tomatoes such as 'Matt's Wild Cherry' (60 days) or 'Gardener's Delight' (65 days). In general, small-fruited cherry tomatoes ripen faster and are easier to grow than other types, and they tend to have high sugar content, too.

Sometimes called a "saladette" tomato, vigorous, disease-resistant 'Juliet' (62 days) bears big trusses of sweet, teardrop-shaped fruits. It is among the easiest tomatoes to grow.

'Early Girl' and award-winning 'Celebrity' start producing round red slicing tomatoes 62 days after transplanting and then keep setting fruits as long as the plants stay healthy. Other proven favorites in the red-round category include 'Rutgers' (75 days),

'Supersonic' (79 days), and many other varieties. Ask around about local favorites, and give them a try.

Diversify colors and flavors by including an orange, yellow, or green tomato in your tomato patch. Varieties that ripen to orange like 'Sweet Tangerine' (68 days) often have a citruslike tang. 'Lemon Boy' (72 days) and other yellow slicing tomatoes usually have a mild flavor, and 'Green Zebra' (80 days) is a sure stunner on the plate and the palate.

'Brandywine' (90 days) is in a class by itself for flavor, but this Pennsylvania heirloom is not the easiest tomato to grow. Its big "potato" leaves need plenty of space, the often huge fruits take a long time to ripen, and they tend to be lumpy or cracked. Despite these flaws, slapping slices of sun-ripened 'Brandywine' on a drippy tomato sandwich is the main reason why some folks bother to keep a garden. Until you try it, you will never know if you are part of this tribe.

Do not wander too deeply into the wonderfully diverse world of heirloom tomatoes until you spend a season or two learning tomato-growing basics. Hybrids are generally faster and more disease resistant than older varieties, and some excel in terms of flavor, too. Open-pollinated strains often taste great, but they can be unpredictable in terms of productivity and offer less disease resistance compared to hybrids. Start with good-tasting hybrids, then try open-pollinated varieties. By mixing them up, you will enjoy many seasons of productive, interesting tomato gardening.

WANTED: COLD-CLIMATE TOMATOES

Fast-maturing hybrids for cold climates have been around for a while, but except for fast-maturing cherry tomatoes, speedy varieties typically fall short in the flavor department. Relatively recent arrivals from Eastern Europe have changed all that, making it possible to grow fine-flavored tomatoes in short-season climates. 'Stupice' and 'Sasha's Altai' (both 55 to 60 days) are excellent choices if you live in a cold climate where ripe tomatoes are the stuff of which dreams are made. Should you luck into an unusually long, warm growing season, the plants will keep producing until frost shuts them down.

Turnip

Brassica rapa Rapifera group

Please set aside any prejudices you have against turnips and allow them into your garden. In spring, try fast-growing salad turnips like snow white 'Hakurei' (38 days) or red-skinned 'Scarlet Ohno Revival' (55 days), and pull the little darlings when they are the size of tennis balls. Don't worry—they will pop to the surface when they're ready. In fall, try a yellow-fleshed turnip like 'Golden Ball' (about 55 days); many garden cooks think yellow turnips are best for braising or roasting.

Any variety of turnip will produce delicious greens, which are at their best in cool weather. Crops sown seven to eight weeks before your first frost in fall will bear abundant greens worthy of blanching and freezing. For top greens production, old varieties like 'Seven Top' and 'Purple Top White Globe' (both 50 to 60 days) develop numerous crowns on the tops of the roots. With these varieties, you won't need but a few plants to have plenty of garden-fresh greens.

Watermelon

Citrullus lanatus

Watermelons need a full summer of warm weather, but they resist insect pests better than other types of melons. They also develop deep roots that help them stand up to drought. In most climates, watermelons are direct-seeded in late spring or early summer, after the soil has warmed. If you live in a cool climate, you can add time to your growing season by starting watermelon seeds indoors and setting out the seedlings when they are three weeks old.

Two important factors limit the planting of watermelons in home gardens: They need lots of warmth *and* lots of space. Assuming you have both—or you just plain love watermelons—start with a small-fruited variety like 8- to 10-pound 'Sugar Baby' (76 days), an old open-pollinated favorite that grows in a wide range of climates. Many gardeners who save and replant their own seed work with selected strains of 'Sugar Baby'. 'Yellow Doll' hybrid (76 days) is similar but with yellow flesh. Disease-resistant hybrid 'Crimson Sweet' (85 days) is a bigger melon (20 pounds), but it's the taste and productivity leader to beat if you live in a warm climate and have plenty of space where watermelon vines can sprawl.

The seedlings of seedless watermelons can be a bit finicky, but once the plants get going you can expect great results from red-fleshed 'Harvest Moon' (90 days) or 'Yellow Buttercup' (90 days). When growing seedless watermelons, one or more normal (seeded) plants must be included for pollination purposes. Seeds of a pollinator like 'Sugar Baby' or 'Ace' (78 days) are usually included in the packet, and they are the reason why some of your "seedless" watermelons will have plenty of seeds.

GARDENER'S BASIC LINGO

People have been speaking the language of gardening for thousands of years, and in modern times the science of horticulture has contributed numerous terms as well. Refer to the alphabetical list of words and phrases below to find an explanation of any terms that are unfamiliar to you. You will catch on in no time, because food garden lingo is easy to learn.

annual. A plant that completes its life cycle within one year, by sprouting from seed and then producing seeds. Most vegetables are annuals, but some require a period of cold temperatures to trigger strong flowering; these are called hardy annuals (spinach) or biennials (carrots). Warm-season annuals such as beans, squash, and tomatoes complete their life cycle in one summer.

beneficial insects. Insects that benefit crop plants by providing pollination services, by preying upon problem insects, or simply by filling a small niche in the food chain. Most of the insects you encounter in your garden are either beneficial or neutral. In fact, beneficial species are so numerous and varied that it is far simpler to get to know problem species (which are relatively few) than to recognize hundreds of beneficial ones. See Top Ten Insect Pests (page 166) for more information on helpful and harmful garden insects.

berm. A linear mound of soil along the edge of a bed that helps retain moisture inside the bed. Indigenous peoples of the American Southwest have long used slightly sunken beds surrounded by berms to make the most of a scant water supply.

blanch. In the garden, blanching means to deprive a plant part of light to enhance its eating quality. For example, leeks become extra long and tender when their bases are blanched with deep mulch. When cauliflower heads form in hot weather, old-fashioned varieties are often blanched by tying or pinning the topmost leaves together to shade the ripening head.

In the kitchen, blanching means to cook briefly. Many vegetables are blanched in steam or boiling water before they are frozen or dried. Blanching preserves nutrients and color, and it enhances the quality of most frozen veggies.

bolting. When low-growing leafy greens and members of the cabbage family switch from vegetative (leafy) to reproductive (flowering) mode, they suddenly grow tall, as if they were bolting for the sky. Once the bolting process begins, it cannot be stopped, and plants' eating quality declines as the process becomes more advanced. Unless you want to save seeds, it is best to pull up bolting plants and compost them.

botanical name. Plants can have many common names but only one botanical name. The first word in the botanical name is the plant's genus, the second is its species. Some food plants, particularly cabbage cousins, are further divided into botanic groups, or subspecies. For example, cabbage is *Brassica oleracea* Capitata group, and broccoli is *Brassica oleracea* Italica group. Botanical names help avoid confusion, and they also tell you which plants are genetically compatible. In general, plants of the same species can cross-pollinate in the garden, but plants of different species cannot.

cloche. A cover used to protect plants from weather-related stresses such as frost, wind, or even hail. See Stretching the Seasons (page 186) for information on using cloches.

cold frame. A structure used to protect plants from weather-related stresses such as frost and wind. An important season-stretching device, a cold frame can have rigid sides made of lumber, or its walls can be made of bales of hay. All cold frames have transparent or translucent tops, which you can make from reconditioned windows, shower doors, or plastic. Ventilation is crucial, because closed cold frames can quickly overheat on sunny days. You can place a cold frame over plants in a bed or use it as a place to harden off seedlings you have started indoors. See Stretching the Seasons (page 186) for information on using cold frames.

compost. Decomposed plant matter and/or animal manure. When plant parts are piled together and kept moist until they rot, the resulting crumbly, dark brown or black material is compost. Compost is an excellent soil conditioner, but few gardeners make as much compost as they need. In a closely managed vegetable garden, you should enrich soil with compost before each planting, so you will probably need to buy compost during prime planting seasons. Every gardener should set aside a convenient space for making compost in the garden, because a garden generates an abundance of raw materials for compost—pulled weeds, dead plants, old mulches, and daily doses of veggie trimmings. In a garden where appearance is important, using an enclosed composter will keep your garden's waste out of sight.

cover crop. Plants that are grown to benefit the soil (as opposed to being eaten). Cover crops can add huge amounts of organic matter to the soil. Organic farmers often use cold-hardy cover crops such as vetch, rye, and annual clovers to build soil fertility during the winter months. But digging deeply rooted cover crop plants into the soil by hand can be very hard work. You can reap the benefits of cover cropping—without a lot of extra work—by pulling up or chopping down cover crop plants when they are young.

cultivation. The process of breaking up the top 10 to 12 inches of soil. Cultivation incorporates air into the soil, improves drainage, and mixes in surface debris. When done prior to planting, cultivation incorporates fertilizer, compost, or other soil amendments into the soil as well.

direct-sowing. Planting seeds in the garden where you want them to grow, also called direct-seeding. For certain success, soil temperatures must be in an acceptable range for the vegetable you are planting, and the soil must be kept moist until the seeds sprout. A few weeks after they sprout, most direct-sown crops need to be thinned to proper spacing. See Direct-Seeding in Your Garden (page 115) for more information on direct-sowing seeds.

double-digging. A special method of long-lasting soil improvement in which the soil is excavated to 18 inches or more. Double-digging adds depth to plants' root zones, so they can forage more effectively for nutrients and moisture. See A Bountiful Border: Year One (page 47) for more information.

drainage. The speed with which water passes through soil. Drainage can be affected by site and soil type. Low spots naturally drain slowly, while high slopes drain fast. Clay soils drain much slower than light sandy soils. Vegetables and herbs appreciate good drainage, so if you have a poorly drained site or compacted clay soil, raised beds may be in order. Raised beds combined with double-digging can transform any sunny site into a good place to grow food plants.

family. In plant science, families are groups of closely related plants; family is the classification group just above genus. For example, cucumbers, melons, pumpkins, and squash belong to the cucumber family (Cucurbitaceae). Similarly, eggplant, peppers, and potatoes belong to the tomato family (Solanaceae). Plants of the same family often share similar preferences for site, soil, and weather and may be prone to damage by similar pests and diseases.

fertilizer. Substances added to soil (or sometimes sprayed upon leaves) that are intended for the direct benefit of plants. Organic fertilizers also benefit the soil because they break down into bits of organic matter. See Fertilizing Your Garden (page 156) for more information.

footprint. The area of a garden, measured from the outermost edges of the beds.

furrow. A shallow trench made in the soil for the purpose of planting seeds or seedlings.

germination. The process of sprouting, which begins when a dormant seed absorbs moisture within a favored temperature range. The embryo inside comes to life, the seed coat splits, and a tiny seedling equipped with root, stem, and leaf tissues emerges. Depending on species, germination time ranges from two days (arugula, mizuna) to two weeks (parsley, parsnip).

hardening off. The adjustment process seedlings should undergo as you prepare to move them from indoor or greenhouse conditions to your garden. During hardening off, plants are gradually exposed to increasing levels of light, wind, and fluctuating day/night temperatures to minimize stress when they are transplanted. See Guaranteed Seedling Success (page 114) for more information on hardening off and transplanting seedlings.

hardy. A general term indicating that a plant can withstand cold. Plants described as half-hardy can usually survive only short periods of freezing weather, whereas hardy perennials such as asparagus and rhubarb tolerate soil that stays frozen for months. Hardiness of plants is a matter of degree; it is rated according to USDA Hardiness Zones. (See box on page 103.)

hybrid. A vegetable, herb, or flower variety that is created by crossing two specially selected parent plants, sometimes indicated by (F1) after the name. The first generation after hybrid crosses are made (the F1 hybrid generation) often brings improved productivity and disease resistance. See Open-Pollinated vs. Hybrid Varieties (page 194) for more information.

intercropping. Growing two or more vegetables or herbs side by side in the same bed or row or intermingled in shared space. This approach works especially well in small gardens or in any garden where you are growing vegetables that stay small for several weeks in early summer and then suddenly grab space.

mulch. Any material used to cover the soil's surface. Plastic mulches will prevent weeds and reduce moisture lost to evaporation, but biodegradable mulches offer bigger benefits. They improve the soil as they rot, provide great habitat for earthworms, and help keep soil cool when the weather turns hot. See The Magic of Mulch (page 146) for more information.

open-pollinated. Vegetable, herb, or flower varieties that were created and refined and are maintained through the selection process. Open-pollinated varieties often feature flavors and colors that are missing from comparable hybrids, but they may be second rate in terms of disease resistance or overall productivity. See Open-Pollinated vs. Hybrid Varieties (page 194) for more information.

organic matter. Fully decomposed plant or animal matter. It is the destiny of any material that was once plant or animal tissue to rot into bits of organic matter in or on the soil. These bits of organic matter hold nutrients in the soil and improve its structure. When soil is enriched regularly with organic matter from compost and decomposing mulches, it gradually becomes dependably fertile, so that all plants grow more vigorously. See What's Inside the Bag? (page 23) for information on choosing types of organic matter to add to your soil.

perennial. A plant that comes back year after year, with a resting or dormant period between growth cycles. Hardy perennials like asparagus survive very cold temperatures, while tender perennials such as marjoram are so easily damaged by cold that they are handled as annuals.

pH. The measurement of where soil falls on the acid to alkaline scale. With 7.0 as the neutral point, soils with a pH below 6.0 will not produce bumper vegetable crops unless treated to modify acidity, while those that measure above 7.5 are too alkaline for some plants. See Lime Enlightenment on page 160 for more information on modifying soil pH. Always test your soil before taking steps to alter its pH.

relay planting. When a planting of one vegetable is immediately followed by another (often in the same day); also called succession planting. For example, in most climates you can grow a relay crop of salad greens or even bush beans after garlic is harvested in midsummer. Similarly, you might be able to follow spring lettuce with summer squash. When timing is tight, using seedlings that are poised to make rapid growth helps ensure the success of relay plantings.

row cover. A cloth or clothlike barrier that excludes insects and may provide frost or shade protection, depending on its weight. Midweight, spunbonded row covers buffer wind and retain a little heat, so they are useful for stretching the spring season. In summer, switch to very lightweight row covers, or make your own using wedding net (tulle) or any featherweight cloth that will exclude insects without trapping heat. See Stretching the Seasons (page 186) for more information.

shade cover. A temporary cover that shields transplanted seedlings or newly sown seedbeds from excessive sun. Upturned flowerpots, bushel baskets, cardboard boxes, or a piece of cloth (such as an old sheet or thrift-store sheer curtains) held aloft with hoops or stakes make good shade covers. See Guaranteed Seedling Success (page 114) for more information.

spacing. The distance between plants. Spacing varies from as little as 2 inches for scallions to as much as 2 feet for big tomatoes or cabbages. Crowded plants often suffer from stunted growth, and overly tight spacing invites problems with diseases by limiting good air circulation. If you're not sure about spacing, follow the recommended spacing between plants printed on most seed packets.

thinning. The removal of plants to achieve proper spacing. You can thin by pulling plants or use small cuticle scissors to clip off unwanted seedlings that are so close together that pulling might ruin all of them. Most crops that are direct-sown should be thinned a week or two after the seeds germinate. You can gradually thin most leafy greens by harvesting plants as baby greens once or twice a week.

variety. A name that describes a particular strain or hybrid with a definable plant form, size, color, flavor, and many other characteristics. Part 3 discusses varieties and variety choices for garden vegetables and herbs.

WHICH PLANTING PLANS ARE RIGHT FOR YOU?

Dreaming of your future garden is almost as much fun as growing it, so spend plenty of off-season time exploring the possibilities. As you plan, make decisions based on what you want from the time and energy you will invest in your garden. In the following key, I've sorted the planting plans in this book in keeping with their purposes.

SOURCES FOR SEEDS AND PLANTS

Baker Creek Heirloom Seeds
417-924-8917
www.rareseeds.com

Fedco Seeds
207-426-9900
www.fedcoseeds.com

Gardener's Supply Company
888-833-1412
www.gardeners.com

High Mowing Organic Seeds
866-735-4454
www.highmowingseeds.com

Johnny's Selected Seeds
877-564-6697
www.johnnyseeds.com

Jung Seed Company
800-247-5864
www.jungseed.com

Native Seeds/SEARCH
520-622-5561
www.nativeseeds.org

Nichols Garden Nursery
800-422-3985
www.nicholsgardennursery.com

Nourse Farms
413-665-2658
www.noursefarms.com

Peaceful Valley Farm &
Garden Supply
888-784-1722
www.groworganic.com

Renee's Garden Seeds
888-880-7228
www.reneesgarden.com

Richters Herbs
905-640-6677
www.richters.com

Salt Spring Seeds
250-537-5269
www.saltspringseeds.com

Sand Hill Preservation Center
563-246-2299
www.sandhillpreservation.com

Seed Savers Exchange
563-382-5990
www.seedsavers.org

Seeds of Change
888-762-7333
www.seedsofchange.com

Southern Exposure Seed Exchange
540-894-9480
www.southernexposure.com

Territorial Seed Company
800-626-0866
www.territorialseed.com

Terroir Seeds LLC
888-878-5247
www.underwoodgardens.com

Turtle Tree Seed
800-930-7009
www.turtletreeseed.org

Victory Seed Company
503-829-3126
www.victoryseeds.com

W. Atlee Burpee & Co.
800-888-1447
www.burpee.com

METRIC CONVERSIONS

Unless you have finely calibrated measuring equipment, conversions between US and metric measurements will be somewhat inexact. It's important to convert the measurements for all of the ingredients in a recipe to maintain the same proportions as the original.

TO CONVERT . . .

Ounces to grams	Multiply ounces by 28.35
Grams to ounces	Multiply grams by 0.035
Pounds to grams	Multiply pounds by 453.5
Pounds to kilograms	Multiply pounds by 0.45
Cups to liters	Multiply cups by 0.24
Inches to centimeters	Multiply inches by 2.54
Feet to meters	Multiply feet by 0.3048
Fahrenheit to Celsius	Subtract 32 from Fahrenheit temperature, multiply by 5, then divide by 9
Celsius to Fahrenheit	Multiply Celsius temperature by 9, divide by 5, then add 32

INDEX

Page numbers in *italic* indicate photos or illustrations; numbers in **bold** indicate charts.

GARDEN SUCCESSFULLY
with More Books from
BARBARA PLEASANT

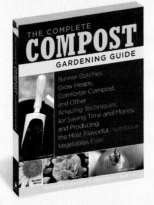

The Complete Compost Gardening Guide
by Barbara Pleasant & Deborah L. Martin

This indispensable handbook shows you the materials and techniques you need to turn an average vegetable garden or flower bed into something extraordinary.

Homegrown Pantry

This one-of-a-kind book shows you how to plan and plant a garden to keep your pantry stocked with homegrown produce throughout the year.

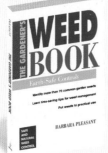

The Gardener's Weed Book

Pleasant reveals everything you need to know to manage weeds in your garden with a minimum of time and effort.